Aldous Huxley: Novelist

Aldous Huxley: Novelist

C. S. FERNS

The Athlone Press
London 1980

Published by
THE ATHLONE PRESS
90–91 Great Russell Street
London WC1
The Athlone Press is an
imprint of Bemrose UK Ltd

USA and Canada
Humanities Press Inc
New Jersey

British Library Cataloguing in Publication Data
Ferns, Christopher S.
Aldous Huxley.
1. Huxley, Aldous—Criticism and
interpretation
823'.9'12 PR6015.U9Z/

ISBN 0 485 11194 2

Printed in Great Britain by
WESTERN PRINTING SERVICES LTD
Bristol

Acknowledgements

I am not at all sure that long hours spent sitting alone in front of a typewriter are entirely conducive to mental health, and I would like to thank all the friends who helped to keep me (relatively) sane during the apparently endless process of writing and rewriting this book. More especially, for much helpful advice during the various stages of its emergence into the light of day, I would like to thank Peter Mudford, Jeannette Mitchell, and Lilian Haddakin. Above all, however, my thanks are due to Barbara Hardy, without whose help and encouragement it would most likely never have been written at all.

REFERENCES

Except where otherwise indicated, all page references are to the Collected Edition of Huxley's works.

Contents

I
Introduction

The purpose of literary criticism is, presumably, to improve our understanding of literature. The critic elucidates what is obscure, draws attention to features of a work whose significance might otherwise escape notice, judges by only the strictest and most discriminating standards. It is because critics delve deeper, read more widely, and bring to the works they discuss a more sophisticated grasp of the processes of literary creation that they are in a position to assist the ordinary reader, to enrich his or her understanding and enjoyment of a work or author.

Yet in practice the critic's reading does not always differ from that of the ordinary reader simply in its depth and completeness. At times the critic's experience would seem to be so radically at variance with that of the public that one is prompted to wonder whether this is merely a reflection of the critic's superior powers of penetration. Where his reading represents not so much an extension, a deepening of the ordinary reader's, as a direct contradiction of it, is the latter's experience therefore invalidated? Does the critic always know best?

Huxley's is a case where this kind of divergence between the critical and the public response is particularly marked. My own experience, when I first began working on Huxley, was of being agreeably surprised by the number of people I met who had read his work, yet at the same time puzzled by the extent to which the Huxley they talked about seemed to differ from the one discussed by the critics. They might almost have been two different authors. The first Huxley (and the one whom I felt corresponded most closely to my own experience) was primarily the author of *Brave New World* and *After Many A Summer*, of *The Doors of Perception* and *Island*—a witty, intelligent writer, whose appeal lay partly in his sense of humour, but more in his capacity to stimulate thought and argument. The second, the critics' Huxley, was rather different. Insofar as he was worth discussing at all, he was the author of *Point Counter Point* and *Eyeless in Gaza*—lengthy, complex, serious, and essentially realistic novels which, in the critics' estimation, represented the pinnacle of his achievement. *Point Counter Point* and *Eyeless in Gaza* could be seen as the culmination of the process of development observable in Huxley's earlier, primarily comic fiction; afterwards, as it became increasingly compromised by didacticism, the quality of his work abruptly declined.

The two readings, it seemed to me, were mutually exclusive, representing two entirely different experiences of the author's work, and it was because I felt that the second, critical reading amounted to a denial of the ordinary reader's experience that I began to wonder whether there were not perhaps different *kinds* of reading involved. Was it possible that Huxley's critics brought to their reading expectations and standards which so coloured their experience as to prevent them seeing what the non-specialist public did? Or alternatively, was it the public who had got Huxley wrong? Were they simply not discriminating enough?

In order to answer such questions, it is necessary to examine the assumptions and expectations which are involved in reading a work of literature. For there *are* assumptions and expectations involved: we do not read a work in a vacuum, automatically arriving at an objective valuation of it at the end; from the moment we open a book, a whole range of factors are at work determining our response to it. Some of our expectations are basic, and common to everyone—we expect to read from left to right, and that the lines we read will follow one another consecutively. Where this is not necessarily the case, as in the work of someone like Cortazar, the effect is dislocating in the extreme. More broadly, however, our experience conditions us to expect that what we read will conform to certain recognizable patterns, to each of which we will bring particular expectations. Once we have recognized the pattern, we will read a thriller, a poem, a political pamphlet, an article in a learned journal, not only with different expectations, but with subtly different kinds of attention. And once again, the violation of those expectations, the realization that the kind of attention we are employing is inappropriate, will have a dislocating effect—we should be startled by the appearance of flying saucers in a realistic nineteenth-century narrative, shocked to encounter grossly intemperate abuse in the context of a learned article. (Although it might be added that our expectations can also be violated in a creative way, perhaps in the interest of some satiric or surrealistic effect, and that our conception of the possibilities of a given pattern can thereby be extended.)

These are all expectations which are acquired either in the process of learning to read, or through the experience of reading; there are, however, other factors, external to that process, which can also condition the reader's response. They might be emotional—to use Wayne Booth's example, a man who believed he had good reason to be jealous of his wife could scarcely see 'Othello' without his response being affected by that fact; they might be sexual—a homosexual would clearly be likely to have a very different experience of a novel by James Baldwin than, say, someone who believed that homosexuality ought to be an offence punishable by law; or they might be political—an anarchist would be unlikely to react to Conrad's 'The Secret Agent' in the same way as a conservative.

It may be objected, of course, that these are extraneous considerations. The critic does not allow his judgement to be affected by his emotional state, sexual preferences, or political beliefs—so what relevance can the reactions of a cuckold, a homosexual, a revolutionary have to the practice of literary criticism? Various answers are possible. It is debatable whether such emotional, sexual, political neutrality in fact exists, and still more debatable whether, if it does exist, such neutrality is desirable. For a work of literature to make its maximum impact, it should surely interact as fully as possible with its audience's experience of living, with their emotions and beliefs as well as with their aesthetic sensibility, and to ignore or underplay the importance of such elements is to risk missing a vital part of literature's appeal. However, it is not the critic's emotions or political beliefs which are at issue here, but rather the expectations and assumptions he brings to a work *as a critic*, and which differentiate him from the ordinary reader. For the critic has his own assumptions and prejudices which, though they may not be as deeply felt as sexual jealousy, or strongly-held political convictions, are by no means as natural and commonsensical as the assumption that one reads from left to right, or that a learned article is unlikely to modulate suddenly into pornography. They are aesthetic assumptions and prejudices, rather than emotional or political ones, but that does not necessarily mean that the judgements informed by them are any more likely to be objective.

What, then, are the assumptions and expectations which distinguish the critic from the ordinary reader, and which might be expected to give rise to a different kind of reading? How does the critic approach a work of literature? W. J. Harvey, in his study *Character and the Novel* (London, 1965), suggests that the critical approach is like a lens:

> It enables the critic to see certain things with greater precision and intensity—but only certain things. The same lens may distort or blur other objects; if it does and if the critic, because he has polished the lens, is reluctant to discard it, then he may either deny that the blurred object is not worth observing, or he may deny that the object is blurred at all. If one's critical lens, for example, focusses perfectly on the novels of Virginia Woolf, then one is quite likely not to think very highly of Arnold Bennett. Or again, if one thinks highly of Kafka, then one may try to applaud the novels of Dickens by stressing those elements in his work most assimilable to Kafka. The circumlocution office, for example, may seem less a satire on Victorian bureaucracy and more a symbol of man's helplessness in an alien and incomprehensible universe. To sum up then; a critical system or method may well deal clumsily and unjustly with older types of fiction, simply because of the radical differences wrought by modern experiment.
>
> (pp. 193–4)

Interestingly enough, Harvey is in fact defending the kind of traditional critical approach which, as we shall see, informs most critical discussion of Huxley. He argues that the critical techniques evolved in order to describe modern fictional experiments rapidly become not just descriptive, but prescriptive and normative, and that their use is therefore likely to distort the critic's understanding of more traditional fiction. But it is an argument which works both ways: if a modernist critical approach is detrimental to one's understanding of traditional fiction, then conversely, a traditional approach is likely to interfere with one's understanding of modern experiment. Once it is conceded that certain approaches work well only in certain cases, and that in others they may produce a distorting effect, then the validity of any universal standards is called into question.

As good an example as any of the kind of critical assumptions that are at work in Huxley's case is afforded by Bernard Bergonzi, in an article in *Encounter*.[1] Reviewing a number of critical studies,[2] his conclusion was that 'the writing of more books about Huxley . . . would be a work of supererogation'—a view with which, if one has read much Huxley criticism, it is possible to have a certain amount of sympathy. However, it is clear from the rest of the article that Bergonzi's main animus is directed, not against the critics, but at Huxley himself. If the studies in question are less than inspiring, it is not so much the fault of the critics as a reflection of the poverty of their subject matter—Huxley simply does not merit that much attention. And with this in mind, Bergonzi addresses himself to the question of Huxley's continued popularity, a phenomenon he finds somewhat puzzling. It is, he suggests, rooted in an implicit rejection of the aesthetic canons of modernism on the part of the reading public, who prefer 'simple narratives, wittily told, with a little action, a moderate amount of sex, and a good deal of talk that is clever without being difficult'. It is because he caters for this preference that Huxley remains popular, despite the clumsiness and unoriginality of his work when compared with 'the splendid aesthetic unity achieved by James or Conrad or Joyce or Virginia Woolf'.

Bergonzi is clearly aware of the divergence between the opinion of the reading public and his own as critic, but his explanation of it, his dismissal of Huxley as a sort of highbrow Harold Robbins, writing to a formula, seems more than a little complacent. He points to the mote in the public eye, while conveniently ignoring the beam in that of the critics—attacking Huxley and, by scarcely veiled implication, the public that reads him, yet at the same time remaining remarkably charitable to the authors of four conspicuously mediocre critical studies, perhaps because, unlike both Huxley and the public, those critics share his own assumptions about literature. Their conclusions, of course, are different: their estimation of Huxley's merit is considerably higher, for one thing; but that does not alter the fact that their terms of reference are essentially the same.

The most important basic assumption which both Bergonzi and Huxley's critics share is implicit in the comparison of Huxley's work to 'the splendid aesthetic unity' of James, Conrad, Joyce, and Woolf—the assumption being that these authors set standards by which the work of others can, and should be judged. They are the important, the major novelists of the twentieth century, the writers who may be said to have inherited the mantle of the great novelists of the past—of Austen, of Eliot, of Dickens. In their works can be found the structural complexity, the representational authenticity, the aesthetic unity which are the distinctive glories of the greatest fiction, and it is by their standards that Huxley is found wanting.

Now certainly, if one takes James, and Conrad, and Joyce, and Woolf to be what the modern novel is all about, it is difficult to rate Huxley very highly. One does not go to Huxley for Jamesian subtlety in the depiction of social interaction, or for the fine articulation of individual consciousness to be found in the works of Joyce and Woolf. Nor can it be said that 'aesthetic unity' is one of Huxley's strong points. Yet it is within precisely these terms of reference that Huxley's critics seek to prove that he *is*, after all, an important writer. Though without necessarily citing these particular authors by name, they uniformly attempt to demonstrate that Huxley's best work exhibits the same features which distinguish James and Conrad and the rest—that there *are* novels where he aspires to, and comes near to achieving the formal sophistication, the realism, the unity of the masters.

With such standards, it is perhaps only to be expected that the critics should tend to value most highly those of Huxley's works which approximate most closely to their idea of what fiction ought to be—those which are most complex, most realistic, most apparently sophisticated. Not *Brave New World*, therefore, and certainly not *Island*, but rather *Point Counter Point* and *Eyeless in Gaza*. Huxley's career is seen as describing a sort of parabola. As George Woodcock puts it:

> ... his novels grow in complexity and quality—with the special exception of *Brave New World*—as they proceed from *Crome Yellow* to *Eyeless in Gaza*, and decline just as steadily from that novel through *After Many A Summer* and *Time Must Have A Stop* to the splendidly intentioned bathos of *Island*.
>
> (*Dawn and the Darkest Hour*, p. 20)

Although there may be individual minor qualifications of Woodcock's view (some critics, for instance, believe *Point Counter Point* to be superior to *Eyeless in Gaza*), in general the emphasis of Huxley's critics is clear and uniform: it is in *Point Counter Point* and *Eyeless in Gaza* that Huxley shows himself to be a 'real novelist', and it is those two novels which constitute the apogee of the parabola traced by works as a whole.

Of course, there are other assumptions involved as well—assumptions about the admissibility of the didacticism which most critics see as one of the main defects in his later work, for example, or about the artistic merit of the forms of fantasy and satire which Huxley employed at the same time as producing 'real' novels—and these will be examined in detail in due course. But what needs to be asked first of all is whether the basic assumption about what the Novel is, or ought to be, is in fact a valid one. Should we judge modern fiction by the standards of James, Conrad, Joyce, Woolf? Are they really what the modern novel is all about? Or are we, in using such authors as a yard-stick, ignoring the changes and developments which the Novel has subsequently undergone?

Now it is not just because they correspond to the critics' notion of what the Novel should be that such writers are admired; they do not owe their reputation simply to the fact that their work is complex, realistic, aesthetically pleasing. What both critics and public alike respond to in the work of James, Conrad, and the rest is the fact that it displays in some measure the same kind of depth and power that is encountered in the work of the great writers of the past. Though their achievement may not be of quite the same order as that of George Eliot, of Shakespeare, of Chaucer, they are, at any rate, not disgraced by the comparison: their work does exert at least some of the force that characterizes the greatest art.

Nevertheless, it remains debatable whether their use as an example in the discussion of subsequent writers is, in fact, helpful. Although at the time they were writing theirs were the most interesting experiments, the most important achivements in fiction, a lot has happened since then. It is curious, for example, that in the half-century or so since no novelist or equivalent stature has emerged. There may be those who are capable of emulating certain aspects of their predecessors' achievements, but none whose work is consistently on the same level. While Nabokov, for instance, equals or even excels the earlier writers in sheer technical virtuosity, one looks in vain in his work for the kind of seriousness, for the moral dimension which their novels display. Though Graham Greene, in his evocation of atmosphere, his depiction of character, is very nearly the equal of Conrad, his subject matter is virtually always esoteric by comparison. To an even greater extent, he restricts himself to dealing with the fringes of society, the world of the exile, the criminal, the expatriate, while the crises and preoccupations of his characters, when compared to those of similar figures in Conrad's work, seem private, peripheral. Greene never aspires to the same kind of typicality, to describe the whole world, rather than a small part of it. One might multiply examples, but the real question is why there appears to be not a single modern English novelist who can seriously be said to rival the achievements of the greatest writers of the past.

Now unless one posits some kind of genetic freak, accepting that after a century and a half which produced Richardson, Fielding, Sterne, Austen, Eliot, Thackeray and Dickens, not to mention James, Conrad, etc., there should suddenly occur a prolonged fallow period when not one talent of that order emerges, one is obliged to conclude that something has happened to the Novel itself. Art forms change, after all; they come and go. If no-one has written a new *Middlemarch* or *Bleak House* in the last fifty years, neither has anyone produced an epic poem to rival *Paradise Lost* or a drama to rival *Hamlet*, and it would seem on the whole more reasonable to suppose that the Novel is undergoing a period of transition, with all its attendant problems for its exponents—just as poetry and drama have done several times since the days of Milton and Shakespeare—than to attribute a generally lower level of achievement to the fact that novelists have suddenly and collectively been bereft of ability.

The Novel, after all, is a literary form uniquely responsive to the world in which it exists. It imposes perhaps fewer constraints than any other, and novelists are probably the least preoccupied with formal rules and traditions of all literary artists. As a form, the Novel evolved to deal with a world that was changing more rapidly than ever before, and it was perhaps to its very looseness and flexibility that it owed its success; if one accepts this, that the Novel owes more to the world to which it constitutes a response than to the example of the past, then the present state of affairs becomes more readily explicable. The last fifty years—a period which has witnessed two world wars and the emergence of the threat of a third and final one, as well as the inauguration of an era of high technology and mass communications which even the nineteenth century could barely have conceived of—has seen the most drastic social change of all, and it is perhaps no wonder if in seeking to portray the world in which they live, novelists have to some extent lost their bearings. It is at least arguable that the accelerating pace of the changes in the world around them, outstripping even the capacity of the most flexible of literary forms to respond to them, has deprived novelists of the confidence in their medium which is prerequisite for the production of the finest art.

How far, then, can standards derived from the example of writers of the past usefully be applied to the discussion of more recent novelists? How relevant to the discussion of modern fiction is the 'splendid aesthetic unity' of James and the rest? Clearly there are numerous links between modern fiction and the fiction of the past—no novelist can read the work of the finest traditional exponents of the medium he or she has chosen to work in without being to *some* extent influenced by their example. Thus, leaving aside those modern novelists who continue to adopt a straightforwardly representational approach to the writing of fiction, even the work of the most experimental writers can be seen to have roots in an older tradition. The experiments of Joyce and Woolf in the registration of subjective individual consciousness, for example, can be interpreted as representing a further development of the increasingly sophisticated and complex rendering of character observable in the Novel throughout the nineteenth century. The virtuoso technique of a Nabokov or a Pynchon can be related not only to the idiosyncratic example of Sterne, but also to that fascination with the sheer mechanics of narrative art which is such a distinctive feature of the work of Henry James. To some extent the work of every novelist is an extension, a development, a deprivation from the work of the past: the question is whether the importance of this aspect remains constant at different periods in time.

For in a wider sense there is a dislocation from the fiction of the past. Examined more closely, it becomes increasingly apparent that the fiction of the last fifty years or so is not simply the same kind of fiction as that of the past, only written less well—it is actually different. While in the nineteenth century writers could be seen to be progressively extending and enriching the possibilities of the form, in more recent times neither conservative adherence to a traditional approach nor radical experiment have enabled novelists to avoid the loss and exclusion of many of the elements which have given the greatest novels their vitality. Although in certain respects the Novel may be said to have developed, its development since the time of Joyce and Woolf has almost invariably been a partial and selective one, involving the exaggeration of some features and the atrophy of others, and it is perhaps for this reason that modern experiment so often seems to indicate the *limitations* of the Novel rather than its possibilities.

Thus, among those who continue to write orthodox representational novels, the bewilderingly rapid pace of social change would seem to be reflected in the failure of their work to present any kind of picture of society in its totality. Graham Greene has already been cited as an example, but in the case of other writers the same kind of limitations are even more glaringly apparent. Whereas Eliot, Dickens, even Thackeray were able to convey the sense that the areas of experience which they described were part of a larger whole, one only has to list names more or less at random—Amis, Braine, Drabble, Sillitoe, Angus Wilson—to realize just how far modern novelists have lost their predecessors' comprehensive grasp of the workings of society. However incisive or entertaining their portrayals of the worlds of university, school, theatre, business, of working-class or middle-class experience may be, the reality they create invariably seems narrow, almost provincial. The worlds they describe, even more than those of Greene, are limited, isolated, and exclusive, rather than parts of an implied social totality; the problems which they examine are of local and specialized, rather than universal interest. While such novelists can still portray the areas of their own personal experience, they seem to have lost confidence in their ability to make sense of it in anything other than its own terms; instead of portraying a world which implies the existence of a whole society, they present only isolated groups of people within that society—as though society itself had become too large and complicated to be seen or understood in its entirety.

But if totality no longer appears to be compatible with a traditional representational approach to the writing of fiction, it is certainly one of the aspirations of authors such as Joyce and Virginia Woolf—writers whose links with past tradition in no way prevented them from pointing the way forward with their experiments. The difference, however, is that it is not a social totality which they seek to portray, but a totality of individual consciousness. And while it is perhaps the vitalizing effect of such an aspiration which lends their work its distinctive richness and sense of possibility, together with the kind of excitement which only the exploration of new horizons can generate, such an approach also has its drawbacks. For the preoccupation with subjective consciousness necessarily involves a retreat from the depiction of the social interaction which is normally inextricably bound up with the Novel's shape and form, and this in its turn causes certain structural problems. The traditional novel is usually structured around a narrative sequence, the portrayal of a chain of events which develops through the relationship and conflict of individuals both with each other and with their environment; social interaction, with its patterns of cause, effect, and combination, is the dynamic principle which not only generates the development of most novels, but also determines their shape. The individual consciousness, however, operates as much by free association as by logic, and also tends to reduce both the outside world and the various individuals it contains to mere functions of its own subjective awareness, with the result that the faithful depiction of such consciousness often entails abandoning the dynamic structuring principle of social interaction.

The major disadvantage of this is that if one's subject matter is inherently fluid, shapeless, and undramatic, it cannot generate its own form and order, which therefore have to be imposed from without. It is because of this that the ordering principles employed by Joyce and Woolf, such as the parallel with *The Odyssey* in *Ulysses*, or the time sequence in *The Years* often seems arbitrary and artificial. Because form is consciously imposed on content, instead of being at the same time derived from it, the unity of structure and subject matter which is characteristic of the greatest nineteenth-century novels becomes impossible. In addition, the subordination of the narrative element, which is what most immediately captures the reader's attention, makes the works in question considerably more difficult to read.

Where the predominant concern of the writer is technique, however, a very different problem arises. A fascination with the endless possible ways of telling a story can easily lead to a preoccupation with form which renders content almost an incidental. Fiction then becomes an elaborate game. But while games can be both entertaining and absorbing, the finest novels are always considerably more than a game: the sense of richness and possibility which the novels of Eliot or Dickens convey is partly the result of the reader's participation, not in a game, but in the novelist's own attempt to understand and make sense of the complexities of life. The complexities encountered in the work of Nabokov, of Pynchon, of Borges, on the other hand, seem rather to be *imposed* on the reader, deriving from the nature of the information which the author chooses to give or withold. While works such as *Pale Fire* or *The Crying of Lot 49* are undeniably impressive, they owe much of their effectiveness to the creation of artificial mysteries, and it is because the inventiveness involved seems to be exercised for its own sake, rather than for any particularly serious purpose, that they seem lightweight and insubstantial in comparison with the great novels of the past. Virtuosity can never wholly disguise the scantiness of what one has to say.

What we have, then, is a situation where, in trying to find

the kind of fiction most appropriate to the changing world around them, the modern novelist almost invariably loses more than he or she gains. On the one hand, the traditional approach which informed the greatest fiction of the past has become obsolete (it was E. M. Forster who confessed that 'one of the reasons I stopped writing novels is that the social aspect of the world changed so much. I had been accustomed to write about the old-fashioned world with its homes and family life and its comparative peace. All that went, and though I can think about the new world, I cannot put it into fiction');[3] while on the other, even the fiction of Joyce and Woolf reveals in embryo the problems inherent in more experimental approaches. In such a context, perhaps the most helpful critical approach is one which emphasizes fragmentation rather than continuity, concentrating on the way in which the various kinds of modern fiction *differ*, both from an older tradition and one another. When seen as a continuation of an older tradition, none of the work of the novelists so far mentioned really bears comparison with earlier achievements, a fact which unfortunately reinforces the critical tendency to regard the distinctive features of an older tradition as normative principles according to which fiction should be both written and judged. Seen as part of a process of fragmentation, however, the virtues as well as the flaws of modern fiction become more apparent; it becomes easier to appreciate the extent of the gains as well as the losses involved in each different approach to writing fiction. Once the divergent directions taken by the modern novel are seen as inevitable rather than merely regrettable, it becomes possible to examine more objectively just what each author has to offer, and at what expense.

Perhaps the real difficulty in the discussion of modern fiction is the whole conception of tradition; it is one which is very dear to the heart of literary critics, being imbibed almost unconsciously as soon as they begin studying literature instead of merely reading it. It offers both a structure and a context for the practice of criticism: within the concept of tradition it is possible to trace the influences at work on a variety of different authors, and at the same time to estimate their success relative to one another, their inventiveness in exploiting the possibilities of a common form. The danger of such a conception, however, is that it encourages the critic to stress those elements in an art-form that are most static. The notion of a tradition involves the assumption that a given form has certain distinctive features, and that these features will therefore be apparent in the work of the form's various exponents—which in turn leads those who conceive of such a tradition to give these features particular emphasis, laying stress on the success with which they are deployed by the individual artist.

Of course, where one is dealing with an art-form which is changing and developing only slowly, this presents few problems; where one has a number of artists working within the terms of broadly the same conventions over a long period of time, there are likely to be numerous grounds for useful comparisons to be made between them. But where the art-form in question is one like the Novel, whose characteristics have changed more drastically, and in a shorter space of time, than those of almost any other literary genre, the usefulness of an emphasis on the common and distinctive factors which the form exhibits is considerably lessened. Such an emphasis encourages static, rigid standards of judgement, leading the critic to look for the same kind of qualities in vastly different works, and to take insufficient account of the form's variety and fluidity. By attaching too much importance to the attainment of formal and artistic standards which the concept of a tradition encourages one to think of as the norm, or emphasizing the significance of the common factors in the work of authors of different periods at the expense of their differences, the critic runs the risk of failing to do justice to the extent of the novelist's responsiveness to the world he writes about.

Moreover, the notion of a fictional tradition, of a line of writers working within and developing the same form, lends itself to an accompanying emphasis on the operation of causal influence within that line. Simply because one is looking for common features in the work of different writers, it is easy to attach undue importance to them when they occur, and hence to over-estimate the extent of the direct influence of one novelist on another. The concept of a tradition transforms itself all too readily into that of a family tree, with every development being seen as rooted in what went before, rather than being related to the changing demands of the world which the novelist writes about. To exaggerate the influence of literary example, as the concept of tradition encourages one to do, is once again to risk losing touch with the way in which the Novel constitutes a response to the outside world.

Yet if it is the case that critics are perhaps too prone to allow themselves to be influenced by literary examples which prevent them from accepting an individual author on his or her own terms, are the perceptions of the ordinary reader necessarily any more reliable? If the critic is liable to judge a work or author according to inappropriate criteria, is the ordinary reader likely to fare any better? Generally speaking, the ordinary reader's response to a work of literature is probably more likely to be influenced by the kind of extraneous considerations—emotional, sexual, political, and so on—referred to earlier; in the case of a novel, too, the ordinary reader is probably liable to identify far more strongly with the characters than a critic would. The adolescent who believes that George Eliot's Rosamond is the image of the girl-friend who is giving him a bad time is unlikely to be very bothered by the fact that his reading of *Middlemarch* is not as objective as it might be. On the other hand, however, the ordinary reader's response is far less likely to be governed by the kind of preconceptions which a critic brings to the study of literature. Though he or she may well notice the same kind of aesthetic imperfections that offend the critic, I think it would be fair to say that if a work has other things going for it, such flaws are unlikely to present an insurmountable obstacle to the ordinary reader's enjoyment. If such a reader is less likely to be worried by formal and aesthetic considerations, he or she is also likely to be more interested in those aspects of a work which the critic habitually neglects—the ideas it contains, for example.

In Huxley's case, such an approach has certain advantages, simply because the characteristic weaknesses of his novels (schematic and often unconvincing characterization, or the frequent occurrence of intrusive and badly integrated didactic passages), are ones which are *particularly* antipathetic to the critic—that is, so antipathetic as to interfere with his capacity to perceive counter-balancing merits. The flaws typical of a Huxley novel are more than usually offensive to the critic's notion of what fiction ought to be (especially if he believes it ought to display the characteristic qualities of James, Conrad, Joyce and Woolf). The ordinary reader, on the other hand, would appear to be far less troubled by such things. In my experience, while the reader unschooled in the prejudices inculcated by the academic study of literature recognizes Huxley's faults (and recognizes that they *are* faults), he or she generally attaches far less importance to them. The wordiness of Propter in *After Many A Summer*, for example, or his dramatic irrelevance; the cardboard characterization of *Island*—these are faults which the ordinary reader would certainly acknowledge, but not at the expense of the recognition of the positive merits of the works in question. An interest in Huxley's ideas, a pleasure in particular felicities, in the excellences of individual scenes can often outweigh the flaws which the critic finds unpardonable.

In the terms of Harvey's metaphor, one might perhaps compare the perceptions of the ordinary reader to those afforded by the naked eye. The naked eye is more liable to be distracted from the scrutiny of a single object by extraneous considerations, and can hardly distinguish the fine detail perceptible through a correctly focussed lens, but it is nevertheless far more reliable in its perception of broad outlines than an incorrectly focussed one. The ordinary reader's response may not tell the whole truth about a work of literature, but it can provide a useful corrective in cases like Huxley's, where there are grounds for supposing that the lens employed by the critics is unsuitable.

The problem, then, is to find a critical approach which offers an extension, rather than a contradiction of the ordinary reader's. In the case of a writer like Huxley, whose appeal to the reader would seem to be as much intellectual as aesthetic, such an approach perhaps requires a broader awareness of the variety of ways in which we respond to literature; as Wayne Booth suggests, in *A Rhetoric of Irony* (Chicago, 1974)—

> We can admire a work because it is constructed unusually well (objective or formal criticism); because it expresses its author or his situation effectively (expressive); or because it does something to us with unusual force (rhetorical); or because it contains or conveys a true or desirable doctrine

(didactic, or ideological); or because it culminates or illustrates a tradition or initiates a fashion (historical).

Since every work *is* all of these—a construction, an expression, an action on its audience, an embodiment of beliefs, and a moment in history—a critic stressing any one interest will find all works amenable to his judgements. And there is no reason to expect in advance that judgements generated by any one of these five interests will agree or disagree with judgements coming from the others. While it often happens, for example, that a work everyone sees as 'well-constructed' also produces powerful effects on readers or expresses its author's deepest dreams, we often find that the historically important work, or the truest poetry, or the hard hitter may seem, to expressionist or objectivist critics, seriously deficient. The point is that we should expect different evaluations, each quite possibly valid in its own terms, when critics are dealing with radically different questions. (p. 207)

This already goes some way towards recovering a sense of the complexity of literature's effect on the reader; it is not, like music, a pure, abstract art—its language is either the same, or derived from that in which we conduct our everyday affairs; it represents and discusses the world we live in, and by virtue of that fact is involved in life, and judgements about life in a way that a 'purer' art such as music is not. And because the Novel is, of all literary forms, perhaps the most intimately bound up with the life of its audience, to judge it by purely aesthetic standards is to deny part of its appeal. We do not read novels simply in order to admire the artistry, the aesthetic unity displayed, but also because we wish to learn about the world, about ourselves, about our perceptions and judgements. The greatest novelists have always used the 'impurity' of the Novel as an art-form, the fact that it is more than a game of abstractions, to teach their audience, as well as move or dazzle it.

Through the recognition of the variety of possible approaches to literature, and of the different factors which play a part in determining our response to it, it becomes possible to do justice to those features of the Novel which are commonly ignored by critics who are primarily concerned with its aesthetic aspects.

To its inherent didacticism, for example: the intent to improve, to instruct has been an integral part of the Novel from its earliest beginnings, and yet it is an element which is seldom emphasized in critical discussion. In general, critics seem to be more interested in stressing the artistry with which Richardson, Fielding, Austen, or Eliot integrate their moral concerns into overall design than in discussing their evident intention to edify, as well as entertain their audience. It is easy, in the course of discussing such writers' artistic merits, to lose sight of the fact that their didactic purpose, their desire to inculcate what they saw as desirable moral standards, was one of the reasons *why* they wrote. In Huxley's case it is significant that the didacticism which is generally held to be one of the main causes of his artistic decline, is an element very much played down in the critical discussion of *Point Counter Point* and *Eyeless in Gaza* even though, as we shall see, it is as important, and indeed as intrusive a feature of those novels as it is in the works which are usually condemned for the overtness of their message. Because they conform more closely to standards of artistry acceptable to the critics, the didactic element is passed over. Yet didacticism is an integral part of Huxley's purpose, a crucial factor in determining the strategies he adopts as a novelist, and as such it needs to be examined more objectively than is possible in the context of a purely aesthetic discussion. And for such an examination to be possible, it has to be realized that a didactic design on the reader is not only one of the main purposes of many novelists, but also an important factor in their appeal, in the overall effect their work creates.

The importance of the historical aspect which Booth mentions is likewise minimized by the critic who judges by absolute formal and aesthetic standards. By taking it into account, however, it becomes possible to see Huxley's fiction as part of the process of fragmentation which seems to have been taking place within the Novel, rather than simply as representing a falling off from earlier, higher standards. Once Huxley is seen, not in the context of an older tradition, but as one writer among many, all of whom can be seen to be facing problems created by the changes taking place in the world around them, it becomes possible to appraise his particular experiments more rationally—as representing an honest attempt to deal with those problems, rather than as evidence of innate incapacity, or wilful failure to write like James or Conrad.

Of course, this is not to say that it is *wrong* to judge by aesthetic standards. It is one possible approach: the question is simply how helpful it is in a given instance, how much it allows the reader to get out of a particular work. Booth, as we have seen, leaves room for such standards, but suggests that there are others which are equally valid. Clearly it is *possible* to judge Huxley by the standards of James and the rest—his critics are proof of that—but it is surely more *helpful* to see him as part of a process, perhaps the sort of process which George Steiner suggests in *Language and Silence* (London, 1967):

> Following on the epic and verse drama, the novel has been the third principal genre of western literature. It expressed and, in part, shaped the habits and feelings and language of the western *bourgeoisie* from Richardson to Thomas Mann. In it the dreams and nightmares of the mercantile ethic, of middle-class privacy, and of the monetary-sexual conflicts and delights of industrial society have their monument. With the decline of these ideals and habits into a phase of crisis and partial rout, the genre is losing much of its vital bearing. (pp. 421–2)

Seen in the context of such a process, the extent to which Huxley's work constitutes a response to the world in which he lived becomes clearer. The whole course of his development as a writer can be seen as having been determined by the changing character of that response, for nearly all his formal experiments were dictated by his concern to find the vehicle most appropriate for articulating it. Thus, while he began by adopting the comic format of Peacock's novels as a model, his subject matter rapidly became increasingly alien to the world of Peacockian comedy, and it was in response to the conflicting demands of form and content that he turned to the bleaker realism of *Point Counter Point* and the harsher satire of *Brave New World*; as it became clear that the comic format was unsuitable for the articulation of the kinds of experience in which he was most interested, he began to experiment with other modes. Similarly, it was because he began to doubt whether a straightforward representational approach was an appropriate method of dealing with the horrors of contemporary reality that he deserted realism in favour of fantasy. This kind of process went on throughout his life—yet considered in purely aesthetic terms, his career takes on an entirely different aspect. The picture of a writer exploring the Novel's possibilities, searching for a form suitable for conveying an increasingly radical critique of the society in which he lived, is replaced by the concept of a parabolic development, first towards what might be regarded as the artistic norm, then away from it, yet without any real analysis or understanding of the processes involved.

However, it would be less than fair to suggest that Huxley's critics are wholly unaware of the relevance of other than aesthetic factors to the discussion of his work. Indeed, the majority of critical studies of his work seem to be permeated by an uneasy consciousness that Huxley doesn't quite fit in with the terms of reference employed. This consciousness is reflected in the persistent comparisons made with Peacock and Swift, neither of whom can really be seen as part of the tradition by whose standards Huxley is normally judged, and also in the frequent discussion of the fictional sub-genre of 'the novel of ideas'. Yet it is a consciousness which never actually leads to a reappraisal of the basic critical values involved. Jerome Meckier, in the introduction to his study *Aldous Huxley: Satire and Structure* (New York, 1969), talks of the difficulty of doing justice to the sheer variety of his 'many inter-related aspects', only to conclude rather lamely that the best approach is to treat him 'primarily as a novelist' (p. 4). Keith May opens his discussion of the author by making some play with the descriptive categories of Northrop Frye (pp. 9–10), (suggesting, for example, that his early works are not so much novels as 'Menippean Satire'), but fails to develop this approach; once again, the basic terms of reference remain unaffected.

Similarly, while one finds numerous references to Huxley's topicality, the acknowledgement that he was distinctively a writer of a particular time rarely seems to lead to any real insight. Woodcock suggests that Huxley is 'the social and moral critic; he is—in a way that still makes *Antic Hay* and *Point Counter Point* required reading for those who wish to understand the intellectual temper of the twenties—the historian of attitudes' (p. 87), but it is a suggestion which indicates a failure to *locate* Huxley in his period. His work is seen as reflecting the period, but only like a kind of sociological litmus paper; that he wrote about the world in which he lived is accepted, but the fact that the character of that world, and his attitude towards it determined the *way* he wrote is ignored. (And Woodcock is one of the more perceptive of Huxley's critics: Meckier, for example, is of the opinion that his 'phenomenal sensitivity to his times' is illustrated by the fact that *Point Counter Point* contains many references to Beethoven, having been written only a year after the centenary of Beethoven's death, and also examines a number of unhappy marriages 'in the very year when the rising divorce rate of the twenties reached its graphical peak' (p. 4). Given the notion of socio-historical context which that implies, one perhaps ought to be grateful that Meckier elected to treat Huxley 'primarily as a novelist'.)

What follows is, by contrast, an attempt not only to acknowledge the existence of artistic and historical factors which separate Huxley from an older fictional tradition, but also actually to take them into account in the examination of his work. In doing so I would hope to offer a reading of his work which bears at least some relation to the ordinary reader's experience of what he wrote, yet at the same time a reading which does not simply amount to an apology. In stressing the importance of recognizing the validity of his audience's response, it is not my purpose to direct attention away from a discussion of Huxley's artistry, but rather to show where it actually lies. For artistic excellence does not necessarily have to be defined in relation to a tradition, or the example of other writers—there are other, more basic tests. The definition of artistic excellence which I would offer is that it is a reflection of the extent to which individual excellences combine and fuse to create something greater than the sum of the individual parts. It is not the same thing as perfection, but rather a question of how far the fusing and connecting power is capable of over-riding whatever flaws a particular work may possess. While almost any writer can produce individually striking passages, what distinguishes the genuine artist is the ability to order his experience in such a way as to combine the various elements of a creation into a whole that is more than merely a collection of individual excellences.

The most rational approach to Huxley, it seems to me, is to begin by trying to ascertain what it was that he tried to do, and to follow by determining how far he succeeded in doing it. To judge an author by his success in realizing his own intentions in no way involves excusing his failures, or the adoption of more lenient standards; indeed, where the author is trying to do something new and different, it is perhaps the only way of judging him. It is in this context that I shall be arguing (among other things) that Huxley's artistry, his distinctive ordering capacity, is most evident in works such as *Antic Hay*, *Brave New World*, and *After Many A Summer*—evident, that is, to the extent that the overall effect more than compensates for the observable flaws. It is in these novels that Huxley's finest and most distinctive qualities are apparent, and it is through the recognition of the nature of these qualities that it becomes possible to perceive not only the individual excellences of other, less successful works, but also the real reasons for their failure—their failure by Huxley's own standards, rather than those of a tradition which he never aspired to emulate.

2

Huxley's Non-Fiction from *On the Margin* to *Themes and Variations*

Given the importance of the didactic element in Huxley's fiction, of the ideas his works contain, it might be as well to begin with a discussion of those ideas, of the things he was didactic *about*. In this context, perhaps the best starting point is provided by Huxley's non-fiction: throughout his life he produced a constant stream of non-fictional works—journalism, essays, criticism, popular philosophy, travel books—and in these it is possible to trace the development of his ideas without at the same time being distracted by the kind of aesthetic questions which arise from a discussion of their fictional presentation. Additionally, a study of Huxley's non-fiction serves to expose the fallacy of the widely held belief that he was first and foremost an intellectual, and that as a writer his main problem was that his artistic talent was not commensurate to his brilliance as a thinker—the kind of view implicit in David Daiches' remark (at the conclusion of a disparaging critique of Huxley's fiction) to the effect that 'his real genius is as an essayist. He has a gift for brilliant discussion' (*The Novel and the Modern World*, Chicago, 1939, p. 210).

In fact, the distinction between Huxley the thinker and Huxley the artist is hard to sustain. An examination of his non-fiction tends to reveal the presence of exactly the same strengths and weaknesses as are to be found in his novels. Far from showing him to be a high-powered intellectual, capable of brilliant insights for which he was unfortunately unable to find an appropriate fictional vehicle, such an examination would seem to indicate that the characteristics of his thinking are integral to his successes and failures as a novelist: it is his particular *kind* of perceptiveness which lends his novels their distinction, and it is the inadequacy of his understanding of the world in which he lived that is largely responsible for their shortcomings. At almost every point, in both his fiction and his non-fiction alike, the same kinds of preoccupation are in evidence.

Thus, in his first volume of essays, *On The Margin*, published in 1923, there is to be found the same note of underlying dissatisfaction which, as we shall see, characterizes his early fiction—a persistent sense of disillusion which, just as in his first three comedies, contrasts oddly with the wit and liveliness of his writing. Reflecting on Voltaire in the essay 'On Re-Reading *Candide*', for example, he wonders whether the maxim 'il faut cultiver notre jardin' is in fact applicable in a contemporary world which he regards as far more horrifying than that depicted in *Candide*:

> ... the only trouble is that the gardens of some of us seem hardly worth cultivating. The garden of the bank clerk and the factory hand, the shop-girl's garden, the garden of the civil servant and the politician—can one cultivate them with much enthusiasm? ... 'Il faut cultiver notre jardin'. Yes, but suppose one begins to wonder why? (p. 17)

A similar dissatisfaction with contemporary reality is manifested in the essay on 'Accidie', where he suggests that the mixture of sloth, boredom, and despair which in mediaeval times was regarded as a mortal sin has become one of the most characteristic features of the modern consciousness. What was once seen as an evil to be avoided, he argues, has come to be accepted as an inescapable fact of human experience or even (as in the case of Baudelaire), something to be gloried in. It is a contention which is illustrated in both *Antic Hay* and *Point Counter Point*, where accidie, a soul-destroying boredom, underlies the efforts of Mrs Viveash and Lucy Tantamount to find ever stronger excitements with which to stimulate their jaded appetites. Taking this as a premiss, Huxley goes on, in another essay, to contrast the active recreations of the past, when people were largely dependent on their own devices for entertainment, to the degenerate passivity of the twentieth century, where mass-entertainment provides 'a distraction which shall occupy the mind without demanding of it the slightest effort or the fatigue of a single thought' (pp. 49–50). Seeing a steady decline in people's capacity to do anything for themselves, he gloomily predicts that

> With a mind almost atrophied by lack of use, unable to entertain itself and grown so wearily uninterested in the ready-made distractions offered from without that nothing but the grossest stimulants of an ever-increasing virulence and crudity can move it, the democracy of the future will sicken of a chronic and mortal boredom. (p. 51)

It almost sounds like an early pre-vision of *Brave New World*.

Yet if the most significant feature of *On The Margin* is its mood of disillusion, *Along The Road* (1925), which describes Huxley's travels in Italy, displays a quality no less characteristic, and considerably more idiosyncratic: an almost obsessive concern with different points of view and alternative interpretations of the same phenomena. It is a concern motivated by what appears to be an exclusively scientific curiosity, for he never indicates any preferences for any of the different views which he catalogues with such fascination: it is the simple fact of their variety which interests him. Talking, for example, of his interest in old travel books, he suggests that their main appeal lies in the fact that the tastes of their authors are informed by different conditioning factors than are those of the modern traveller.

> They are morally wholesome reading too, these old books of travel; for they make one realize the entirely accidental character of all our tastes and our fundamental intellectual beliefs. (p. 42)

Huxley is both amused and stimulated by the tastes of earlier travellers in Italy—by Byron's liking for Canova, for example, or by Goethe's ignorance of the work of Giotto—while among the writers of travel books he singles out Veuillot as his favourite, simply because 'his prejudices were unlike those which most travellers bring with them to Italy) (p. 44).

Similarly, in the field of literature, Huxley expresses a liking for Balzac's *Les Paysans*, which he recommends for its sympathetic treatment of landlords, who are represented as

> . . . suffering incessant and unmerited persecution at the hands

> of the peasants. Balzac's reading of social history may not be correct; but it is at least refreshingly unlike that of most novelists who deal with similar themes. (p. 45)

The correctness or otherwise of a point of view does not appear to of much interest to Huxley; indeed, he seems to be doubtful whether any point of view can be termed correct—any single point of view is necessarily exclusive, implying a choice of one out of all the points of view possible—and at this juncture Huxley appears to shy away from exclusivity. Instead, he prefers to stand outside the world of exclusive interpretations, making no judgements, merely observing and relishing the variety of the possibilities he sees.

This preoccupation with the variety of subjective perceptions of reality, and a corresponding doubt as to the possibility of arriving at any objective truth which would make sense of them, was a longstanding one. As early as 1916 he had written a poem on the subject:

> A wagon passed with scarlet wheels
> And a yellow body, shining new.
> 'Splendid!' said I. 'How fine it feels
> To be alive, when beauty peels
> The grimy husk from life.' And you
>
> Said, 'Splendid!' and I thought you'd seen
> That wagon blazing down the street;
> But I looked and saw that your gaze had been
> On a child that was kicking an obscene
> Brown ordure with his feet.
>
> Our souls are elephants, thought I,
> Remote behind a prisoning grill,
> With trunks thrust out to peer and pry
> And pounce upon reality;
> And each at his own sweet will
> Seizes the bun that he likes best
> And passes over all the rest.[1]

This is frivolous enough, taken by itself, but the underlying seriousness of Huxley's concern with the variety of possible perceptions of reality becomes apparent when, in *Along the Road,* he comes to discuss something which really mattered to him at the time. What interested him most in the course of his Italian travels was art—the paintings, sculpture, architecture which he came across, and it is in his discussion of this that the genuineness of his belief in the necessity of recognizing the validity of different, even conflicting interpretations of experience becomes apparent. Our understanding of reality is necessarily partial and limited, he seems to suggest, yet to pretend otherwise is to make it even more so, since by accepting any one interpretation of reality as representing the whole truth about it, one automatically excludes a whole range of other interpretations which may in fact be no less valid. And in this connection he goes on to argue that the discussion of art is more than usually bedevilled by exclusive, and hence misleading theories:

> Most of our mistakes are fundamentally grammatical. We create our own difficulties by employing an inadequate language to describe facts. Thus, to take one example, we are constantly giving the same name to more than one thing, and more than one name to the same thing. The results, when we come to argue, are deplorable. For we are using a language which does not adequately describe the things about which we are arguing.
>
> The word 'painter' is one of those names whose indiscriminate application has led to the worst results. All those who, for whatever reason and with whatever intentions, put brushes to canvas and make pictures are called, without distinction, painters. Deceived by the uniqueness of the name, aestheticians have tried to make us believe that there is a single painter-psychology, a single function of painting, a single standard of criticism. (p. 133)

And because it is a single standard, Huxley believes that it necessarily omits from consideration all those works which do not conform to it:

> In every age theory has caused men to like much that was bad and reject much that was good. The only prejudice that the

ideal art critic should have is against the incompetent, the mentally dishonest, and the futile. The number of ways in which good pictures can be painted is quite incalculable, depending only on the variability of the human mind. Every good painter invents a new way of painting. Is this man a competent painter? Has he something to say, is he genuine? These are the questions a critic must ask himself. Not, Does he conform with my theory of imitation, or distortion, or moral purity, or significant form? (pp. 140–1)

The weakness of all exclusive theories of art, no matter how avowedly objective they may be, becomes apparent, in Huxley's view, as soon as one considers the way in which tastes and standards change over the years. As he observes, people who at the time of writing adored Matisse would very likely, two generations before, have worshipped Landseer.

Yet though his consciousness of the sheer variety which art displays makes for excellent and perceptive criticism, Huxley is at the same time very much aware that the knowledge of different kinds of art creates certain problems for the artist. In modern times there had suddenly become accessible to the creative artist an unprecedented variety of examples of different artistic traditions—primitive, modern, foreign, exotic—which, taken together, could easily have a confusing effect. The modern artist's very openness to different influences, in Huxley's view, makes it more difficult for him to find a form suitable to his talents, and to illustrate this contention, Huxley contrasts the classical tradition of architecture, from Brunelleschi to Nash, within which even the minor artist could achieve beauty, to the chaos of modern art, where genius is essential for the creation of a viable synthesis of the heterogeneous traditions to which the artist is exposed. It is a view which might be seen as having a certain relevance to the predicament of the modern novelist as well.

The variety and conflicting character of individual perceptions, whether of art or of life, is a theme which continues to preoccupy Huxley in *Jesting Pilate*, published in 1926, which gives an account of his travels in India and the Far-East. The travel journal, the reflections of a traveller on the undifferentiated mass of his experiences, provides perhaps one of the most naked examples of the mind's arbitrary processes of selection when confronted by the unfamiliar—what, out of all the new experiences afforded him by a strange land and culture, does the traveller decide is most worth talking about? It is a choice which is likely to tell as much about the traveller as about the country he has visited, and in Huxley's case the choices he makes are particularly interesting. For example, one of the things which he stresses very early on in *Jesting Pilate* is the disquieting tendency of travel to undermine one's most unquestioned assumptions—assumptions one has been conditioned into accepting for so long as to be no longer even aware of them. Soon after his arrival in India, Huxley attends the recital of a poem by Iqbal—a poem about Sicily, which is described as 'a Mohammedan's indignant lament that the island which had once belonged to the Musulmans should now be in the hands of infidels'—and his reaction is interesting:

> I did not say so at the time, but I must confess that the idea of Sicily as a Mohammedan country cruelly ravished from its rightful owners, the Arabs, struck me as rather shocking. For us good Europeans, Sicily is Greek, is Latin, is Christian, is Italian. The Arab occupation is an interlude, an irrelevance. True, the Arabs in Sicily were the best sort of civilized Arabs. But it is hard for us to regard them as anything but trespassers upon Theocritus's island—just as Italians before the war looked on the Trentino and other fragments of *Italia irredenta* —as a fragment of 'unredeemed Araby'. It was asking too much. For the first moment, I felt quite indignant—just as indignant, no doubt, as the poet had felt at the sight of those Mohammedan shores now polluted by the Christians. In the traveller's life these little lessons in the theory of relativity are daily events. (pp. 13–14)

It is this *kind* of experience which interests him on his travels: travel exposes one to the assumptions of a different culture, assumptions whose very unfamiliarity helps one to see one's own in a new light; and in *Jesting Pilate* he testifies to the invigorating effect of travel, challenging as it does one's ignorance and unthinking preconceptions:

> To travel is to discover that every body is wrong. The philosophies, the civilizations which seem, at a distance, so superior

> to those current at home, all prove on a close inspection to be in their own way just as hopelessly imperfect. That knowledge, which only travel can give, is worth, it seems to me, all the discomfort and expense of circumnavigation. (p. 214)

Interestingly enough, one of the features of Indian society which Huxley finds 'hopelessly imperfect' is its religion. While eastern religion may have its appeal for those who live in the materialist societies of Europe or America,

> ... to one fresh from India and Indian 'spirituality', Indian dirt and religion, Ford seems a greater man than Buddha... One is all for religion until one visits a really religious country. There, one is all from drains, machinery, and the minimum wage. (p. 214)

This scepticism concerning religion, and eastern religion in particular, is worth stressing, for although it might seem consistent with his general outlook at the time, it should be remembered that in *Those Barren Leaves*, published in the previous year, Huxley had seemed to suggest that mysticism and contemplation might offer a possible resolution to life's problems and contradictions. *Jesting Pilate*, in fact, reveals the extent of the critical consideration which Huxley gave to religious and mystical solutions before finally coming, as he was to do some ten years later, to accept them.

Huxley begins by criticizing eastern religion on the grounds that the 'true light' has manifestly failed to do anything to improve the appalling conditions under which the majority of Indians have lived from time immemorial. Sharing his train compartment with an unsavoury looking guru, he wonders what the guru actually *does* for his fellow man in return for all the adulation that is bestowed on him; whatever the answer might be (and he does not pretend to pass judgement) he decides that

> ... 'spirituality' ... is the primal curse of India, and the cause of all her misfortunes. It is this preoccupation with 'spiritual' realities, different from the actual historical realities of common life, that has kept millions upon millions of men content, through centuries, with a lot unworthy of human beings. A little less spirituality, and the Indians would now be free—

> free from foreign dominion and from the tyranny of their own prejudices and traditions. There would be less dirt and more food. (p. 109)

Religion, he goes on to suggest, 'is a luxury which India, in its present condition, cannot possibly afford' (p. 129).

Indeed, at this point in time, Huxley seems to see religion as offering no more than consolation for those unable to cope with reality:

> The Other World . . . the world of metaphysics and religion—can never be as interesting as this world, and for an obvious reason. The other world is an invention of the human fancy, and shares the limitations of its creator. (pp. 110–11)

Nevertheless, while he regards religion as being a consolatory invention, he acknowledges that religious and mystical disciplines can confer benefits on those who practise them—benefits which he proceeds to explain in rationalist terms:

> Every symptom of the trance, from the 'sence of presence' to total unconsciousness, can be produced artificially in the laboratory. The drug taker, the epileptic, the suddenly 'inspired' mathematician or artist, the experimental psychologist differ from the religious mystic only in their attitude towards the mystical experiences which they all equally share. Believing them to be divine, the religious mystic cultivates his experiences, makes use of them to bring him happiness and serenity. The others accept them as merely curious sensations like giddiness or the hiccoughs, and do not attempt, therefore, to make a systematic use of their experiences in the conduct of their lives. In this they are wrong.
>
> We are, I think, fairly safe in supposing that religious mystics do not in fact unite themselves with that impossible being, a God at once almighty and personal, limited and limitless. But that does not in any way detract from the value of mysticism as a way to perfect health. No man supposes he is entering into direct communion with the deity every time he does his Swedish exercises or cleans his teeth. If we make a habit of Muller and Pepsodent, we do so because they keep us fit. It is for the same reason that we should make a habit of

> mysticism as well as of moral virtue. Leading a virtuous and reasonable life, practising the arts of meditation and recollection, we shall unbury all our hidden talents, shall attain in spite of circumstances to the happiness of serenity and integration, shall come, in a word, to be completely and perfectly ourselves. (pp. 191–2)

Of course, the kind of mysticism with which Calamy experiments in *Those Barren Leaves*, lacking as it does any specifically religious bias, is by no means incompatible with the attitude expressed here. Nevertheless, the strictures on religion contained in *Jesting Pilate* turn out to be the prelude, not to further attempts to find an underlying unifying reality, but rather to a still more positive emphasis on life's variety. *Proper Studies*, published in 1927, shows signs of the growing influence of D. H. Lawrence, with whom Huxley had recently become friends. It was a friendship which was to have a profound, if only transitory effect on Huxley: after Lawrence's death he paid tribute to him in the following terms—

> To be with Lawrence was a kind of adventure, a voyage of discovery into newness and otherness. For, being himself of a different order, he inhabited a different universe from that of common men—a brighter and intenser world, of which, while he spoke, he would make you free.[2]

In Huxley's case, however, this freedom does not seem to have been an altogether unmixed blessing. Though he continues, as before, to point to the variety of life and its possible interpretations, in *Proper Studies* he appears to do so with intention of affirming not only that such variety exists, but also that it is good. Yet there is a rather strident tone to his affirmations, as though Huxley were protesting a little too much in an effort to convince himself of the validity of a stance which would seem to run counter to his deepest convictions.

> I find incomprehensible the state of mind of those to whom the flux of reality seems something dreadful and repulsive. Enjoying my bath in the flux, I feel no longing for the rock of ages or other similar eternal solidities. I am in my element in the current, and pant for no dry land. There are many people

who feel all the hymn-writer's distress at seeing 'change and decay in all around'. I am not one of them. Nor would it naturally occur to me to seek a comfort, of which I do not feel the need, from the contemplation of something changeless.
(p. 49)

This new, more positive approach seems to have had the effect of leading Huxley to take a more active interest in the affairs of the world. In *Proper Studies* (as in 'the proper study of mankind is man'), he attempts to subject the whole range of social organization—education, religion, government—to a dispassionate critique founded on true objectivity (which is founded in its turn on the acceptance of an infinite variety of subjectives), and also to suggest remedies for the various flaws in society which he sees as being the consequence of the widespread acceptance of unthinking assumptions.

Unfortunately Huxley's grasp of the mechanisms of society is far less sound than his understanding of art or religion: with the exception of his essay on education, which contains a powerful attack on traditional teaching methods, both his critique of social institutions and his suggestions as to how they might be improved are decidedly erratic. In the essays on 'The Idea of Equality' and 'Political Democracy', for example, he sets out to demolish the myth that all men are equal, on the grounds, as might be expected, of human variety: one cannot say that all men are equal when they are, in fact, so manifestly unequal in their capacities. Nevertheless, he appears to be arguing against a largely imaginary opposition, attacking a conception of equality which, in modern times at least, would be held only by the crudest kind of behaviourist. Denouncing the 'myth' that all men are of identically equal capacities, Huxley virtually ignores all the other connotations which the word 'equality' possesses, and ends up falling into the same trap as the hypothetical art-critic in *Along the Road*—that of 'giving the same name to more than one thing, and more than one name to the same thing'. Because there is only one word, 'equality', Huxley deceives himself that there is a single concept which corresponds to it. And since the concept which he chooses to discuss is the equality of ability, all the other kinds of equality, of rights, of opportunity, are passed over; the result is a confused discussion from which there finally emerges the suggestion that the ideal form of government would be an aristocracy based on merit.

What is interesting about Huxley's concept of an ideal form of government at this point in time is the light which it throws on his subsequent Utopian novels: *Brave New World*, where resistance to an undesirable society is seen as doomed to failure, and *Island*, where the take-over of a desirable society by the dictatorship of Rendang is shown as virtually inevitable. For Huxley sees society and its government as existing in a series of essentially static states; the mechanics of social change, which bring about the transformation from one static state to the next, are regarded as being almost wholly fortuitous. Human beings are, by nature, uninterested in politics, and it is only when

> ... government becomes so intolerably bad that it seriously affects the interests of each individual, when it oppressively robs men of the comfort, the prosperity, the personal privileges to which they have been brought up to think themselves entitled... (p. 143)

that people react by taking 'a passionate interest in law-making'. This is seen as being a general rule:

> In different societies governments reach the oppression point at different times; but when the point is reached, the reaction, in the shape of intense political interest, is always the same. When the particular grievances which brought dissatisfaction to a head have been remedied, the sustained interest in politics dies down. (p. 144)

It is perhaps because he sees the answer to this cycle of interest and apathy, this oscillation between static states, as being the creation of a static state which is desirable, i.e. meritocracy, that he fails to consider that it too might have its own dynamic which would ultimately lead to change: the possibility that an aristocracy based on merit might be less than fully sympathetic to the needs and desires of the less meritorious, or that it might stratify society to the extent where further accesses of merit from below might be seen as a threat to the ruling elite is never even discussed.

Human nature, too, is seen as static and unchanging:

> The doctrine of Original Sin, in the shape of anti-social tendencies inherited from our animal ancestors, is a familiar and observable fact. Primitively, and in a state of nature, human beings were not, as the eighteenth-century philosophers supposed, wise and virtuous: they were apes. (p. 19)

For this reason, it is a mistake for human beings, when they *do* seek to change society, to aspire to impossible ideas—

> For example, the ideal of communism in property and women is an impossible ideal . . . the average man has at all times been keenly interested in private property and marriage, and no ideal which denies the existence of such an interest can be pursued with profit. (p. 262)

The unregenerate nature of humanity has to be taken into account by anyone who seriously wishes to understand society, and it is perhaps for this reason that Huxley suggests (far cry from *Island*!) that 'there must be discipline, a hierarchy, the subjection of many and the dominion of few' (p. 20).

But if Huxley's analysis of society and its institutions is often confused, his suggestions for possible improvements are considerably more than that. Among the reforms he proposes is the institution of an examination system for parliamentary candidates, together with corresponding intelligence tests for the voters, while among the dangers to be avoided is the prospective degeneration of the human race caused by faster breeding amongst the lower orders of society. He cites with approval a book entitled *The Need of Eugenic Reform*, by one Major Leonard Darwin, who maintained that the best indicator of eugenic fitness was wage-earning capacity:

> We regard as desirable the qualities that make for social success; these qualities must therefore be fostered. Major Darwin has elaborated a scheme for the systematic discouragement of fertility among the ill-paid and its encouragement among the well-paid. I need not go into the details here.
> (p. 279)

One would hope not.

In *Do What You Will* (1929), however, although the feeling

that Huxley is somehow writing out of character remains, there is far less political and social theorizing. Instead, Huxley appears in the guise of a 'Life-worshipper', given to such pronouncements as 'The greatest sins, perhaps the only sins, are the sins against Life' (p. 151). (Life is frequently written with a capital L.) Throughout *Do What You Will*, in fact, Huxley seems to apportion praise and blame to the various historical figures he discusses according to their attitude towards Life: at times one is embarrassingly reminded of Burlap's editorial policy in *Point Counter Point*. Baudelaire, Pascal, St Francis, and above all, Swift are roundly condemned for their refusal to accept the realities of Life, whereas Rasputin, whom Huxley erroneously believed to be an advocate of salvation through the vigorous practice of sin, is commended for his Life-enhancing outlook.

Yet Huxley's life-affirmation is not simply a pose: essentially he still argues that it is important to do justice to the infinite variety present in every human being and in the world they inhabit, rather than passively accepting some limiting account of what human beings ought to be, or of the world they ought to inhabit. In his essay on Pascal, Huxley laments that

> . . . such is man's pride, such his intellectually vicious love of system and fixity, such his terror and hatred of life, that the majority of human beings refuse to accept the facts. Men do not want to admit that they are what in fact they are—each one a colony of separate individuals, of whom now one and now another consciously lives with the life that animates the whole organism and directs its destinies. (p. 234)

Likewise, in 'One and Many', he argues persuasively in favour of the merits of polytheism over the worship of a single god, inasmuch as it encourages human beings to feel reverence for more aspects of experience, to see divinity as inherent in nature, rather than as a remote authority figure.

With these concerns in mind, Huxley goes on to reiterate the dissatisfaction with contemporary society which he had expressed in *On the Margin*, with the difference that he now begins to suggest why it is that the life of the individual in modern society is so unsatisfactory:

> In a society like ours the successful are those who live intensely with the intellectual and voluntary side of their being, and as little as possible with the rest of themselves. The quietly Good Citizens are those who live as little as possible on any plane of existence. While those who live fully and harmoniously with their whole being are doomed to almost certain social disaster. (p. 36)

Society permits the individual to realize only a fraction of his or her potential, to live only a partial, shoddy existence. In 'Holy Face' and 'Silence is Golden' Huxley once again condemns modern popular culture for its encouragement of a degenerate passivity, and sees it as symptomatic of a lifeless and sterile civilization, while in his essays on 'Revolutions' he remarks that 'the real trouble with the present social and industrial system is not that it makes some people very much richer than others, but that it makes life fundamentally unlivable for all'. (pp. 224–5)

Huxley's discussion of revolution sheds further light on his conception of the mechanisms of social change: he sees revolution not so much as a struggle for power, as a manifestation of a deep-seated human urge for justice:

> In the depths of the human soul is something we rationalize as a demand for justice. It is an obscure perception of the need for balance in the affairs of life; we are conscious of it as a passion for equity, a hungering after righteousness. An obvious lack of balance in the outside world outrages this feeling for equity within us, gradually and cumulatively outrages it, until we are driven to react, often extravagantly, against the forces of disequilibrium. (pp. 216–17)

It is an interpretation which, seeing political unrest as proceeding from a latent conception of ideal harmony, is essentially spiritual in character, and also intensely individualistic: revolution is seen, not as the result of an organized struggle, but as being in some mystical way the outcome of the simultaneous arousal of a passion for justice among a mass of individuals.

At this stage, however, Huxley shows no inclination to rationalize his tendency to see society and politics in individual and spiritual terms into any kind of specifically religious philosophy. He continues to criticize religion on the grounds that it imposes a limiting, and consequently falsifying interpretation on reality, and though he admits the possibility of obtaining some kind of religious insight or illumination, he sees this as being very difficult to integrate with the experience of everyday living:

> ...even if it were not so difficult to arrive at the vision of what philosophers and mystics assure us, for reasons, however, which can never be wholly convincing, to be the Truth; even if it were easy for us to pass in the spirit from the world of distinctions and relations to that of infinity and unity—we should be no nearer to being able to *live* in that higher world. For we live with our bodies; and our bodies grossly refuse to be anything but distinct and relative. (p. 64)

Religious insight is useful only insofar as it increases the intensity of one's awareness, not if it interferes with one's capacity to recognize other aspects of reality.

In fact, almost anything that is conducive to living more intensely meets with Huxley's approval, even revolution:

> The hopes of revolutionaries have always been disappointed. But for anyone who values life as life, this is no argument against attempting revolutions. The faith in the efficacy of revolutions (however ill-founded events may prove it to be) is a stimulus to present living, a spur to present action and thought. In the attempt to realize the illusory aims of revolution, men are induced to live more intensely in the present, to think, do, and suffer with a heightened energy; the result of this is to create a new reality... (p. 249)

Nevertheless, this insistence of the importance of living as fully and intensely as possible, of doing justice to the full variety and range of human potential can be seen as a logical development of the characteristically Huxleian view that there is too much to life for it to be encompassed by a single, limiting interpretation of reality. The sense of strain caused by Huxley's rather self-conscious adoption of what he conceived of as a Lawrentian position only really becomes apparent when his emulation of Lawrence leads him to argue against what would seem to be his own instincts, as for example when he launches a violent attack on Swift, denouncing his pathological distaste for the body, and the jaundiced idealism it implies, as signs of an inability to come to terms with the realities of life. For Huxley's own temperamental affinities were closer to Swift's than to those of Lawrence. His own novels consistently display a revulsion from physical pleasure, and a fascination with disease, death, and suffering which is certainly more akin to the world of Swift than to that of *The Rainbow* or *Women in Love*. The fact that Huxley was later to acknowledge Swift as the chief literary influence on both *Brave New World* and *After Many A Summer* is perhaps a fair indication of just how far Lawrence's example led him to the adoption of attitudes to which he was temperamentally unsuited; certainly, the spectacle of Huxley attacking a writer who, more than anyone, was his mentor, is both surprising and more than a little distasteful.

But the influence of Lawrence was relatively short-lived: of his novels, only *Point Counter Point*, with its exceedingly thinly veiled portrait of Lawrence in the guise of Mark Rampion, is really affected by it; while in the works that succeed *Do What You Will* there is apparent a reversion to more characteristic preoccupations. In *Music at Night* (1931), his essay on 'Tragedy and the Whole Truth' argues that tragedy, in the interests of achieving an effect of grandeur and nobility, distorts reality by the exaggeration of certain aspects of it, along with the exclusion of others; Huxley expresses a preference for authors like Chaucer and Fielding who, by contrast, tell us all the truth, including the all-too-human details which the tragedian would be likely to omit, as detrimental to the effect he was seeking to achieve. 'On Grace' repeats Huxley's attack on the idea of equality, while 'Ethics in Andalusia' contains yet another expression of Huxley's insistence on the relative nature of moral standards, describing the notoriety, in Granada, of a play which would seem quite blameless to an English audience, but which seems, in the moral atmosphere of a Catholic society, thoroughly scandalous. He also notes how the particular taboos and conditioning of Western society have led to the attachment of a far greater social stigma to sexual immorality than, say, to avarice and gluttony, despite the fact that they are all sins which, in theory at least, the Christian religion condemns equally. But perhaps most characteristic of all is the essay entitled 'And Wanton Optics', in which he contrasts the scientist's way of looking at the world with other modes of perception. It is a contrast which he finds faintly disquieting:

> We live in a world of non-sequiturs. Or rather, we would live in such a world, if we were always conscious of all the aspects under which any event can be considered. But in practice we are almost never aware of more than one aspect of each event at a time. Our life is spent first in one watertight compartment of experience, then in another. The artist can, if he so desires, break down the bulkheads between the compartments and so give us a simultaneous view of two or more of them at a time. So seen, reality looks exceedingly queer. Which is how the ironist and the perplexed questioner desire it to look.
>
> (pp. 40–1)

'The ironist and perplexed questioner' is in many ways a fair description of the author of *Brave New World*, which appeared in 1933, and it is interesting to note how many of its themes are first adumbrated in *Music at Night*. In 'Obstacle Race' he discusses Stendhal's *Armance*, contrasting the fierce emotions of Stendhal's lovers, whose passions are inflamed by the obstacles they have to overcome, with the jaded appetites of the modern lover, to whom everything is permitted. In 'Liberty and the Boundaries of the Promised Land', he speculates on the likelihood of a future where machines will assure everyone of unlimited freedom and leisure, at the same time gloomily forecasting that such an eventuality would prove to be a disaster rather than a blessing, since no-one would know how to make use of the freedom and leisure they had acquired. And in 'History and the Past' he develops his favourite theme, demonstrating the different ways in which people have interpreted history in order to make the facts fit in with their own assumptions. The same applies to prophecy, too: Utopias are only a reflection of the assumptions current at the time when they were written; thus the Utopias of the twentieth century are no longer based on the assumptions of More or Morris, but on the very latest scientific and eugenic theories. It is these which inform H. G. Wells' visions of the elitist societies of the future, and which prompt Huxley himself to suggest that

> . . . we can imagine our children having visions of a new caste system based on differences in native ability and accompanied by a Machiavellian system of education, designed to give members of the lower castes only such instruction as it is profitable for society at large and the upper castes in particular that they should have. (p. 152)

All of which coalesces in *Brave New World*, first intended as a parody of the Wellsian Utopia, which depicts a society where sexual permissiveness, technological development, selective breeding, and the debasement of popular culture are carried to the limit, creating a world of insipid, conformist mediocrity.

But if *Music at Night* anticipates many of the concerns of *Brave New World*, Huxley's next non-fictional work, *Beyond the Mexique Bay* (1934), is chiefly remarkable for its discussion of war, which in many ways foreshadows the pacifism of *Eyeless in Gaza*. War, or the threat of war, was one of the overriding concerns of the 1930s, and for Huxley it was the symbol of all that was foolish and irrational in society. In the course of his travels in Central America, which are described in *Beyond the Mexique Bay*, one of the most important questions he asks himself is why an area which had known almost uninterrupted peace while subject to the Spanish Empire should have been plagued by incessant wars ever since being broken up into independent capitalist nation states. It was a question he found hard to answer: capitalists, so he reasoned, must surely be aware that war, harming trade as it did, was not worthwhile; equally, the rulers of capitalist countries must surely realize that the power of the small ruling oligarchy could only be threatened by war, which brought with it the risk of the overthrow and destruction of its power base, the nation. In the end, his conclusion is that war is caused by the fact that 'all capitalist rulers are bound by a theology of passion' (p. 77)—once again, an essentially spiritual explanation of a social phenomenon.

War, in fact, was something which Huxley simply could not understand. It is perhaps to his credit that he was unable to comprehend *why* people fought—a sign of rationality, of civilization—but this lack of comprehension is also symptomatic of a wider failure of understanding. Because he saw war as irrational, he was unable to see any rational component in it at all, and hence tended to ignore the extent to which comprehensible political and economic factors also played a part in causing wars. To Huxley, the irrational was not an extension from the rational, but something wholly alien; people fought wars, not because they were unable to see beyond the logic of the social and economic pressures which led them to fight, but because they were in the grip of some incomprehensible passion. Yet, incomprehensible though it was, it was nevertheless a fact of human nature, and hence something to be taken into account by anyone wishing to suggest rational ways of improving society. And it is when Huxley comes to make such suggestions, discussing in a rational manner something which he does not really understand, that the limitations of his approach become most apparent. Rational his suggestions may be, but they are at the same time informed by a curious kind of silliness, which perhaps reflects just how far his rational approach is out of touch with the realities of the subject he is discussing.

Thus, having decided that war has its roots in mankind's irrational, and frequently anti-social, emotional impulses, he concludes that the way to prevent wars is by dealing with these impulses at their source, by setting up

> . . . a World Psychological Conference, at which propaganda experts should decide upon the emotional cultures to be permitted and encouraged in each state and the appropriate mythologies and philosophies to accompany these emotional cultures. (p. 86)

The cure for was is something to be imposed on mankind by the experts, by those capable of seeing what is best for their fellow men. To deal with humanity's irrational instincts, a new culture must be artificially contrived, while to deal with recalcitrant individuals—those who reveal powerful anti-social impulses, such as the desire to dominate other people—Huxley suggests that

> . . . one of the minor tasks of our conference will be to provide born adventurers and natural slave-drivers with harmless and unharmable blackamoor Ersatzes, human but satisfying Putomayo substitutes. (p. 105)

Paternalistic, patronizing in its attitude to the mass of humanity who don't know what's good for them, Huxley's philosophy is hardly distinguishable from that of Mustapha Mond in *Brave New World*.

Seeing society as a mass of infinitely variable individuals, and history as no more than the chronicle of their random activities, Huxley regards the widespread adoption of particular beliefs at particular stages in history as simply fortuitous coincidence—the clear implication being that history is not so much a process of development, as a succession of passing and unrelated fashions. The ideas of Luther, say, or Marx, are only influential because they happened to catch the fancy of large numbers of individuals (who might equally well have been attracted by something else); ideology is the product of a simple coincidence between propaganda and circumstance. In *The Olive Tree* (1936), he suggests that

> The mechanism of successful propaganda may be roughly summed up as follows. Men accept the propagandist's theology or political theory, because it apparently justifies and explains the sentiments and desires evoked in them by the circumstances. The theory may, of course, be completely absurd from a scientific point of view; but this is of no importance so long as men believe it to be true. Having accepted the theory, men will work in obedience to its precepts. . . (p. 15)

Political theory and theology finally become practically interchangeable: in the essay on 'Justifications' Huxley reiterates the view that ideology is simply the rationalization of fortuitous desires—

> A complete history of justification would be, to a great extent, identical with a history of thought. Most political, ethical, and even cosmological systems have been essentially justificatory. They are the work of men in rebellion against the existing system, or of the scrupulous, or of the defenders of orthodoxy. (p. 153)

The significant thing is that Huxley so far identifies the political and the theological that he seems to regard his statement as being adequately illustrated by examples which are exclusively of religious eccentrics who used theology to justify sexual licence.

Much the most interesting aspect of *The Olive Tree*, however, is the discussion of literature contained in the essay 'Writers and Readers', where Huxley examines the nature of the relationship between the writer and his public, investigating both the function of literature and its effect. Huxley divides what he calls 'non-scientific literature' into three main categories. The first is that of mindless entertainment, literature which exists merely 'to fill a gap of leisure, to kill time and prevent thought, to deaden and diffuse emotion'—the kind of writing which prompts him to reflect that 'reading has become, for almost all of us, an addiction, like cigarette smoking' (p. 2). Next comes literature which is designed to modify the reader's opinions, to change the social, political, economic, and moral thinking of its audience, and hence to alter their patterns of behaviour—in other words, propaganda. And finally there is imaginative literature, ostensibly purer and more disinterested, but which can often condition the reader even more effectively into sharing the author's assumptions.

Imaginative literature does not, in Huxley's opinion, offer any kind of objective account of reality: it interprets reality according to the assumptions, even prejudices of the author, selecting, excluding, and almost inevitably distorting. While, in *The Olive Tree,* he distinguishes between propaganda and imaginative literature, he nevertheless argues that the latter may be no less partisan, and it is this contention which he goes on to develop in *Ends and Means*, which was published in 1937.

> Literary example is a powerful instrument for the moulding of character. But most of our literary examples . . . are mere idealizations of the average sensual man. Of the more heroic characters the majority are just grandiosely paranoiac; the others are good, but good incompletely and without intelligence; are virtuous within a bad system which they fail to see the need of changing; combine a measure of non-attachment in personal matters with loyalty to some creed, such as Fascism or Communism or Nationalism, that entails, if acted upon, the commission of every kind of crime. There is a great need for literary artists as the educators of human beings.

> Unfortunately most literary artists are human beings of the old type. They have been educated in such a way that, even when they are revolutionaries, they think in terms of the values accepted by the essentially militaristic society of which they are members. (pp. 209–10)

This, with its talk of non-attachment and militarism, is no longer the language of the dispassionate ironist or of the life-worshipper, but of a man converted to a firm belief in pacifism and mysticism. Mysticism, in fact, is in some ways the logical conclusion of Huxley's individualism: individual enlightenment is seen as being of supreme importance, the one thing from which all else follows. Increasingly, Huxley seems to be saying that it is impossible for anyone who has not first achieved enlightenment to do good in a wider sphere, and that the actions of the unenlightened, however well-intentioned, can lead only to a compounding of the problems which they try to solve. It is an essentially inward-looking philosophy: truth lies within the individual, and its pursuit is scarcely compatible with any kind of involvement in the world; the enlightened man is 'non-attached', immune to the lures and demands of an unenlightened society.

Nevertheless, 'non-attachment' was an ideal which Huxley was anxious to reconcile with his continued to desire to try to improve the world in which he lived, and *Ends and Means*, which Huxley described as 'a practical cookery book for reform' addresses itself primarily to social, rather than individual problems. Unfortunately, however, Huxley's recipes are jumbled to the point of incoherence, perhaps because of an underlying contradiction in his thinking which he never really resolves. Huxley's main problem is that, despite his conviction of the importance of attaining individual enlightenment, he sees human nature as something given and unalterable, a factor which will always remain an obstacle in the path of all attempts to improve society. Thus, in the chapter on 'The Efficacy and Limitations of Large Scale Social Reform', Huxley first of all suggests that 'economic and political reform is a branch of what may be called preventive ethics', in that such reform can help to create a society where the possibilities for doing evil are minimized. However, since human nature is unalterable, such reforms will only succeed in deflecting evil into new channels: humanity's evil instincts are a constant, varying only in the way in which they express themselves. Because of this, Huxley argues that political reform is not enough—human nature must be changed first. But human nature is something given and unalterable. . .

Unable to decide whether or not human nature *can* be affected, uncertain as to whether or not social reform serves any useful purpose, Huxley's discussion of social problems in *Ends and Means* is inevitably confused. Although the list of contents gives a clear enough indication of the topics to be discussed, in the body of the text Huxley darts back and forth, raising all manner of issues, but never really dealing with any of them. Lacking any kind of organizing framework for his observations, he also seems to lack any sense of proportion with regard to them, consistently failing to distinguish between those of his arguments which are relevant and those which are merely specious. Thus we suddenly find him, for example, upholding the supreme necessity of sexual continence:

> . . . I have described the kind of political, economic, educational, religious and philosophical devices that must be used if we are ever to achieve the good ends that we all profess to desire. The energy created by sexual restraint is the motive power which makes it possible for us to conceive those desirable ends and to think out the methods for realizing them. (p. 318)

Uncertain as to how society works, or indeed, as to whether it can be made to work at all, Huxley is continually liable to seize on some implausible hypothesis and make it the cornerstone of his generalizations.

Yet out of the confused arguments of *Ends and Means* there emerges a fairly clear expression of the basically individualist ideal which was to set the tone both for *After Many A Summer* and for much of his subsequent non-fictional writing. However confusing the affairs of the world might be, there was still an ideal of individual behaviour on which those who aspired to enlightenment could model themselves. But it was not a merely human ideal: human values, in Huxley's view, were ephemeral, transient.

> Every age and class has had its ideal. The ruling classes in Greece idealized the magnanimous man, a sort of scholar-and-gentleman. Kshatriyas in early India and feudal nobles in mediaeval Europe held up the ideal of the chivalrous man. The *honnete homme* makes his appearance as the ideal of the seventeenth century gentleman; the *philosophe*, as the ideal of their descendants in the eighteenth century. The nineteenth century idealized the respectable man. The twentieth has already witnessed the rise and fall of the liberal man and the emergence of the sheep-like social man and the god-like Leader. Meanwhile the poor and downtrodden have always dreamed nostalgically of a man well-fed, free, happy and unoppressed. (p. 2)

And to these various ideals, he contrasts the permanent and unchanging vision of the mystics:

> . . . among these freest of human beings there has been, for the last eighty or ninety generations, substantial agreement in regard to the ideal individual. The enslaved have held up for admiration now this model of a man, now that; but at all times and in all places, the free have spoken with only one voice. (p. 3)

It is this voice which we find recorded in *The Perennial Philosophy* (1946): the voice of those individuals who have achieved their own salvation through the apprehension of an absolute and trenscendent reality. The confused social analysis of *Ends and Means* is replaced by the mystic's vision of ultimate reality. With the outbreak of the Second World War, Huxley had succumbed to a profound despair about the possibility of achieving anything at all on other than an individual basis, and it is significant that prior to *The Perennial Philosophy* he had produced a work, *Grey Eminence*, which amounts to an extended illustration of his conviction of the impossibility of combining enlightenment with action. *Grey Eminence* (1941) is a historical study of Père Joseph, the Capuchin monk who became Cardinal Richelieu's adviser, and it tells the story of a man who, in attempting to combine spiritual life with a political career, succeeded only in jeopardizing his own mystical insights, while at the same time assisting in the prosecution of the appalling barbarities of the Thirty Years War. Even for the enlightened, social action was ultimately futile, even dangerous. As Huxley put it, in a letter to Kingsley Martin written as early as 1939,

> Religious people who think that they can go into politics and transform the world always end up by going into politics and being transformed by the world (e.g. the Jesuits, Père Joseph, the Oxford Group). Religion can have no politics except the creation of small-scale societies of chosen individuals outside and on the margin of essentially unviable large-scale societies, whose nature dooms them to self-frustration and suicide.[3]

The Perennial Philosophy is an anthology of mystical writings, the words of those sufficiently enlightened to have achieved a perception of the unity which underlies the infinite variety of appearances, a glimpse of the truth which Calamy had so tentatively sought in *Those Barren Leaves*. This truth, Huxley believed, could be grasped only by those who undertook the difficult task of 'dying to self', and who were capable of the discipline required in order to perceive the illusory and irrelevant nature of the merely material world. It is a belief which is entirely concerned with the modification of the individual nature, the nature which he had once regarded as unalterable.

For Huxley the only real problems were ultimately individual ones, and in discussing these he seems able to talk with far greater clarity and credibility than when dealing with the more confused affairs of society. Seeking the cool, impersonal unity of transcendent reality, Huxley no longer speaks in the strained tones of the Life-worshipper, while the silliness which marred much of his discussion of social problems also disappears. Although at this time, as he tells us in *The Doors of Perception*, mystical perception was still a closed door to him, his discussion of it gains in force from his evident conviction that such experience was both possible and worthwhile. While bathing in 'the flux of reality' and extolling the infinite variety and disunity of life, there seemed to be something both false and limited about the positive attitudes that Huxley felt called upon to adopt. In

The Perennial Philosophy, by contrast, there is nothing insincere about his aspirations; nor does the unity which he seeks, implying and containing as it does all manner of variety, involve any feeling of limitation.

Even so, Huxley's convictions do not seem to have been sufficient to prevent him from periodically turning his attention back to worldly matters. Despite his declaration that 'religion can have no politics', he also seems to have been convinced that

> The world would be even more horrible than it actually is, if it were not for the existence of a small theocentric minority working along quite other lines than the anthropocentric majority. (*Letters*, p. 470)

Quite how the influence of this theocentric minority operates remains unclear: neither *After Many A Summer* nor *Time Must Have A Stop*, in which members of that minority appear, throw much light on the subject. Nevertheless, it is perhaps as a result of some residual feeling that even those who pursue individual enlightenment should try to make the world less horrible that he returns, in *Themes and Variations* to a consideration of the society in which he lives.

The results, as usual, are erratic. There is still evidence of a continued capacity for intelligent and perceptive comment, particularly in 'The Double Crisis', an alarming prophecy of ecological disaster which anticipates by some years the contemporary preoccupation with the subject, and in his discussion of the dangers of the way in which the criterion of excellence in the machine, efficiency, is increasingly being applied to human beings. Nevertheless, his remedies for social ills remain much the same ever: there is a similar reliance on World Conferences to sort things out, and the same expectation that governments, composed though they are of unregenerate human beings, will somehow be persuaded to implement necessary reforms. Once again the spectre of racial degeneration is raised, only this time it is the high birth-rate of the poorer countries rather than the poorer classes which disturbs him; in fact, the only new suggestion that emerges from Huxley's discussion of society is to be found in the essay, *Science, Liberty, and Peace*, published in 1947, where he argues in favour of the setting up of an international organization of scientists. Technology is the key to power in the modern world, and power, therefore, is effectively in the hands of the scientist; if the scientist resolves to use this power only for good ends, then, all will be well. The solution, Huxley concludes, is for all scientists to take the equivalent of a Hippocratic oath!

What, then, are we to conclude about Huxley's capacities as a thinker? His limitations should not be allowed to obscure his strengths: his consciousness of the variety and independence of individual perceptions helped him to see through the follies consequent on a belief in the existence of only one reality, perceptible to commonsense, and this in its turn gave him the capability for producing excellent destructive satire which challenged and demolished accepted assumptions. The freshness, wit, and sharpness of Huxley's best work is largely due to this particular quality of mind. But while this is a strength, this particular preoccupation of Huxley's is also responsible for one of his main weaknesses. He did not feel that it was enough merely to satirize, to criticize, to expose. Discussing Proust, in *Proper Studies*, Huxley remarked that

> No author has studied the intermittences of the spirit with so much insight and patience, and none has shown himself so placidly content to live the life of an intermittent being . . . the idea of using his knowledge to make himself better never seems to have occurred to him. (p. 247)

And it is this notion of using one's knowledge to improve oneself and others that is the source of the difficulties which are not only responsible for Huxley's characteristic weaknesses, but are also in many ways the key to his development as a writer. Huxley was, like Henry James, a man of keen aesthetic sensibility; saw himself, like James, as a spectator rather than as an actor in the affairs of the world; and was obsessed, like James, with the varieties of human perception. That, unlike James, he did not proceed on this basis to write novels of a Jamesian representational complexity and self-sufficient artistry may be attributed, leaving aside questions of technical capacity, to his refusal to accept either his own behaviour or that of the society in which he lived as desirable. For Huxley the conduct of human beings in society was not sufficiently morally neutral for him to wish simply to represent them; although the representational novel can obviously imply moral standards by which the actions represented can be judged, Huxley clearly felt that merely to imply such standards was not enough.

Unfortunately, the effect of this attitude was to emphasize and bring to the fore the weaknesses of Huxley's social analysis. Seeing each individual as having a purely subjective perception of reality, and seeing the reality to which individual perceptions relate as either illusory or incommunicable, he found it difficult to understand the processes of social interaction, since he was unable to believe in the possibility of real communication between individuals whom he saw as isolated in their own subjectivity. As he remarked in *Proper Studies*,

> Few things are more disquieting than to discover, on the evidence of some casual remark, that you are talking to a person whose mind is radically alien to your own. Between one easy chair in front of the fire and another a gulf suddenly yawns; you must have a strong head to be able to look into it without feeling giddy. (p. 51)

Generalizing from such experiences, Huxley found difficulty in understanding, or even perceiving the relationships between one individual consciousness and another, and it is this, more than anything, which made it so hard for him to conceive how society worked on a larger scale. As C. P. Snow pointed out,

> ... the combination of social pessimism and individual romanticism is more common than we think. It is a serious disqualification for social thinking for a rather curious reason. It means that one is constantly trying to think, or idealize, the individual into a non-social context. Huxley has always been tempted to do this. He has never had any feeling for the social plasma in which we, as human beings, really live our lives.[4]

Unable to believe in the possibility of communication between individuals, and hence equally unable to understand any form of social organization based on such communication, Huxley can only understand individuals on an individual, out-of-context basis. It is perhaps because of this that he tends to resort to various arbitrary systems of classification in order to organize his discussion of the infinite variety of individual consciousness. In *Proper Studies* he classifies human beings as extravert and introvert, and talks of a grid for measuring intelligence, with one axis labelled kind of intelligence and the other labelled degree—a system which was soon superseded by his discovery of W. H. Sheldon, an American psychologist who had evolved a formula for classifying people according to their temperament and physique.[5] From *Ends and Means* onward Sheldon's terminology, with its categories of cerebrotonic, somatotonic, viscerotonic, of ectomorph, mesomorph, and endomorph, becomes an integral part of Huxley's vocabulary; while the basic notion of different *types* of human being only serves to reinforce Huxley's belief in the existence of essential and irremediable differences between individual human beings. Yet for all this, the order imposed by such systems of classification scarcely seems to serve any useful purpose; the fact that the essential differences between human beings were, to Huxley's satisfaction at least, scientifically proven does not appear to have assisted his understanding of how the various differently classified individuals relate to one another.

In addition, Huxley's conviction that everyone is ultimately alone, beyond the reach of other people, leads him to minimize not only the effect which human beings have on one another, but also (the conditioning processes of *Brave New World* notwithstanding) the extent to which they are influenced by the society in which they live. Although he always claimed to recognize that character was equally the product of heredity and environment, his antipathy towards behaviourism, with its emphasis on conditioning, in fact led him to think in geneticist terms no less extreme. One's character is what one is born with, and there is little scope for doing anything about one's biological inheritance. This made it still more difficult for Huxley to envisage the possibility of meaningful human relations, for if human nature is something given, it is unlikely to be modified by interaction. The effects of one person on another, the changes and development of character which are the stuff of so much fiction, were things which Huxley found it difficult to believe in, for all his presentation, in *Eyeless in Gaza* and *Time Must Have*

A *Stop*, of characters who are converted by the example of others. As Louis Kronenburger observed, as early as 1928, 'His people are created statically, they almost never develop, they almost never influence one another, they almost never work together in the interests of a central theme or story.'[6]

So long as Huxley is writing comedy or satire, which depend for much of their effect on the fact of non-communication, this creates few problems; the difficulties only really arise when he also seeks to embody positive standards of behaviour in his work. For Huxley's ideals are nearly always voiced by an isolated individual, whose ability to influence either society, or the individuals of which it is composed always seems to be strictly limited. However much he may believe in the ideals advocated by characters such as Propter, Rampion, Miller, or Rontini, Huxley is never able to portray their influence on other characters with much conviction.

Nevertheless, Huxley's difficulties are not simply the product of his idiosyncratic and pessimistic view of human relations: they are also grounded in historical conditions which would have made it difficult for any writer to embody his moral positives in a single character. Now the notion of a good individual exerting a beneficial influence on other people and on society is hardly a new one in literature—one need only think of Dorothea in *Middlemarch*:

> The effect of her being on those around her was incalculably diffusive; for the growing good of the world is partly dependent upon unhistoric acts; and that things are not so ill with you and me as they might have been, is half owing to the number who lived faithfully a hidden life, and rest in unvisited tombs. (*Middlemarch*, Finale)

The effect of Dorothea's being is, of course, convincingly portrayed, as well as stated, but it should be pointed out that it is not just George Eliot's superior artistry that makes Dorothea's portrayal so much more satisfactory than that of, say, Rampion or Propter. For Dorothea is an individual who works for the good of others in the context of a society whose basic premisses are accepted; she acts in accordance with moral standards which owe much to a Christian ethic which, though by no means universally acted on in her society, was nevertheless tacitly accepted as a desirable ideal of behaviour. And it is partly because Dorothea operates within the context of normal social behaviour and normative social principles that her capacity for doing good can be plausibly portrayed.

Huxley's good characters, on the other hand, generally uphold ideals which imply the need for radical changes both in society and in individual behaviour—changes whose desirability is by no means widely accepted, tacitly or otherwise. The normative standards in Huxley's fiction, therefore, are hardly ever enshrined in the society which he describes, but only in the words and actions of lone individuals, whose capacity to affect either their environment or their fellow human beings is seldom convincingly depicted, partly because the society in which they live is unwilling to accept their moral standards, and partly because Huxley himself did not really believe that even the most perfect human beings could exert much influence on an unregenerate world. Of all Huxley's novels, *Island* is the only one of which it can be said that desirable moral standards are embodied in the society portrayed, rather than in a single individual. And the society in *Island* is, of course, an imaginary one.

In fact, as we shall see, in the last years of his life Huxley went some way towards resolving the difficulties and contradictions which we have been examining; but it is their effect on the bulk of his fiction, on the kind of fiction he wrote, as well as its quality, to which I now propose to turn.

3
Crome Yellow, Antic Hay and *Those Barren Leaves*

It would be hard to imagine a greater contrast than that between the Huxley of the 1940s—the compiler of *The Perennial Philosophy,* which Gerald Heard described as being an expression of 'Hinayana Buddhism, that stone-cold and ultra-honest faith, that more than stoical disciplinary order that manages to stand on the very brink of suicidal despair'[1]—and the Huxley who was the author of *Crome Yellow,* a first novel whose predominant mood is of gentle, untroubled comedy. That two works so disparate in subject, tone, and intention could come from the pen of the same man might well be taken as confirmation of Huxley's belief in the intermittent and inconsistent nature of personality—it would certainly seem, at any rate at first sight, that the two works were the product of what Huxley himself described as 'watertight compartments of experience'.

Nevertheless, it is worth looking to see what links, if any, exist between the comic world of Huxley's early fiction and the austere mysticism which informs not only *The Perennial Philosophy,* but also such novels as *After Many A Summer* and *Time Must Have A Stop.* Remote though *Crome Yellow* may seem from Huxley's later preoccupations, it represents a starting point from which he developed, and on closer examination it may be seen that the seeds of that development are present even in his earliest novel. The bulkhead dividing the world of comedy from that of Hinayana Buddhism is by no means as watertight as it might seem.

Huxley was quite explicit about the main influence on his early work—that of Thomas Love Peacock, an author whose outlook on life is about as far from Hinayana Buddhism as it is possible to get. And while *Crome Yellow* is perhaps the closest in mood to Peacock, all of Huxley's first three novels conform closely to the Peacockian model. Both *Crome Yellow* and *Those Barren Leaves* employ the classic Peacockian country-house setting, using the house-party as a mechanism for assembling a cast of characters whose widely differing attitudes and obsessions can then be brought into conflict; while *Antic Hay*, despite its urban setting, brings a similar kind of cast into a similar kind of interplay. As in Peacock, there is in all three works a toying with contemporary ideas, as well as a series of thinly veiled portraits of contemporary figures, the correspondences between Scogan and H. G. Wells in *Crome Yellow*, between Coleman and the composer Philip Heseltine in *Antic Hay*, and between Lilian Aldwinkle and Ottoline Morrell in *Those Barren Leaves* all being very much in the Peacockian tradition. Above all (and this is perhaps the main reason for Huxley's choice of Peacock as a model), there is the same kind of reliance, for comic effect, on the spectacle of non-communication, on the failure of the various characters to get outside the world created by their own obsessions.

As has already been suggested, the comparison of one author to another in itself implies a kind of judgement: to return to Harvey's example, the critic who compares Dickens to Kafka is articulating a radically different experience of his work from that of someone who examines his work purely in the context of a nineteenth-century tradition. This being so, it might be as well to define the function of a comparison between Huxley and Peacock; though we have, so to speak, Huxley's own authority for making it, it is nevertheless a comparison which indicates a particular *kind* of approach.

Now obviously the comparison is not a new one: almost every critic makes at least *some* reference to the influence of Peacock. What is interesting, however, is that in the majority of cases the comparison of Huxley to a non-naturalistic comic novelist does not, in fact, affect a critical approach which is already dictated by a more basic implicit comparison with the James-Conrad-Joyce-Woolf continuum which we have already discussed. The comparison with Peacock is made, but it is not integral to the critical discussion of Huxley's work. On the other hand, when the comparison with Peacock *is* a functional one, it nearly always tends to be misleading. For in the latter case, the stress is laid, not on Huxley's use of Peacock's novels as a formal model for his own, but on the fact that both were exponents of 'the novel of ideas'. Peter Bowering, for example, suggests that

> ... it is not the least of Huxley's achievements that he has revived an outmoded form, to which only one major English novelist has previously aspired, and blessed it with a touch of his genius. Under Huxley the 'novel of ideas' has approached the status of a major art form.[2]

What precisely is meant by the term 'novel of ideas' can perhaps be adduced from the following:

> Walter Allen, commenting on Peacock's dramatization of the intellectual notions of his age wrote: 'For anything comparable in our time we would need to imagine a novelist intellectually powerful enough to satirize in one book the exponents of, say, Marxism, psycho-analysis, the psychology of Jung, logical positivism, neo-catholicism, Existentialism, Christian Science, abstract painting.' It is a measure of Huxley's achievement that in the nineteen-twenties he came close to realizing that ideal. (p. 2)

The trouble with this (leaving aside for the moment the view of Huxley which is implied), is that, without wishing to denigrate Peacock's capability as a comic novelist, the claim which is made for him is a ridiculously inflated one. The notion that Peacock offers a serious, or even a particularly intelligent examination of the thinking of his contemporaries is simply untenable. Although, taken purely as caricatures, his portraits of Coleridge, Shelley, Byron are amusing enough, they can hardly be said to constitute a serious comment on what any of them actually *thought*. In fact, Peacock's fundamentally unserious treatment of his subject matter makes it difficult to regard him as a satirist at all. A satiric treatment of the philosophy of the Romantics would surely involve some kind of exposure of falsities and contradictions inherent in it, and this Peacock does not provide. Nor, to be fair, does he attempt to: the nearest he comes to suggesting the existence of a contradiction in the Romantic position is when he portrays its representatives as sharing, for all their professed ideals, his own preference for good food and good wine. Peacock's attitude is a cheerful, hedonistic, and basically philistine one: ideas are presented as being, if anything, a distraction from the more serious business of pleasure. What he makes fun of is not so much specific ideas, as the fact of having any ideas at all. Ideas are, at best, no more than a form of entertainment: the thinkers whom Mr Crotchet invites to his home are a stimulant of the same order as the thousand dozen bottles of wine he has laid down in his cellar; the only mistake one can make is to take ideas too seriously. Peacock's most sympathetic characters are not the men of ideas, but the men of robust commonsense, like Dr Folliott, the emphasis being on the 'robust'.

It is the basically unserious treatment of ideas, and of those who have them, that accounts for the absence of venom which characterizes Peacock's work, and which is responsible for its distinctive lightness of touch. The picture of Peacock as an intellectual, a man of ideas, is ultimately misleading, and to base a comparison between Huxley and Peacock on such a misconception is to risk ending up with a view of Huxley which is equally distorted. In the first place, the exaggerated claims made for Peacock's intellectual stature tend to encourage an equivalent valuation of Huxley, which in turn leads to the mistaken view of Huxley as some kind of supreme intellectual, whose weaknesses as an author are attributed, not to a grasp of ideas which is often confused and superficial, but to simple artistic incapacity. Additionally, the view of Peacock as a 'novelist of ideas' is responsible for the critical tendency to see Huxley's increasingly serious treatment of ideas as representing a development of the Peacockian model. In fact, the case is quite the reverse: it is in his early novels, with their comic, essentially unserious handling of ideas that Huxley is closest to Peacock; as his treatment of ideas and their implications becomes increasingly serious, as in *Point Counter Point* and *Eyeless in Gaza*, he abandons both the mood and all but the vestiges of the form characteristic of Peacock.

Crome Yellow, *Antic Hay*, and *Those Barren Leaves*, with their elegance, clarity, and lightness of touch, owe a great deal to Peacock's example; yet even in these works Huxley begins to explore the limitations of the form which he had consciously adopted as a model. As we shall see, Peacock's novels achieve their comic effect at the expense of the exclusion of large areas of human experience, and the same is true, to a lesser extent, of Huxley's early fiction. Nevertheless, it was not long before Huxley began to find that the model he had chosen was becoming less and less appropriate for dealing with the areas of experience which he wanted to articulate, and as this became clear, he began to abandon it. That his novels, as a result, became clumsier in construction and more ponderous in their treatment of ideas is partly attributable to his failure to find or evolve a new model suitable for dealing with his changing preoccupations—a fact which cannot be grasped so long as one continues to adhere to the concept of Huxley developing rather than abandoning the Peacockian format.

Peacock's art was not only limited, but also essentially static: his style, standards, and preoccupations remained virtually unchanged from the publication of *Headlong Hall* in 1816, to the completion of *Gryll Grange* forty- four years later. The difference between Huxley's first and last novels, on the other hand, could scarcely be more marked; despite the importance of Peacock's influence on his early fiction, it is Huxley's divergence from the Peacockian model, not his development of it, which provides the key to his evolution as a novelist.

Crome Yellow, as has already been observed, is the novel most obviously influenced by the Peacockian model. It has an almost pastoral quality, which is only fleetingly apparent in his subsequent works, and its treatment of the foibles and eccentricities of its characters is generally indulgent. Even the most fatuous behaviour is presented comically, without the venom characteristic of the later Huxley: one need only contrast the amused portrayal of the bogus spirituality of Mr Barbecue-Smith and Priscilla Wimbush with the violently hostile depiction of the Rani's similar preoccupations in *Island*. In *Crome Yellow* Huxley is not so much interested in the shortcomings of life-styles based on limiting obsessions, as in their humorous possibilities; thus, for example, it is not so much the stupidity of Lady Priscilla's twin passions for astrology and gambling that is emphasized, as their ridiculous consequences:

> She betted on football too, and had a large notebook in which she registered the horoscopes of all the players in all the teams of the league. The process of balancing the horoscopes of two elevens one against the other was a very difficult and delicate one. A match between the Spurs and the Villa entailed a conflict in the heavens so vast and complicated that it was not to be wondered at if she sometimes made a mistake about the outcome. (p. 9)

This is very much in the style of Peacock, whose world is one in which even the grossest idiocies are merely amusing. And the characters who inhabit Crome indulge in characteristically Peacockian pastimes. They listen to stories: the poignant, but at the same time faintly absurd tale of the dwarfish Sir Hercules; or the more farcical account of George Wimbush's courtship of Lapith sisters, who felt that eating was 'unspiritual', yet gorged themselves in secret. They while away the hours in the pursuit of not terribly serious love affairs, or in fantastic speculative discussions: what were the works of the imaginary writer Knockespotch really like? How should modern lovers free themselves from their repressions? Just as in Peacock, almost any subject can serve as a starting point for the exposition of the various characters' pet theories. Confronted with a pig-sty, Gombauld extols the breeding of animals, with all its connotations of increase and fertility, as being conducive to Life. Scogan sees pig-breeding as an illustration of the principles of the rational scientific state, where everything is geared to maximum efficiency; whereas Anne is appalled by 'the indecency and cruelty' of raising animals merely so that they may be killed and eaten. And the whole discussion is brought back to earth in the best Peacockian tradition by Rowley, the old farm-hand, whose only comment as he looks into the pen is to remark, 'Rightly is they called pigs' (p. 29).

Yet even in *Crome Yellow* there are elements which would never have been admitted into the purely comic world of Peacock, which has a perfection and completeness that could easily be destroyed by the introduction of extraneous material. In *Music at Night* Huxley pointed out how tragedy depends for its effect on the exclusion of details which, however realistic, might detract from the overall impression—on the exclusion, as he put it, of the 'Whole Truth', which consists of 'the great oceans of irrelevant things, events, and thoughts stretching endless away in every direction from whatever island point (a character, a story) the author may choose to contemplate' (p. 16) And much the same could be said of Peacock's own particular brand of comedy: just as, in tragedy, the introduction of intrusive realistic details might undermine the grandeur and dignity of the proceedings, so in Peacockian comedy, too much realism can endanger the sense of detachment which makes the misfortunes and disasters which befall the characters seem merely amusing.

In Peacock's world no-one ever gets hurt. Though people may occasionally drown or get shot, such misfortunes are reserved for relatively insignificant figures (such as the retainers in *The Misfortunes of Elphin*, or the robbers in *Crotchet Castle*), and are invariably described in such farcical terms that it is impossible to think of anyone actually dying. And it is one of the features of this comic world that its inhabitants can undergo experiences which in real life would be likely to prove uncomfortable, injurious, or even fatal, yet emerge from them unscathed. Peacock's novels are full of people who get themselves blown up, knocked down, hit over the head, or precipitated into deep water from great heights without any apparent ill-effect, while the possibility that the comic effect of such incidents might be undermined by too realistic a description is consistently guarded against by the provision of dehumanizing details. When, for example, Scythrop Glowry and Mr Toobad collide with one another and fall downstairs, in *Nightmare Abbey*, they are described as dropping 'like two billiard balls into one pocket' (the episode being still further distanced by being immediately fitted into Mr Toobad's obsessive scheme of things, his interpretation of the accident being that it is 'one of the innumerable proofs of the temporary supremacy of the devil').

Unpleasant emotions are similarly distanced. Scythrop Glowry's outrageously melodramatic behaviour makes his disappointments in love seem purely comic. His conduct is based on an outlook which, even in the grotesque world of a Peacock novel, appears conspicuously unrealistic, and his amorous misfortunes can be seen as an appropriate reward for his wilful preference for gloom and melancholy over the pleasures of Peacockian conviviality.

The world of *Crome Yellow*, on the other hand, though in many respects similar, is one where there is at least some awareness of the exclusions on which comedy depends. Scogan, for example, points out that

> At this very moment . . . the most frightful horrors are taking place in every corner of the world. People are being crushed, slashed, disembowelled, mangled; their dead bodies rot and their eyes decay with the rest. Screams of pain and fear go pulsing through the air at the rate of eleven hundred feet per second. After travelling for three seconds they are perfectly inaudible. These are distressing facts; but do we enjoy life any the less because of them? Most certainly we do not. We feel sympathy, no doubt; we represent to ourselves imaginatively the sufferings of nations and individuals and we deplore them. But after all, what are sympathy and imagination? Precious little, unless the person for whom we feel sympathy happens to be closely involved in our affections; and even then they don't go very far. And a good thing too; for if one had an imagination vivid enough and a sympathy sufficiently sensitive really to comprehend and to feel the sufferings of other people, one would never have a moment's peace of mind.
>
> (pp. 111–12)

Obviously, the way in which Scogan describes such matters helps to distance them: his hyper-rational attitude to horror and suffering is in itself an aspect of a Peacockian character, whose obsession in this case happens to be rationality. Nevertheless, the fact that the exclusion of pain and suffering is consciously made, that it is actually *mentioned*, is significant. By the very fact of admitting the existence of an outside world where there are such things as fear and horror, the innocence characteristic of Peacockian comedy is compromised. It is the presence of this element of consciousness, and also of self-consciousness that makes *Crome Yellow* different both in feeling and in tendency from the Peacockian novel on which it was modelled.

In addition, there are, throughout the novel, all kinds of touches, or irrelevantly realistic details which, when taken together, tend to undermine the stable world of comedy. Huxley's characters, and the world in which they live, continually hover on the edge of being believable in a way in which Peacock characters are not. The presentation of Denis, for example, is full of details which create a certain feeling of verisimilitude, and which also make for a degree of emotional involvement on the part of the reader. Although there is certainly something comical about his rather pathetic love for Anne Wimbush, it is not comical in the same way as Scythrop Glowry's agonized indecision, which causes him to lose both the women he loves. The faithful description of Denis's moments of embarrassment, of his feelings of inferiority, and above all, of his self-consciousness is far removed from the kind of theatricality which makes Scythrop's plight appear simply amusing. If Denis's weaknesses are also comical, they are still the weaknesses of a realized, rather than a stylized character.

Denis's self-consciousness, in fact, is the crucial factor which distinguishes *Crome Yellow* from the comedies of Peacock. Although, like Peacock's novels, *Crome Yellow* depends on the inability of characters to communicate for much of its comic effect, an added dimension is given to the comedy by the fact that one of the characters, at least, is aware of the fact of non-communication. It is an awareness which makes for a kind of unhappiness which is never found in Peacock, an unhappiness which almost amounts to a sense of alienation. Denis, as he tries to hold a conversation with Jenny, who is deaf (which, in a world where no-one really pays attention to what anyone else says, is not a terribly serious handicap), is prompted to reflect that human beings are like parallel straight lines, which meet only at infinity—'We are all parallel straight lines. Jenny was only a little more parallel than most' (p. 21).

Nevertheless, it is Jenny, ironically, who makes Denis realize that his is not the only consciousness, and that he has an existence in other people's eyes. Jenny has a notebook, in which she makes unflattering sketches of other people, and when Denis unthinkingly leafs through it, he discovers that he features prominently—an experience which brings with it a kind of awareness that would be quite impossible for any of Peacock's characters. To Denis, Jenny and her notebook represent

> ... all the vast conscious world of men outside himself; they symbolized something that in his studious solitariness he was apt not to believe in. He could stand at Picadilly Circus, could watch the crowds shuffle past, and still imagine himself the one fully conscious, intelligent, individual being among all those thousands. It seemed, somehow, impossible that other people should be in their way as elaborate and complete as he in his. Impossible; and yet, periodically he would make some painful discovery about the external world and the horrible reality of its consciousness and its intelligence. The red notebook was one of these discoveries, a footprint in the sand. It put beyond doubt the fact that the outside world existed.
>
> (p. 174)

It is this kind of awareness which makes Huxley's characters more complex, on the whole, than the monomaniacs whom Peacock loves to depict. For Denis is by no means the only character for whom experience brings awareness. Mary, for example, who is first presented as a caricature, obsessed with the ideal of sexual freedom, becomes something more than that when she begins to realize that sexuality has emotional implications. At first she is a purely Peacockian figure, acting on principle rather than inclination; feeling that she ought to have some sexual experience, she selects first Denis, then Gombauld as prospective partners, only to settle for Ivor when it turns out that neither of her first choices are interested. But when Ivor leaves, her realization that she has got herself involved in something more than a rational experiment is portrayed with a degree of pathos that makes her seem a believable human being, and not just an instrument capable of playing only one tune.

Of course, within the conventions of Peacockian comedy, such complications of character create problems. Though comically portrayed, both Denis and Mary exhibit a degree of awareness which seems slightly out of place; Denis's feelings of loneliness and alienation, the implications of Mary's adherence to false but fashionable moral standards—neither of these are subjects with which Peacockian comedy is really equipped to deal, and the faintly incongruous nature of their presence in *Crome Yellow* is perhaps an indication of an essential contradiction between

Huxley's preoccupations—the things he was interested in talking about—and the limitations of the model he had chosen.

The presence of characters who are humanized by their confused glimmerings of awareness tends, on occasions, to make the spectacle of non-communication appear sad, rather than comical. Though Mary's initial rebuffals by Denis and Gombauld are purely comic, her meeting with Denis after Ivor's departure is a melancholy occasion. She has become aware of the existence of emotions which she did not know she possessed; he has just had the traumatic experience of seeing himself through Jenny's eyes: both are anxious to articulate their new awareness. Yet what might have been the occasion for the first real communication in the book lapses into the familiar spectacle of people talking at one another. Despite their mutual unhappiness, Denis and Mary remain interested only in themselves. Nevertheless, as one never finds in Peacock, there is a definite sense of loss, a feeling that a chance has been missed.

Perhaps because of this element of complication, of an accumulation of realistic, humanizing details which compromise the overall comic effect, the tone of *Crome Yellow* is, in places, almost elegiac. As though in reaction to the complexities of the modern world, Huxley seems to hark back to a past which is seen as both simpler and happier. Scogan, for example, suggests that sexuality has been irrevocably blighted by the hypocrisy of the Victorian age:

> The only century in which customs were not characterized by . . . cheerful openness was the nineteenth, of blessed memory. It was an outstanding exception. And yet, with what one must suppose was a deliberate disregard of history, it looked upon its horribly pregnant silences as normal and natural and right; the frankness of the previous fifteen or twenty-thousand years was considered abnormal and perverse. (pp. 104–5)

As a result, humanity has lost its natural attitude towards sexuality: although Scogan concedes that in the twentieth century a degree of openness has returned, but a cold, clinical openness: 'It was to scientific openness, not to the jovial frankness of the past, that we returned.'—the attitude, in effect, whose deficiencies are illustrated by Mary.

Henry Wimbush, too, looks to the past with approval. Studying the old histories of the district, he reads of all kinds of fascinating occurrences, events whose singularity only serves to emphasize the dreariness of the present.

> In Manningham's Diary for 1600 there was a queer passage, he remembered, a very queer passage. Certain magistrates in Berkshire, Puritan magistrates, had had wind of a scandal. One moonlit summer night they had ridden out with their *posse* and there, among the hills, they had come upon a company of men and women, dancing, stark naked, among the sheepcotes. The magistrates and their men had ridden their horses into the crowd. How self-conscious the poor people must have felt, how helpless without their clothes against armed and booted horsemen! The dancers are arrested, whipped, gaoled, set in the stocks; the moonlight dance is never danced again. What old, earthy, Panic rite came to extinction here, he wondered? Who knows—perhaps their ancestors had danced like this in the moonlight ages before Adam and Eve were so much as thought of. He liked to think so. And now it was no more. These weary young men, if they wanted to dance, would have to bicycle six miles to the town. The country was desolate, without life of its own, without indigenous pleasures. The pious magistrates had snuffed out for ever a little happy flame that had burned from the beginning of time. (pp. 127–9)

It would be wrong, of course, to over-emphasize the elements of suffering, of complexity, of sadness and nostalgia. The summery world of Crome is for the most part a happy one. If anguish is present, it is more often than not the object of mirth rather than sympathy. Denis's tormented reflections are made to appear ridiculous by contrast with Anne's commonsense Peacockian attitude. Life, he complains

> . . . life, facts, things were horribly complicated; ideas, even the most difficult of them, deceptively simple. In the world of ideas everything was clear; in life all was obscure, embroiled. Was it surprising that one was miserable, horribly unhappy? (p. 24)

But Anne puts his self-pity into perspective with her characteristically Peacockian response:

> I've always taken things as they come . . . it seems so obvious. One enjoys the pleasant things, avoids the nasty ones. There's nothing more to be said. (p. 25)

Anne is scarcely a Dr Folliott, but her view is one which Huxley appears, in the main, to support, using it as a yardstick by which other attitudes towards life are judged. Henry Wimbush's reflections on the sterility of modern life are more in the nature of a sub-theme, their disillusionment offering a contrast to the predominantly cheerful tone. Yet it is a theme which is to sound increasingly clearly in Huxley's works, and when one looks at *Crome Yellow* with his later works in mind, or even in the light of the kind of attitudes expressed in *On The Margin*, it is Henry Wimbush's words that stand out, as he laments the old days, when people had 'social amusements in which they would have partaken as members of a conscious community. . .'—

> . . . now they had nothing, nothing except Mr Bodiham's forbidding Boys Club, and the rare dances and concerts organized by himself. Boredom or the urban pleasures of the metropolis were the alternatives that presented themselves to these poor youths. Country pleasures were no more. . .
> (p. 128)

With *Antic Hay*, Huxley, too, turns to the urban pleasures of the metropolis. London, rather than a country house, is the setting for his portrayal of a gallery of characters who once more display a fine range of Peacockian obsessions. Nevertheless, the setting does make a difference: it is impossible to paint city life in quite the tranquil tones which are characteristic of both *Crome Yellow* and the novels of Peacock; with the change of scene from the country to the town, there is an immediate increase in tension. In the city it seems to be that much harder to ignore the unpleasant aspects of reality which the world of comedy necessarily excludes.

From the outset, the intrusion of reality is harsher and more insistent. Gumbril's whimsical musings during school prayers, for example, soon give way to the vivid recollection of his mother's death from cancer. Pain and death were subjects with which Huxley was to become almost obsessionally preoccupied in his later fiction, and they represent areas of experience which are beyond the scope of Peacockian comedy. In *Antic Hay*, while the subject of death does not recur, it is nevertheless the precursor of a series of intimations of the existence of a distinctly un-Peacockian world of suffering and squalor. In the city, however well insulated one may be by the comforts of food, drink, money, and intellectual conversation, it is difficult to ignore the fact of other, less comfortable existences. Coleman demands of his companions whether it has occurred to them

> ... that at this moment we are walking through the midst of seven million distinct and separate individuals, each with distinct and separate lives, and all completely indifferent to our existence? Seven million people, each one of whom thinks himself quite as important as each of us does. Millions of them are now sleeping in an empested atmosphere. Hundreds of thousands of couples are at this moment engaged in mutually caressing one another in a manner too hideous to be thought of, but in no way differing from the manner in which each of us performs, delightfully, passionately and beautifully, his similar work of love. Thousands of women are now in the throes of parturition, and of both sexes thousands are dying of the most diverse and appalling diseases, or simply because they have lived too long. Thousands are drunk, thousands have overeaten, thousands have not had enough to eat. And they are all alive, all unique and separate and sensitive, like you and me. It's a horrible thought. (pp. 56–7)

It is an idea which is more forcibly illustrated in the ensuing scene at the all-night coffee stall, where Mrs Viveash's flirtation with Shearwater is counterpointed by the carter's tale of misfortune, sickness, and unemployment. On his way home afterwards, Gumbril reflects on the infinite variety of human misery and suffering:

> ... there were the murderers hanged at eight o'clock, while one was savouring, almost with voluptuous consciousness, the final dream-haunted doze. There was the phthisical char-

> woman who used to work at his father's house, until she got too weak and died. There were the lovers who turned on the gas and the ruined shopkeepers jumping in front of trains. Had one a right to one's education and good taste, a right to knowledge and conversation, and the leisurely complexities of love? (p. 69)

A right, in other words, to all the things that make the world of Peacock go round.

Nor do pain and suffering merely remain in the background: they are realities which impinge on even the most theatrically Peacockian of the characters. Lypiatt, windbag though he is, on occasions communicates the genuine unhappiness which his love for Mrs Viveash causes him; while Shearwater, the single-minded scientist whose gradual realization that he is in love is so comically portrayed, also displays an unexpected intensity of feeling. His final appearance, pedalling madly on a stationary bicycle in the laboratory as he tries desperately to exorcise his infatuation, is more akin to nightmare than to comedy. Suffering is a reality from which no-one, no matter how eccentric or comical their behaviour, is immune; even so minor a figure as Porteous, with his blameless obsession with the poetry of Notker Balbulus, has his life ruined by his son's gambling excesses.

The possibility of real suffering makes for complications; to a much greater degree than in *Crome Yellow*, the characters display an awareness born of experience. Even in the Peacockian set-pieces, such as the scene in the Soho restaurant, the comedy is not simply dependent on the portrayal of conflicting obsessions, but on the depiction of affectation as well. Huxley's characters are far more self-consciously theatrical than those of Peacock: unlike Peacock's aimiable lunatics, figures such as Coleman and Mercaptan appear to have chosen the roles they play. Coleman's blasphemies and Mercaptan's elegance are calculated, and it is this element of calculation which makes Huxley's characters appear to be less one-dimensional than Peacock's: the element of self-conscious calculation implies the existence of a person behind the mask.

In fact there is, in *Antic Hay*, an intensification of nearly all the qualities which, in *Crome Yellow*, seemed almost to work against the basic comic tendencies of the novel as a whole. The main character, Gumbril, suffers even more than Denis from self-consciousness and doubts about his own identity. Where Anne humiliated Denis merely by telling him he was 'sweet', Mrs Viveash more bluntly refers to Gumbril as 'the weak, silent man'. Comparing himself with his acquaintances, Gumbril sees himself as a pale reflection of the more definite personalities of others, following the example now of one person, now of another, like a sheep following the shepherd. Yet even then, he lacks the comforting sense of belonging to a herd, since he is unsure which herd he belongs to:

> Shearwater's herd, Lypiatt's herd, Mr Mercaptan's herd, Mrs Viveash's herd, the architectural herd of his father, the educational herd (but that, thank God! was no bleating on distant pastures), the herd of Mr Bojanus—he belonged to them all a little, to none of them completely. Nobody belonged to his herd. How could they? No chameleon can live with comfort on a tartan. (p. 93)

Unlike Denis, however, Gumbril is not prepared just to drift passively through life. Perhaps because his feelings of self-doubt are so much more intense, perhaps because the world of *Antic Hay* is more complex and problematic, he determines to do something about his unsatisfactory existence, and attempts self-transformation through disguise. Gumbril's idea is that the adoption of a definite identity will enable him to forget his usual uncertainties, but his choice of disguise is a significant one—the identity he adopts is that of the Rabelaisian 'Complete Man':

> Great eater, deep drinker, stout fighter, prodigious lover; clear thinker, creator of beauty, seeker of truth and prophet of heroic grandeurs. (p. 94)

Yet although Gumbril's ideal is avowedly Rabelaisian, his 'Complete Man' bears more than a passing resemblance to the splendidly self-assured heroes of Peacock. Allowing for the compromises necessary to an Anglican clergyman, Dr Folliott is the archetypal 'Complete Man', able to dispose of armed robbers, well-stocked cellars, groaning tables, and radical arguments as a matter of course.

Nevertheless, playing the role of the no-nonsense Peacockian hero in the more complicated world of *Antic Hay* fails to resolve Gumbril's problems. True, his disguise gives him the confidence to act decisively both as a businessman (successfully bullying Boldero into offering acceptable terms for a share in his invention), and as a lover, seducing women whom he would previously never have dared to speak to, but it does little to alter his essential nature. Though his disguise enables him to form relationships with both Rosie and Emily (instead of just dreaming about them), the nature of those relationships is dictated, not by the Complete Man, but by the woman. For all his veneer of assertiveness, he goes along equally happily both with Rosie's pretentiousness and Emily's rather cloying sentimentality: his essential passivity remains unchanged. His disguise is, literally, only skin-deep.

Of course, the contradiction between Gumbril's real and assumed selves is all part of the comedy. Just as Peacock found the spectacle of normal human beings acting against their own basic instincts because of their specious intellectual preoccupations a comic one, so Huxley found there was something irresistibly amusing about the idea of a neurotic intellectual pretending to be something other than himself. The only difference is that, whereas for Peacock the obsessions of his characters are aberrations, departures from a self-evident norm which he assumes that his audience also accepts, in *Antic Hay* there is no concept of normality to relate to. Whereas the melancholy and alienation of a character like Scythrop are portrayed as a wanton affectation, Gumbril's anxiety and self-doubt are seen as perfectly genuine. His neuroses may be comical, or even undesirable, but they are not regarded as unnatural; if anything, it is the commonsense extravert behaviour of the Complete Man which is false. In Huxley's world, while feelings of alienation, unhappiness, self-consciousness may be comically portrayed, there is never any suggestion that they are abnormal. Unhappiness, which in Peacock's novels is nearly always seen as self-inflicted, the result of a failure to conform to the norms of behaviour which would make happiness possible, is presented by Huxley as an inevitable fact of experience.

Once again, it is possible to over-emphasize the importance of

Huxley's portrayal of the unpleasant aspects of experience; though Gumbril's unhappiness is genuine enough, his quest for a new and better life, with its paraphernalia of false beards and inflatable trousers, remains a primarily comic one—his efforts to resolve his anxieties and dissatisfactions scarcely serve to make him a precursor of such later Huxleian seekers after truth and enlightenment as Calamy, in *Those Barren Leaves* or Beavis, in *Eyeless in Gaza*. Despite the intrusiveness of an unpleasant reality, Huxley is not yet concerned to make any positive suggestions as to how the individual ought to deal with it; the real advance which *Antic Hay* represents over *Crome Yellow* is primarily an artistic one, lying not so much in its more serious treatment of the predicament of the characters, as in the greater success with which Huxley succeeds in reconciling the conflicting elements of comedy and realism. While in *Crome Yellow* the effect of the realistic details, such as those surrounding the characterization of Denis, remained faintly incongruous, at odds with the overall comic effect, in *Antic Hay* realism and comedy are more evenly balanced, each working to heighten the other.

One of the most distinctive features of *Antic Hay*, in fact, is its constant juxtaposition of contrasting moods and styles. The frivolity of the hedonistic pursuits of the various characters is continually underlined by the insistence on the most unsavoury aspects of urban civilization; ludicrous though the misunderstandings between the characters are, the comedy is given an added edge by the fact that the puppets can also feel pain. Indeed, pain and suffering are not so much an intrusion, as an essential element in an altogether richer and more complex kind of comedy than is to be found in *Crome Yellow*. Huxley himself indicated that he felt he was articulating a new *kind* of experience in *Antic Hay*, describing it as

> . . . intended to reflect—fantastically, of course, but none the less faithfully—the life and opinions of an age which has seen the violent disruption of almost all the standards, conventions, and values current in the previous epoch. (*Letters*, p. 224)

This new kind of experience, he felt, also demanded a new kind of treatment:

> Artistically, too, it has a certain novelty, being a work in

which all the ordinarily separated categories—tragic, comic, fantastic, realistic—are combined so to say chemically into a single entity, whose unfamiliar character makes it appear at first sight rather repulsive. (ibid.)

Certainly, even though the basic theme of people living out parallel existences, lives which never touch, is similar to that of *Crome Yellow*, the comedy in *Antic Hay* often has a rather strange flavour. Thus, while life is shown as having its own meaning for each character, depending on the nature of their particular obsessions, Huxley seems concerned to stress, not so much the comic possibilities of the clash between conflicting obsessions, as the way in which each individual reality becomes unreal as soon as it is seen in the context of another. Mrs Viveash's appearance in Shearwater's laboratory is construed by him as a hallucination induced by the physical strain of pedalling his bicycle. When Lypiatt, incensed by Mercaptan's review of his exhibition, bursts into the critic's cosy, Second Empire-style apartment the extent to which he seems out of place is emphasized by Huxley's description of his entering 'like a Goth into the elegant marble vomitorium of Petronius Arbiter' (p. 197). Gumbril, after making love to Rosie, whom he believes to be a total stranger, is alarmed to discover that she is in fact Shearwater's wife, and that what had been a new, and intensely romantic experience had been taking place in the prosaic setting of a friend's house. Forced to reinterpret his experience, he wonders

Could Shearwater be wholly unaware of what she was really like? But for that matter, what *was* she really like? (p. 110)

This sense of dislocation is continually emphasized throughout *Antic Hay*: his characters stumble through life equipped with interpretations of reality which are always hopelessly inadequate, with assumptions that are always liable to be undermined, leaving them staring over the brink into nothingness. Yet because so many different interpretations of reality are possible, the same experience can be presented in different ways—sympathetically, or farcically, as a subject for pathos, or for comedy—and one of the most remarkable things about *Antic Hay* is the assurance with which Huxley shifts from one approach to another. Mrs Viveash, for example, is shown wandering through London one lunchtime, lost in a reverie about her lover, who was killed in the war; her languor, her inability to feel anything, have hitherto been comically presented, but here we are shown the reasons for her behaviour—she has been emotionally crippled by the war, and we are at last allowed to share the pathos of her attempts to regain the intensity of feeling which she has lost. Yet just as the mood of melancholy and nostalgia seems about to become firmly established, Huxley once again reminds us that there is more than one way of looking at the same thing. Mrs Viveash's forlorn murmur of 'never again' is misheard by an old military gentleman who is passing, and the pathos immediately gives way to farce:

> 'I beg your pardon?' queried the martial gentleman, in a rich, port-winey, cigary voice.
>
> Mrs Viveash look at him with such wide-eyed astonishment that the old gentleman was quite taken aback. 'A thousand apologies, dear lady. Thought you were addressing... H'm, ah'm.' He replaced his hat, squared his shoulders and went off smartly, left, right, bearing preciously before him his pigeon breast. Poor thing, he thought, poor young thing. Talking to herself. Must be cracked, must be off her head. Or perhaps she took drugs. That was more likely: that was much more likely. Most of them did nowadays. Vicious young women. Lesbians, drug-fiends, nymphomaniacs, dipsos—thoroughly vicious, nowadays, thoroughly vicious. He arrived at his club in an excellent temper. (p. 158)

Better still is the scene where Lypiatt is shown writing a farewell letter to Mrs Viveash. It begins ridiculously enough: Lypiatt is obliged to write in pencil because his ink has dried up, and the first part of his letter is given over to a characteristically melodramatic outburst of self-pity; yet in the midst of his maudlin reminiscences about happier days, his theatrical quotations from Michaelangelo, the tone suddenly changes. The picture of Lypiatt as a pompous charlatan dissolves into that of a man who has finally realized that he is a complete failure:

> . . . I have come to admit everything. That I couldn't paint, I couldn't write, I couldn't make music. That I was a charlatan and a quack. That I was a ridiculous actor of heroic parts who deserved to be laughed at—and *was* laughed at. But then every man is ludicrous if you look at him from outside, without taking into account what's going on in his heart and mind. You could turn Hamlet into an epigrammatic farce with an inimitable scene where he takes his adored mother in adultery. You could make the wittiest Guy de Maupassant short story out of the life of Christ, by contrasting the mad rabbi's pretensions with his abject fate. It's a question of point of view. Every one's a walking farce and a walking tragedy at the same time. The man who slips on a banana skin and fractures his skull describes against the sky, as he falls, the most richly comical arabesque. . . And what am I? A charlatan, a quack, a pretentious, boasting, rhodomontading imbecile, incapable of painting anything but vermouth posters. . . I was all that—and grotesquely laughable. And very likely your laughter was justified, your judgement was true. I don't know. I can't tell. Perhaps I am a charlatan. Perhaps I'm insincere; boasting to others, deceiving myself. I don't know, I tell you. Everything is confusion in my mind now. (p. 214)

Through the very intensity of his misery, Lypiatt arrives at last at some kind self-awareness; with his illusions stripped away, he sees himself as others see him. But even as he reaches this bleak realization, the mood changes yet again: overcome by self-pity, Lypiatt reverts to his more usual, exaggeratedly theatrical tone of voice, ranting melodramatically about death—only to be interrupted by the arrival of Boldero, who wants to commission him to design some posters to advertise pneumatic trousers, and gets booted unceremoniously downstairs for his pains.

This fascination with the different possible interpretations of the same events is, as we have already seen, a characteristic one. Huxley's concern to demonstrate the paradox that tragedy is simply farce seen from another angle is a reflection of his preoccupation with the relative nature of perception. And it is this which largely dictates the way in which Huxley develops the model he has chosen. In his hands, the Peacockian comedy of conflicting obsessions becomes something altogether more complex; while *Antic Hay* remains primarily a comedy, the collisions between conflicting outlooks are not just there for comic effect, but are part of a more serious exploration of the nature of our perception of reality. Far more than in *Crome Yellow*, Huxley extends the possibilities of the Peacockian model, and for the most part his greater ambition is rewarded by a corresponding degree of success; without sacrificing the lightness of touch which characterized the earlier novel, he succeeds in producing a comedy which is substantially more than a mere entertainment.

In *Antic Hay*, the real world is always just around the corner, its presence serving to give an added edge to the portrayal of those characters who seek to ignore it. The images which Huxley conjures up of a surrounding world of pain, suffering, and poverty are sufficiently vivid to reflect adversely on anyone who tries to pretend that it does not exist. When Opps complains that

> 'I hate everyone poor, or ill, or old. Can't abide them; they make me positively sick.' (p. 62)

and Mercaptan rejoins

> 'Quelle ame bien-née . . . how well and frankly you express what we all feel and lack the courage to say.' (ibid.)

there is implied a moral criticism of the whole coterie to which they belong. (It is significant that none of Mercaptan's companions make any objection to being included in his approval of Opps' sentiments.) Unlike Peacock's characters, whose world, limited though it is, is the only one portrayed, Huxley's men and women move, in their pursuit of pleasure, amongst dangerous realities—and it is the presence of these realities which exposes the limited nature of their response to life.

Unlike his later fiction, however, *Antic Hay* offers no solution to the problems his characters face; at no point does Huxley suggest how the individual might comes to terms with the complex realities of the modern world. Instead, like *Crome Yellow*, *Antic Hay* looks to the past for its images of peace and harmony. Henry Wimbush's nostalgia for country pleasures has its equivalent in Gumbril senior's realization of Wren's plans for rebuilding London after the Great Fire. The characters in *Antic*

Hay live purposeless lives amid squalid surroundings, but against the realities of Shearwater's ghastly suburban maisonette, of Lypiatt's seedy lodgings, of the sordid Soho restaurant, is set a vision of what London might have been, had Wren's plans not been rejected. As Gumbril senior laments, Wren offered the people of London

> . . . open spaces and broad streets; he offered them beauty, order and grandeur. He offered to build for the imagination and the ambitious spirit of man, so that even the most bestial, vaguely and remotely, as they walked those streets, might feel that they were of the same race—or very nearly—as Michaelangelo; that they too might feel themselves, in spirit at least, magnificent, strong and free. He offered them all these things; he drew a plan for them, walking in peril among the still smouldering ruins. But they preferred to re-erect the old intricate squalor. . . (p. 135)

Huxley's characters are the descendants and inheritors of those who rejected Wren's vision, and it is significant that Huxley uses the ideal world of Wren's vision as a standard by which to condemn the squalor of everyday reality. It is the reverse of what we find in Peacock, whose every instinct rejected the idealist, visionary outlook. When, in *Antic Hay*, Gumbril senior is forced to sell his model of Wren's London to help buy back some of the books which his friend Porteous has been obliged to sell in order to pay his son's gambling debts, the sacrifice of the grandeur which it represents is not so much a commentary on the ideals of Wren and Gumbril senior, as a reflection on the unpleasantness of the world with which both had to compromise.

But if *Antic Hay* represents an advance over *Crome Yellow*, achieving a balance between comedy and realism which the earlier novel lacked, the mixture in Huxley's third novel, *Those Barren Leaves*, is rather different. Both longer and, with its combination of first and third person narration, formally more ambitious, it constitutes Huxley's first attempt not just to synthesize comedy and realism, but also to integrate into his fiction some kind of suggestion as to what might be done to resolve the problems which his characters face.

Nevertheless, the influence of Peacock is still very much in evidence; it would seem likely that it was *Those Barren Leaves* to which Huxley was referring when, as early as 1921, he wrote to his brother Julian of

> ... a plan to do a gigantic Peacock in an Italian scene. An incredibly large castle—like the Sitwells' at Monte Gufone, the most amazing place I have ever seen in my life ... which will be occupied, for the purposes of my story, by the most improbable people of every species and nationality. Here one has the essential Peacockian datum—a houseful of oddities. (*Letters*, p. 202)

With *Those Barren Leaves*, Huxley returns to the classic house-party formula; that it is an Italian palazzo rather than an English country house is largely incidental, since little attempt is made to explore the possibilities of a foreign setting. It is English society with which Huxley is dealing—the Italian location provides only a certain amount of local colour.

Huxley's use of the contrast between the magnificence of the setting and the absurdity of the characters is, however, somewhat double-edged. The former glories of the palace of the Cybo Malaspina, far from being a symbol, like Wren's London, of man's highest aspirations, turn out to be largely a figment of the imagination of the ageing society hostess who has bought the place:

> In Mrs Aldwinkle's enthusiastic imagination what marvellous symposia had been held within these walls—centuries even before they were built—what intellectual feasts! (p. 22)

In her day-dreams, Mrs Aldwinkle fabricates a past history for the palazzo, with a list of previous house-guests which includes Aquinas, Boccaccio, Dante, Michaelangelo, Galileo, and Luca Giordano, and envisages herself at the centre of a company of their modern equivalents:

> She saw herself, unofficially a princess, surrounded by a court of poets, philosophers and artists ... the palace of Vezza should re-become what it had never been except in Mrs Aldwinkle's fancy. (p. 23)

The reality, however, seems to have been rather different, if one is to judge by the faces of the busts in the Saloon of the Ancestors:

> From circular niches set high in the walls of the huge square room the lords of Massa Carrara looked out, bust after bust, across the intervening centuries. Right round the room they went, beginning on the left of the fireplace and ending, with the penultimate Malaspina, who arranged the room, on the right. And as marquess succeeded marquess and prince, prince, an expression of ever profounder imbecility made itself apparent on the faces of the Ancestors. The vulture's nose, the formidable jaw of the first robber marquess transformed themselves by gradual degrees into the vague proboscises of anteaters, into criminally prognathous deformities. The foreheads grew lower with every generation, the marble eyes stared ever blanklier and the look of conscious pride became more and more strongly marked on every countenance. It was the boast of the Cybo Malaspina that they had never married beneath them and that their heirs had always been legitimate. One had only to look at the faces of the last three Princes to feel sure that the boast was amply justified. Were these the Muses' friends? (ibid.)

Appropriately enough, Mrs Aldwinkle's entourage turns out to be more in keeping with the actual past than with her fantasies: her 'court of poets, philosophers and artists' is in fact chiefly remarkable for its mediocrity, the glittering company including such figures as Mary Thriplow, the second rate novelist; Mr Falx, the political hack; Lord Hovenden, his feeble-minded protégé, who only comes to life when he is behind the wheel of a car; Francis Chelifer, a dilettante who earns his living by editing *The Rabbit Fancier's Gazette*; and Cardan, who can only be described as a professional guest. Far from presiding over the intellectual renaissance of which she dreams, Mrs Aldwinkle succeeds only in assembling a household full of Peacockian caricatures.

But although *Those Barren Leaves* re-unites a Peacockian cast with a Peacockian setting, the more unpleasant aspects of reality continue to intrude on the comedy. Thus, for all her absurdity,

Mrs Aldwinkle is portrayed as having an only too realistic horror of old age; though she is devoid of both dignity and intelligence, the sheer desperation of her feelings—of her ludicrous passion for Chelifer, of her pathetic faith in the rejuvenating powers of skin foods and electric massage machines—makes her far too real to work simply on the level of caricature.

Still harsher than the reality of old age, however, is the reality of death, and it is Cardan, perhaps the most Peacockian of all Huxley's characters, who is brought face to face with the unpalatable fact of mortality by the death of Grave Elver, a harmless idiot whom he had been intending to marry for her money. It is an experience which prompts him to some extremely un-Peacockian thoughts:

> It had been a disgusting sort of death. Pains, vomiting, collapse, coma, then the coffin—and now the busy ferments of putrefaction and the worms. (p. 333)

It is about as far removed as possible from Peacock's delight in the humorous possibilities of the macabre, as exemplified in *Nightmare Abbey*, where Christopher Glowry selects his servants according to 'one of two criterions—a long face, or a dismal name' and ends up employing a butler called Raven, a pair of grooms called Mattocks and Graves, and a footman with the name of Diggory Deathshead.

But while such morbid preoccupations were, for Peacock, no more than an amusing eccentricity, Cardan's reflections are clearly designed to expose the limitations of the hedonistic outlook which constitutes the Peacockian norm.

> Sooner or later every soul is stifled by the sick body; sooner or later there are no more thoughts, but only pain and vomiting and stupor. . . The wise man does not think about death lest it should spoil his pleasures. But there are times when the worms intrude too insistently to be ignored. Death forces itself sometimes upon the mind, and then it is hard to take pleasure in anything. (pp. 334–5)

Until Grace's death, Cardan is, like Dr Folliott, singlemindedly committed to the cheerful pursuit of pleasure wherever it is to be found—particularly at other people's tables; like Dr Folliott, too, he appears impervious to any criticism of his resultant life-style. Yet, confronted by the reality of death, he is forced into a realization of the inadequacy of his philosophy; like Scogan, in *Crome Yellow*, he finds comfort in the belief that pain and suffering are only real when they are directly experienced, and that otherwise they can safely be ignored—only to discover, too late, that it is an attitude which has little to commend it when pain and suffering come too close.

In fact, the hedonism of which Scogan and Cardan are the most overt exponents can be seen to underlie the behaviour of nearly all the characters in Huxley's first three novels, and it is perhaps because its limitations are so clearly exposed in *Those Barren Leaves* that, for the first time, we find someone consciously searching for a more satisfactory philosophy of life. Ironically, it is Calamy, who appears to be very much at home in the world of mindless hedonism, who first begins to wonder who he is, and what he is doing, and it is he who, at the end of the book, abandons his old life, in favour of a hermit-like existence in the mountains. Like Huxley, Calamy is obsessed by the sheer variety of different ways of looking at things, and the main purpose of his retreat from civilization is to find the solitude in which he can pursue his search for the ultimate reality which, he feels sure, underlies infinite variety of the world of appearances—a reality which will enable him to make sense of a life which he has come to see as aimless and futile.

Unfortunately (and this is one of the book's main weaknesses), Calamy's search for truth does not carry a great deal of conviction. While he is obviously sincere enough, neither what he is looking for, or its relation to the problems which he and the other characters encounter are at all clear. Explicable though his dissatisfaction with the life he has been leading may be, the alternatives he explores seem extraordinary abstract.

Seeing the whole of his previous life as having been somehow unreal, Calamy seems to be seeking something which is real, something which he can hang on to, and use as the basis for constructing a new philosophy of life. This reality, he believes, lies beyond what we normally interpret as being 'real'. Even the most prosaic object turns out, on closer examination, to be 'real' in a number of different ways; what Calamy wants to discover is the underlying reality to which all the ways of being real relate. Looking at his own hand, for example, he wonders about

> ... all the different ways in which these five fingers ... have reality and exist. All the different ways ... if you think of that, even for five minutes, you find yourself plunged up to the eyes in the most portentous mysteries. (p. 346)

Even something as simple as a human hand exists

> ... simultaneously in a dozen parallel worlds. It exists as electrical charges; as chemical molecules; as living cells; as part of a moral being, the instrument of good and evil; in the physical world and in the mind. (ibid.)

Beyond these parallel worlds, however, Calamy is convinced that there is something else:

> I believe that if one could stand the strain of thinking really hard for several days, or weeks, or months about one thing, this hand for example, one might be able to burrow one's way right through the mystery and really get at something—some kind of truth, some explanation. (p. 340)

Yet there is something curiously unsatisfactory about Calamy's enunciation of the problem; while his revulsion from the mindless hedonism of the world in which he has been living is something with which it is possible to sympathize, it is hard to avoid feeling that there is more to his dissatisfaction than the purely intellectual issue which he makes of it. Calamy has, after all, come to the conclusion that, in effect, his whole past life has been a mistake, and that the assumptions by which he has been living have no basis in reality—and the suggestion that the problems thus created can be resolved by 'thinking really hard' is one which seems, in the context of the novel as a whole, distinctly unconvincing.

Essentially, there are three main problems with Calamy's presentation. In the first place, it is improbably idealized: Huxley may perhaps have felt that the unworldliness of Calamy's proposed solutions could be taken as a sign of an inability, on his part, to cope with the real world, and it is as though to forestall the possibility of such a criticism that Calamy is portrayed as being very much a man of the world. Gone are the self-consciousness and neuroses of Denis Stone and Theodore Gumbril: Calamy has all the social graces, knows what to do and when to do it, and appears in addition to have almost limitless appeal to the opposite sex—it is certainly not personal weakness or incapacity which leads him to foresake the world. Unfortunately, however, Huxley's efforts at portraying a character who is strong and self-assured are all too often grossly overdone. As Mary Thriplow looks at him, for example, we are told that

> He looked insolent still, still arrogantly conscious of power; but all the drowsiness and indolence that had veiled his look were now fallen away, leaving his face bare, as it were, and burning with a formidable and satanic beauty. (p. 197)

Nor is this all; in addition to resorting to such cheap romantic magazine clichés, Huxley, in attempting to emphasize Calamy's self-sufficiency, succeeds only in making him appear egostistical and conceited. Thinking of Mary Thriplow (whom he sees as a distraction from the important business of searching for truth and reality), he reflects that

> Woman is made by nature to be enslaved—by love, by children. But every now and then a man is born who ought to be free. For such a man it is disgraceful to succumb under the torture. (p. 270)

('Torture' is Calamy's rather less than gracious description of his sexual relations with Mary Thriplow.)

At such moments it is tempting to wonder if it is not Huxley the satirist who is at work, but unfortunately it is impossible to interpret his portrayal of Calamy as being anything other than straightforward and approving. We are evidently intended to take passages such as the above seriously; even the amusing parody of Calamy's ideas which Mary Thriplow's rapid conversion to his point of view affords is clearly aimed only at her. However, this is not to say that Calamy's *ought* to have been a satiric presentation—merely that, as it stands, it becomes difficult to believe in Calamy's conviction that

> If I could free myself . . . surely I could do something; nothing

useful, no doubt, in the ordinary sense, nothing that would particularly profit other people; but something that for me would be of the last importance. (ibid.)

When the novel closes, with Calamy looking out across the mountains from his solitary retreat, it is not so much his qualified optimism that one shares, as a sense of disparity between the author's intention to communicate something which he believes to be important, and his success in actually doing so.

But, even if one were able to accept as valid the solutions which Calamy proposes, a further problem is created by their *nature*. As in Peacock, the comedy in *Those Barren Leaves* is primarily one of non-communication. Mary Thriplow's attempts to remedy the effects of her initial misconception of Calamy's character; Mrs Aldwinkle's ludicrous attempts to convince herself that Chelifer returns her love; Hovenden's jealous suspicions of Irene: all owe their comedy to the conflict between private fantasy and reality—a conflict which the reader is able to appreciate, through being in a position to tell which is which. But whereas, in Peacock, the lunatic notions of the characters tend to imply the existence of some sort of commonsense and normality, in the light of which their lunacy becomes evident, the difficulty with Huxley's world is, as has already been suggested, that there is no such implicit norm. The alienation of the characters, their inability to communicate, is presented as natural and inevitable—which in its turn serves to make the plight of the characters seem that much more real. In *Those Barren Leaves*, however, Huxley is suggesting for the first time that there may be an answer, that there may be a way out of the difficulties with which his characters are confronted—and it is this which is the second main problem. The trouble with the solution which Calamy explores is that it is so *private*; to find reality, he believes it necessary to have absolute solitude. Yet the problems of a world where there is no communication is surely one of loneliness and isolation: the bleakest moments in *Those Barren Leaves* are when, faced with the realities of old age and death, characters such as Cardan and Mrs Aldwinkle realize that they are fundamentally alone, that they have no-one to turn to. To these problems, Calamy's speculations have no answer, or indeed relevance—it is no sort of resolution to the problems of loneliness and isolation to be told that one should find total solitude in which to think. Instead of offering a contrast to the novel's more pessimistic tendencies, Calamy's positive suggestions only serve to reinforce them; in his view, other human beings are merely a distraction, and the intellectual stimulation or bodily pleasure they may offer no more than diversions from the pursuit of reality, which can only be undertaken by the individual on his own.

Yet perhaps the biggest difficulty with the presentation of Calamy is that it is fundamentally irreconcilable with the comic character of the rest of the novel. For, despite the intrusion of the realities of pain and suffering, and the problems they pose, *Those Barren Leaves* remains primarily a comedy. Yet it is on the evidence of a world that is comically presented that Calamy reaches his serious solutions. Because the world is like *this*, he seems to be saying, it may be worth exploring the kinds of problems he believes need to be investigated. Calamy is seriously disillusioned with a world which is primarily a comic one, and it is this contradiction between the seriousness of his message and the comic character of the material which illustrates it that creates the greatest problems for the reader. To take Calamy seriously involves extending an equivalent degree of seriousness to the world which gives him grounds for his behaviour, and this is to give a degree of weight to the comedy which it is not really designed to bear. Absurd though the behaviour of most of the characters is, it hardly amounts to the kind of tirade against human folly which might justify Calamy's adoption of a hermit's existence. There would seem to be a basic conflict between the tendencies of the message which Huxley clearly intends to convey, and the vehicle he uses to express it: while it is impossible to see Calamy as simply another figure in the comedy, it is equally difficult to interpret the comedy as an illustration of Calamy's message. The balance between comedy and realism which Huxley achieved in *Antic Hay* is upset by the introduction of alternatives to the world he creates—a third element which he is unable to integrate with the other two.

But if the presentation of Calamy is problematic, it is not nearly so unsatisfactory as Huxley's handling of Chelifer.

Chelifer, unlike Calamy, is another of Huxley's acutely self-conscious intellectuals, and besides figuring as a character, he also acts as narrator for part of the time. He is firmly convinced (once again, unlike Calamy) that life has no meaning whatsoever, and, as if on principle, tries to lead a life which will confront him as often as possible with the absurdity of existence. It is with this in mind that he decides to take up residence in an appalling boarding-house, and to earn his living in the meantime by editing *The Rabbit Fancier's Gazette.*

Taken simply as a Peacockian caricature, one of a 'houseful of oddities', whose ruling obsession happens to be with the meaninglessness of existence, Chelifer works well enough; the real problem is that he also narrates nearly a quarter of the book. For it is difficult to see what function Chelifer is supposed to serve in his capacity as narrator; while there are obvious advantages to be derived from the combination of first and third person narration, Huxley fails to exploit any of them. Chelifer's narrative throws no new light on the action: his point of view appears to be almost exactly similar to that implied by the third person narration, and in any event he is primarily interested in talking about himself—no use is made of the different angle which a first person narrator might provide. Nor does Chelifer's narration offer any significant variety in tone: his style differs from that of the third person narrative only in being considerably more prolix—as the following sample may indicate:

> This little digression will suffice, I hope, to show that I labour, while writing, under no illusions. I do not suppose that anything I do has the slightest importance, and if I take so much pains in imparting beauty and elegance to these autobiographical fragments, it is chiefly from force of habit. You may ask why I write at all, if I regard the process as being without importance? It is a pertinent question. Why do you do this inconsistent thing? I can only plead weakness in justification. On principle I disapprove of writing; on principle I desire to live brutishly like any other ordinary human being. The flesh is willing, but the spirit is weak. I confess I grow bored. I pine for amusements other than those legitimate distractions offered by the cinema and the Palais de Danse. I

> struggle, I try to resist the temptation; but in the end I succumb. I read a page of Wittgenstein, I play a little Bach; I write a poem, a few aphorisms, a fable, a fragment of autobiography. I write with care, earnestly, with passion even, just as if there were some point in what I were doing, just as if it were important for the world to know my thoughts, just as if I had a soul to save by giving expression to them. But I am well aware, of course, that all these delightful hypotheses are inadmissible. In reality I write as I do merely to kill time and amuse a mind that is still, in spite of all my efforts, a prey to intellectual self-indulgence. . . (pp. 85–6)

And so on. The fact is, Chelifer is a *bore*, like most people whose favourite topic is their own idiosyncracies, and while bores have a great deal of comic potential, there are obvious dangers involved in making one the narrator. The longer Chelifer's narrative continues, the drearier his world-weariness and continual self-deprecation become. The comic possibilities afforded by *The Rabbit Fancier's Gazette* and by his residence at Gog's Court are almost entirely wasted through the sheer heavy-handedness of Chelifer's narration, while what little sympathy he commands is forfeited in the end by his complacent reaction to the death of Grace Elver. Mrs Aldwinkle, who has been making an embarrassing protestation of her love for him, is obliged to desist and leave his room because of a commotion outside, and Chelifer observes that

> The commotion was caused by the beginning of Miss Elver's death agony. Providence, having decided that my education had gone far enough, had broken off the lesson. The means it employed were, I must say, rather violent. A vain man might have been gratified by the reflexion that one woman had been made miserable in order that he might be taught a lesson, while another had died—like King John, of a surfeit of lampreys—in order that the lesson might be interrupted before it was carried too disagreeably far. But as it happens, I am not particularly vain. (p. 329)

It is a characteristically egocentric reaction—what happens is only important to Chelifer insofar as it affects *him*—and it is one that opens up the possibility that his narrative has perhaps some satiric purpose, that Chelifer is intended to condemn himself out of his own mouth. Yet as an explanation of Chelifer's function, this is not very satisfactory either. A first person narrative, by its very nature, nearly always commands an initial assent on the part of the reader, a feeling that what is said is to be trusted; if it was really Huxley's intention to satirize Chelifer, he fails to give his readers the cues which might prompt them to adjust their attitude accordingly. Although, as we have seen, Chelifer's style is rather an irritating one, so much of his narrative consists of straightforward reminiscence, without any apparent satiric intent on Huxley's part, that it is impossible to see him as having been designed as a satiric creation. While Chelifer's tone is too jaded and self-indulgent for him to command much sympathy, his point of view, his opinion of the other characters, is so very nearly that of the third person narrative that it is difficult to see him from the distance necessary to make him appear as an object of satire.

Nonetheless, it would be wrong to judge *Those Barren Leaves* too harshly; though it is, on the whole, the least successful of Huxley's early novels, it contains many memorable episodes. It is not the novel's flaws which make the most lasting impression, but rather such *tours de force* as the account of the journey to Rome, where each successive scene is described as though seen through the eyes of a different painter; as Lord Hovenden's mad drive around Lake Trasimene, as he attempts to terrorize Irene into marrying him; or the description of Mrs Aldwinkle's proprietorial love of all things Italian:

> . . . how she appreciated the Italians! Ever since she had bought a house in Italy, she had become the one foreigner who knew them intimately. The whole peninsula and everything it contained were her property and her secret. She had bought its arts, its music, its melodious language, its literature, its wine and cooking, the beauty of its women and the virility of its Fascists. . . Nor had she forgotten to buy the climate—the finest in Europe—the fauna—and how proud she was when she read in her morning paper that a wolf had devoured a Pistoiese sportsman within fifteen miles of home!—the flora—

> especially the red anemones and the wild tulips—the volcanoes —still so wonderfully active—the earthquakes...
> (pp. 18–19)

The weaknesses of *Those Barren Leaves* are not the result of a decline in Huxley's abilities as a comic writer, but are rather due to a fatal imbalance between the work's different elements. Both *Crome Yellow* and *Antic Hay* were primarily conceived as comedies, and in the latter, as we have seen, Huxley allowed reality to intrude as far as he dared. But in *Those Barren Leaves,* he appears to be undecided as to whether the primary mode was to be comic, even though with serious implications, or serious, with comedy used as light relief. The result is confusion, and it is confusion, in its turn which seems to be largely responsible for the crucial failure in the presentation of the novel's two main characters, Calamy and Chelifer. Uncertainty of purpose robs the work of the connecting power necessary to create a satisfactory whole.

Huxley himself testified to a sense of dissatisfaction in a letter written in the same year as his third novel appeared, referring to *Those Barren Leaves* as being

> ... tremendously accomplished, but in a queer way, I now feel, jejune and shallow and off the point. All I've written so far has been off the point. And I've taken such enormous pains to get off it; that's the stupidity. All this fuss in the intellectual void; and meanwhile the other things go on in a quiet domestic way, quite undisturbed. I wish I could afford to stop writing for a bit.
> (*Letters*, p. 242)

The immediate result of this dissatisfaction would seem to be a change, or perhaps changes in direction, for in the novels which ensure he begins to explore two different and distinct approaches to writing fiction. In *Point Counter Point* (1928), and *Eyeless in Gaza* (1936) he deserts Peacockian comedy in favour of greater realism, formal complexity, and seriousness in the treatment of ideas; while in *Brave New World* (1932), and *After Many A Summer* (1939) he turns from comedy to a brand of satire which is characterized both by a greater economy of utterance than is to be found in his earlier fiction, and also by a far more fantastic kind of humour and invention. And though the two approaches could scarcely be more dissimilar, both can be seen as the fruits of Huxley's search for a fictional format which would allow him not only to explore the values of the society in which he lived, but also to suggest ways in which they might be changed.

Yet even in his early novels there is evidence of Huxley's desire to create a kind of fiction more responsive to his needs than any model furnished by another author could be. Even as he modelled himself on Peacock, he began to extend the scope of the model he had chosen, increasingly including material whose presence would be unthinkable in one of Peacock's novels. By the time he came to write *Those Barren Leaves*, where his concern with the reality of death, and with the possibility of there being some kind of ultimate explanation of the world is combined with a tendency towards increasing narrative complexity and depth of characterization, the outlines of the original model were already becoming blurred.

Huxley's development, then, is not so much a development *of* Peacockian fiction, as a development away from it. A comparison with the author who was by far the most powerful influence on his early fiction serves primarily to highlight the dissimilarity of Huxley's temperament and outlook—a dissimilarity which helps in turn to explain the direction of Huxley's development.

Most notably, perhaps, Huxley lacks Peacock's characteristic delight in the physical world. In his fiction one finds none of the loving descriptions of pleasure, particularly the pleasures of the table, that are so prominent a feature of Peacock's novels. When Denis Stone upholds the virtues of alcohol, he does so largely in order to illustrate the virtues of the more heady intoxication of words; in any event, his speech hardly bears comparison with Dr Folliott's panegyric on the delights of lobster for breakfast, or the many illustrations of Prince Seithenyn's single-minded devotion to wine. When Huxley uses mealtimes as occasions for conversation, descriptions of the food are generally omitted, whereas in Peacock such an omission would be unthinkable. Indeed, Peacock often contrives to use the demands of the physical world to undermine the ideal world of discourse—Mr MacQuedy's exposition of his educational theories stands not the slightest chance of being taken seriously, what with the repeated interruptions of Dr Folliott, drinking toasts, or demanding such delicacies as 'a slice of lamb, with lemon and pepper'. The nearest we get to this in Huxley is in the restaurant scene in *Antic Hay*, where Coleman, on discovering that Shearwater is a kidney specialist, celebrates the fact by ordering a whole plate of kidneys, *sautés*. Food evokes not so much relish, as disgust.

If anything, Huxley seems more concerned to stress the deleterious effects of physical pleasure. Drink does not make one merry—it makes one sick—witness Lord Hovenden's trepidation about drinking too much in *Those Barren Leaves*. Food is no better: when Bruin Opps and Mrs Viveash are found at the coffee stall, they recount their experiences at a restaurant at Hampton Court, where

> Everything tasted as though it had been kept soaking for a week in the river before being served up—rather weedy, with that delicious typhoid flavour of Thames water.
>
> (*Antic Hay*, p. 59)

Grace Elver, in *Those Barren Leaves*, gluttonizes disgustingly on chocolate, and dies from eating bad fish. It is very different from the world of Peacock, where even over-indulgence is merely seen as an excuse for comedy, as for example in *The Misfortunes of Elphin*, where Prince Seithenyn's retainers loyally emulate not only their master's drinking habits, but also his inebriated collapse to the floor.

Huxley's lack of sympathy with the pleasures of the body extends into the realm of sexuality (an area with which Peacock, unsurprisingly, refrained from dealing), and here Huxley's descriptions become almost pathologically distasteful. In *Antic Hay*, Rosie's feelings after her experiences with Coleman, despite having at the time been 'overcome by a pleasure more piercing and agonizing than anything she had ever felt before' (p. 51), are of horror and shame; while Mary Thriplow (making love with whom was regarded by Calamy as 'torture') is portrayed as lying 'extenuated, limp and shuddering, like one who had been tormented on the rack' (p. 269). And this is only a foretaste of the kind of descriptions which are to be found in *Point Counter Point* or *After Many A Summer*. Sexuality does not bring people into contact, it only serves to emphasize the extent of their alienation.

For Peacock, the physical world was a source of comfort, of pleasure, of consolation, but above all it was *real*—and he almost invariably used the contrast between the physical and the intellectual world as a means of deflating the pretensions of the latter. Huxley, on the other hand, scarcely ever does this. Although, in *Crome Yellow*, he uses Anne's hedonism to poke fun at Denis's intellectual anxieties, Huxley never seems to find the physical world either comforting or real. In *Music at Night*, he remarks significantly (attacking those who believe that moral behaviour is only possible if one has faith in a life after death) that

> These moralists seem to forget that there are many human beings who simply don't want to pass their time eating, drinking and being merry. . . The deadly tedium of Horatian life . . . would be quite enough, survival or no survival, to keep me . . . unswervingly in the narrow way of domestic and intellectual labour. (p. 107)

Seeing pleasure for its own sake as merely tedious, and being as yet unclear as to the nature of the positives by which one *should* lead one's life, it is perhaps unsurprising that Huxley, in his early novels, conveys a sense of prevailing dissatisfaction. Whereas, for Peacock, dissatisfaction with the existing order of things was something to be either satirized (as in the case of Scythrop Glowry), or resolved (as with Captain Fitzchrome, in *Crotchet Castle*, whose resentments, caused by a combination of poverty and an unsuccessful love affair, are quickly dispelled by his reconciliation with Lady Clarinda), the dissatisfaction exhibited by Huxley's characters frequently seems to be endorsed by the author. The world is too complicated, too unstable, too full of misery simply to be ignored in favour of the pursuit of pleasure. And if any sense is to be made of the chaos caused by the body and its instincts, it can only be through the intellect.

As a result, we tend to find in Huxley's first three novels an increasingly serious treatment of ideas. From his portrayal of Calamy onwards, Huxley is engaged in a search for some kind of meaning or reality which will make sense of the world, and in the course of that search he shows himself prepared to re-examine even those ideas which he had previously satirized or dismissed. In *Point Counter Point,* for example, the portrayal of Rampion constitutes a serious examination of a philosophy which seeks meaning and satisfaction in the sheer fact of living—despite the fact that Huxley had earlier satirized a similar outlook through his depiction of Lypiatt's empty posturings in *Antic Hay*. And Huxley likewise treats more seriously points of view which he has come to see as wrong and dangerous: the comic portrayal of Coleman's satanism in *Antic Hay* gives way to the much more damning analysis of Spandrell's conscious pursuit of evil for its own sake in *Point Counter Point*.

Nearly all of Huxley's most basic tendencies can be seen to lead away from the world of Peacock, and while some of the techniques of presentation used in his later novels still appear to reveal Peacock's influence, the context in which they are employed is so radically altered as to make them something altogether different in kind. By the end of *Those Barren Leaves* Huxley has already left the world of Peacock behind, and where, in his subsequent fiction, he continues to employ fictional devices derived from Peacock's example, their use becomes incidental rather than central. From *Point Counter Point* onward, as we shall see, Huxley was driven to seek new and different techniques with which to structure and make sense of the world he was beginning to explore.

4
Point Counter Point and *Eyeless in Gaza*

With *Point Counter Point* (1928) and *Eyeless in Gaza* (1936), the comic format of the earlier fiction gives way to a primarily realistic approach. Comedy becomes a wholly incidental element, with the result that the tensions and contradictions apparent in Huxley's first three novels largely disappear. The witty, detached tone of the early fiction gives way to a flatter, more naturalistic presentation, and the incongruities which, in the earlier novels, arise from the fact that characters who are believable are also seen and portrayed as amusing caricatures likewise vanish.

In *Point Counter Point*, we are plunged at the outset into the midst of a tawdry domestic row—a quarrel between a man and his mistress, both of whom are painfully aware that their relationship has irretrievably broken down, but are at the same time too cowardly to admit it. Alienated from one another, they share only a sense of shame and failure in their relationship, together with a common awareness of their weakness in being unable to put an end to it. Yet for all their feebleness, their plight arouses a greater sense of sympathy and involvement on the part of the reader than is created by the more distanced, stylized presentation of character typical of the early fiction. Compared with the elegance of the opening chapters of *Crome Yellow*, *Antic Hay* and *Those Barren Leaves*, it is a drab, depressing beginning, but it nonetheless succeeds in eliminating the feeling of distance which had proved a major obstacle to Huxley's previous attempts at realistic characterization.

But it is in the following scene that it really becomes apparent just how far Huxley has moved on from *Crome Yellow* and *Antic Hay*. Lady Tantamount's musical evening, introducing a large and varied cast of characters, is an episode which still betrays the influence of Peacock, but the overall context is one in which the techniques of the older writer are transformed almost beyond recognition. Thus, while Huxley's prefatory account of the origins of the wealth and position of the Tantamount family is superficially reminiscent of Peacock's own description of Ebenezer MacCrotchet's background, it differs markedly both in its tone and its effect. Where Peacock's hints of a past history of financial double-dealing remain at the level of comedy, Huxley's recital of the misdeeds of the Tantamount family adds up to a harsh indictment of their greed, dishonesty, and meanness—an indictment which, in its turn, serves to put the frivolity of the ensuing proceedings at Tantamount House into a different perspective. While, in the course of the evening, Huxley contrives to introduce a whole gallery of characters, many of whom verge on the caricatured, there nearly always proves to be some kind of complicating factor at work. Even in the most Peacockian scene of all—the confrontation between Webley and Lord Edward, whose respective obsessions with politics and ecology cause them to talk at total cross-purposes—the comedy is to some extent modified by what we know of the characters involved: of Lord Edward's emotional immaturity, of the fact that Webley is a fascist.

Even the simplest, one-dimensional caricatures, such as the fatuous Mrs Betterton, or the pompous General Knoyle, are more than just figures of fun. The reader does not merely see Mrs Betterton being characteristically fatuous, or the General being characteristically pompous, for Huxley introduces other angles, allowing the reader to enter into other characters' experience of them. We are shown Walter's father's irritation at Mrs Betterton, Illidge's hatred of General Knoyle, even the General's own vexation at being made fun of by Lady Tantamount. Unlike Peacock's characters, who hardly seem to be aware of one another's existence, and scarcely ever take offence, Huxley presents the spectacle of a world where people *are* affected by one another, if not to the extent that communication actually takes place between them, at least far enough to allow them to annoy one another.

As in both *Antic Hay* and *Those Barren Leaves*, we also encounter the complicating factor that even the most apparently caricatured behaviour may be the result of a consciously adopted pose which implies the existence of a person who has adopted it. Molly d'Exergillod, for example, whom Huxley describes as 'a professional athlete of the tongue', is presented in a distanced, ironic fashion reminiscent of the earlier novels. We are told that

> ... like all professional talkers Molly was very economical with her wit and wisdom. There are not enough *bons mots* in existence to provide any industrious conversationalist with a new stock for every social occasion... A good housewife, she knew how to hash up the conversational remains of last night's dinner to furnish out this morning's lunch. Monday's funeral baked meats did service for Tuesday's wedding. (p. 119)

Yet at the same time we are also made aware of the element of calculation involved: the very self-conscious artificiality of her conversation makes her more than the kind of obsession brought to life that we find in Peacock. Instead, she is shown as someone who has *chosen* to play a certain part—a method of presentation which is at once subtler and more depressing.

With Burlap, there is an even stronger sense that there is a man behind the mask. While there is a strong element of caricature in the depiction of his posturings about Art, about the Spirit, about Life, it is backed up by a great deal of detail about the characteristics which lie behind the public personality—about his meanness and greed, for example, about the way in which he loves to wallow in emotion for its own sake, about his revolting sexual habits—to the extent that he becomes less a caricature than a study in hypocrisy. In addition, there is a streak of viciousness in Huxley's portrait (which evidently bore a sufficiently close resemblance to Middleton Murry for the latter to consider challenging Huxley to a duel), which, once again, cuts down the reader's sense of distance from the action. Huxley clearly *dislikes* the character he has portrayed and, equally clearly, he intends that the reader should share that dislike: hence such scenes as Burlap's seduction of Beatrice while continuing to pretend that they are both little children, which, by the feeling of revulsion it evokes, serves to heighten the reader's sense of involvement in the action.

While Huxley is still concerned to portray the variety of ways in which it is possible to interpret experience, it is noticeable that the particular interpretation afforded by the detached, ironic observer is far less in evidence. A man slipping on a banana skin and fracturing his skull might, as Lypiatt suggested in *Antic Hay*, be seen to describe 'the most richly comical arabesque' as he fell; *Hamlet* could be retold as a farce; but in the context of *Point Counter Point* the kind of detachment which might make such interpretations possible would be inappropriate. It is grimmer, as well as more realistic than Huxley's earlier novels, and its world is one where a Peacockian attitude would seem frivolous and irresponsible; even in a scene of Peacock-style slapstick, as when Illidge slips on the stairs in the full view of the audience at the Tantamount's concert, the focus is not so much on the spectacle he presents to those who find it funny, as on his own consciousness of being that spectacle, of being made to look ridiculous.

Throughout *Point Counter Point*, Huxley consistently sacrifices the comic possibilities of his material in favour of a subtler and more complex presentation, which gives a degree of depth to even the most minor characters, and it is against this background that he proceeds to conduct a far more serious investigation of the implications of the behaviour of his central characters than would have been possible in the context of his earlier fiction. If we look, for example, at Lucy, or Spandrell, we find what was only fleetingly apparent before: a serious examination of particular philosophies of life, and of the life-styles that follow from them.

Lucy's attitude towards life is similar to that of Anne Wimbush in *Crome Yellow*, or Mrs Viveash, in *Antic Hay*, but it is clear from Huxley's successive portrayals of a hedonist outlook that his attitude towards it was rapidly changing. Where Anne appears to enjoy authorial approval, her uncomplicated attitude serving to make Denis's anxieties and confusions seem all the more ridiculous. Huxley's treatment of Mrs Viveash is more equivocal; while her languid pursuit of distractions from the boredom of everyday existence is amusingly enough portrayed, it is also clear that it is a pursuit which involves her in causing a considerable amount of unhappiness to others. Although her past history helps to explain her behaviour, it does not altogether disguise the fact that it is irresponsible. In Lucy's case, however, there is no question of equivocation: her hedonism is quite clearly seen as not only amoral, but wrong. In her affair with Walter, for example, the callousness she displays goes far beyond what might be seen as justifiable annoyance at his pathetic behaviour; while it is clear that his view of their relationship is a wholly unrealistic one, her final letter, in which she describes to him in the greatest possible detail her sexual encounter with a total stranger, reveals a viciousness which is her characteristic reaction to the implication that she has responsibilities to another person.

Spandrell, with his conscientious abandonment of moral standards, might be seen as an example of the Peacockian character whose behaviour is ruled by an obsession, but once again Huxley in interested in the reality of a life-style rather than its comic possibilities. While Spandrell's philosophy bears certain similarities to that of Coleman in *Antic Hay*, it is presented very differently. Coleman's blasphemy and debauchery are only briefly seen (through Rosie's eyes) as something disgusting: for the most part his vigour and theatricality combine to make his views seem amusing. But while in comedy there can be a liveliness about such perversity, Spandrell is anything but lively. Corrupt, slothful, and bored, his wilfully negative attitude towards life finally leads him to a logical enough conclusion—suicide. Seeing himself in grandiose terms, the explorer of all that becomes permissible when morality is jettisoned, his behaviour amounts to little more than posturing. He boasts to Rampion and his wife of his seduction of young girls, but the reality behind his claims is merely sordid, while his efforts to free himself from the tyranny of convention are put into perspective by the petty details of his existence—drinking too much, not getting up until the afternoon, cadging money from his mother. Even when, in search of the ultimate sensation, he commits murder, he finds the experience strangely unreal. Killing Webley solves nothing and reveals nothing; it is just another pointless act. Seeking to abandon all standards and scruples, Spandrell becomes obsessed by the need to find something which will give his life shape and meaning, only to realize that his exploration of evil is rendered meaningless by his inability to accept any moral code which would enable him to see it as evil. In despair, he engineers his own death at the hands of Webley's thugs.

Both Lucy and Spandrell live one-sided, limited lives—lives from which, as they themselves are only too well aware, there is something missing. In their attempts to define it, however, they only contrive to illustrate the extent of their own degeneracy:

> Lucy frowned. 'I'm so sick of the ordinary conventional sorts of liveliness. Youth at the prow and pleasure at the helm. You know. It's silly, it's monotonous. Energy seems to have so few ways of manifesting itself nowadays. It was different in the past, I believe.'
>
> 'There was violence as well as love-making. Is that what you mean?'
>
> 'That's it.' She nodded. 'The liveliness wasn't so exclusively . . . so exclusively bitchy, to put it bluntly.'
>
> 'They broke the sixth commandment too. There are too many policemen nowadays.'
>
> 'Many too many. They don't allow you to stir an eyelid. One ought to have had all the experiences.'
>
> 'But if none of them are either right or wrong—which is what you seem to feel—what's the point?'
>
> 'The point? But they might be amusing, they might be exciting.'
>
> 'They could never be very exciting if you didn't feel they were wrong.' (pp. 214–15)

Spandrell's search for excitement leads, as we have seen, to murder and death. Lucy's leads to—what? Presumably to an ever more desperate search for new experience, for more and more unconventional forms of liveliness; the directions she intends to explore can only be guessed at from her last letter to Walter, where she describes her experiences with the young Italian she picks up:

> 'He came at me as if he were going to kill me. I shut my eyes, like a Christian martyr in front of a lion. Martyrdom's exciting. Letting oneself be hurt, humiliated, used like a doormat—queer. I like it.' (p. 493)

But the squalor of the lives of Lucy and Spandrell is by no means exceptional: the world portrayed in *Point Counter Point* is a sordid one, full of horror and suffering. Where only one death intruded on the comedy of *Those Barren Leaves, Point Counter Point* features two murders, a suicide, and the death of a small child from meningitis. The distaste for physical experience which was observable in Huxley's earlier fiction is transformed into an exaggerated revulsion: with the exception of the disgusting account of the Quarles' culinary experiences in India, food is mentioned mainly in connection with John Bidlake's growing incapacity to digest it; drink has only unpleasant effects, leaving Spandrell's mouth 'haunted by a taste like the fumes of heated brass', making Walter ill, and causing Carling to get disagreeably drunk. Sexual activity evokes nothing but aversion: besides Lucy's and Spandrell's experiments, we are also treated to unappealing descriptions of Sidney Quarles' lechery, and of Burlap's infantile fumblings with Beatrice.

With this kind of emphasis on the most negative aspects of experience, it is scarcely surprising that Huxley's characters appear even less able to cope with reality than was the case in his earlier novels. Walter shares Denis Stone's feebleness and ineffectuality, but their effects are far more disastrous; Chelifer's emotional poverty is nothing compared with that of Philip Quarles. Characteristics which Huxley might once have treated comically are now seen as indicative of a drastically limited and inadequate response to life. But it is not just the weak characters who suffer: even the most virile and energetic figures are ultimately powerless. John Bidlake's creative powers fade with the onset of illness and old age, while Everard Webley, for all his vigour and authority, can do nothing to prevent his murder.

Where even the most determined and capable characters are vulnerable, the weaker ones, the Walters and the Philips, seem completely at the mercy of a harsh and uncaring world. Elinor's timid hesitations over whether or not to have an affair with Webley are rendered pathetic and irrelevant by his murder, and the almost simultaneous death of her son. Sidney Quarles, unable to face up to the problems created by his mistress's pregnancy, takes to his bed under the pretence that he is dying, and leaves his wife to deal with the matter. Unable to cope with life, the characters in *Point Counter Point* are obliged to take refuge instead in illusions and compensatory fantasies. Sidney Quarles tries to convince himself that he is a great writer; Illidge attempts to disguise his weakness by advocating violent revolution; Walter maintains, in the face of all the evidence to the contrary, an illusion of Lucy's tender and loving nature. No-one has the courage or the vision to live more than a partial, limited existence, or to see the world other than through a protective haze of subjective illusion.

No-one, that is, except Rampion. Just as, in *Those Barren Leaves,* Huxley had sought to balance his exposure of human weakness by the delineation of possible alternatives to the undesirable norms of behaviour he saw around him, he clearly felt that the far harsher depiction of human inadequacy in *Point Counter Point* also called for the inclusion of character who had at least some answers. Rampion's philosophy of life, however, is far removed from Calamy's rather vague mysticism—he constitutes, in fact, an extremely thinly veiled portrait of D. H. Lawrence, and expounds what Huxley took to be Lawrence's views.

At the same time, Rampion also illustrates Huxley's growing inclination to re-examine and re-assess ideas which he had previously satirized. Rampion's insistence on the necessity of leading a whole, harmonious existence bears more than a passing resemblance to the philosophy expounded by Lypiatt in *Antic Hay*. But whereas Lypiatt is made to look ridiculous by the fact that for all his high ideal and grandiose visions, he is essentially a mediocrity, a man whose denunciations of the modern world are somewhat undermined by his aspirations to success in the terms of that world, Rampion is obviously intended to be taken seriously. Unlike Lypiatt, he is portrayed as possessing genuine artistic talent: his vision is harsh and clear, free from the vulgarity and self-indulgence which prompted Mrs Viveash to compare Lypiatt's paintings to Vermouth posters. Nor does he dissipate his energies in the way that Lypiatt does—unlike Lypiatt, he has a certain sense of proportion, and sees the world too clearly to be seduced by it. Yet he is not a mere spectator, either: he has the vitality to become involved in living, and to preserve him from the arid intellectualism of characters like Chelifer and Quarles.

Rampion is practically the only character in *Point Counter Point* whose life can be seen as the product of a balance between mind and instinct, between intellect and emotion, and it is balance which is the essence of his message, of the alternative he offers. Amid all the partial, unbalanced, incomplete lives of the people who surround him, he stands for wholeness and harmony, for living the whole of life to the full, not part of it to excess. He is able to enjoy himself, but his life is not just an aimless pursuit of pleasure; he works, but not, like Philip Quarles, to the exclusion of living. Significantly, too, his marriage is the only successful relationship portrayed in the whole book—he and his wife complement one another, rather than protecting or exploiting each other. And it is from the standpoint of his own satisfactory, fully achieved existence that Rampion puts forward his ideas as to what life ought to be like.

Man, according to Rampion, is

> . . . a creature on a tight rope, walking delicately, equilibrated, with mind and consciousness and spirit at one end of the balancing pole, and body and instinct and all that's unconscious and earthy and mysterious at the other. Balanced. (p. 560)

Or at least, that is what man ought to be. Unfortunately, Rampion finds himself surrounded by people who are less than fully human, people who

> . . . could have been perfectly decent human beings if they'd just gone about behaving naturally, in accordance with their instincts. But no, they wanted to be more than human. So they just became devils. Idiots first and then devils, imbecile devils. (p. 563)

In Rampion's view, those who deny their own essential humanity by attempting to transcend it are, in the truest sense of the word, perverts:

> . . . And all perverted in the same way—by trying to be non-human. Non-humanly religious, non-humanly moral, non-humanly intellectual and scientific, non-humanly specialized and efficient, non-humanly the business man, non-humanly avaricious and property-loving, non-humanly lascivious and

> Don Juanesque, non-humanly the conscious individual even in love. All perverts. Perverted towards goodness or badness, towards spirit or flesh but always away from the central norm, always away from humanity. The world's an asylum of perverts. (pp. 563–4)

And, in the context of *Point Counter Point*, it seems a justifiable enough view, particularly since the audience to whom he addresses his remarks consists of Burlap, Quarles, and Spandrell, all of whom can be seen to bear them out. Unlike Calamy, Rampion has more than enough material to substantiate his criticisms of the world in which he lives.

Turning to *Eyeless in Gaza*, we find much the same tendencies at work: if anything, the picture of society it paints is even bleaker, the alternatives it puts forward still more explicit. While, unlike *Point Counter Point*, it is essentially the story of one man, centring on the experiences of Anthony Beavis, it is a work of equivalent narrative complexity, relying on a dislocation of the time sequence to achieve the kind of juxtapositions and contrasts which, in the earlier novel, resulted from the counterpointing of different story-lines.

Perhaps the main advantage of the novel's extended time-span is that it allows Huxley to explore more thoroughly than before the implications of the different attitudes and life-styles of his characters; while, as we have already seen, one of his chief preoccupations is with what happens when the individual is forced to confront a fact of life (pain, suffering, old age, death) which he has previously managed to ignore, the time-scale of *Eyeless in Gaza* allows him to go into greater and more uncomfortable detail. In the earlier novels some of the characters, at least, are able to avoid such confrontations, but in *Eyeless in Gaza* almost everyone is forced, sooner or later, to face up to the consequences of the life-styles they have chosen to adopt. One need only contrast the portrayal of Lucy, in *Point Counter Point* with that of her equivalent in *Eyeless in Gaza*, Mary Amberley. While Lucy's irresponsible hedonism is quite clearly seen as wrong, it is only in *Eyeless in Gaza* that Huxley goes on to portray what he takes to be the inevitable consequences of such an attitude to life.

It is this more exhaustive examination of inadequate, limited ways of living that makes the world of *Eyeless in Gaza* even more nightmarish than that of *Point Counter Point*. Not only are the characters, as in *Point Counter Point*, incapable of coping with reality—they become progressively more incapable of coping with it as times goes on. Anthony's father, for example, is a pathetic enough figure at the outset, with his melodramatic displays of grief for his dead wife, and his distasteful attempts to keep alive her memory, but it is only in the course of his subsequent marriage to the gluttonous Pauline that the full extent of his emotional immaturity becomes apparent. At the same time, his inability to communicate with people becomes increasingly embarrassing, as his confidential little linguistic jokes fall steadily flatter and flatter. Similarly, his brother James, despite his more generous nature, is shown becoming progressively more irascible and neurotic through being forced to repress his homosexual impulses; a militant atheist for most of his life, he ends up seeking comfort and refuge in Catholicism.

Anthony's father and uncle, however, are comparatively minor figures; it is the limitations of the attitudes of the central characters which Huxley exposes most ruthlessly. Brian Foxe, for example, dominated by his mother, becomes the victim of his inability to come to terms with his own sexuality. The neuroses this induces first sap his health, then undermine his mental stability. On learning of his fiancée's unfaithfulness, he commits suicide. Mark Staithes, a far more forceful and energetic figure, likewise alters for the worse: the determination and assertiveness he displays as a schoolboy is gradually transformed by his increasing cynicism into bitterness and misanthropy. His instinctive compulsion to excel is thwarted by his inability to believe that there is anything worth excelling in, and he gradually turns in on himself until he becomes as twisted and negative as Chelifer or Spandrell. He ends up crippled in body as well as spirit after losing a leg during an abortive attempt to take part in a revolution in Mexico.

Mary Amberley is seen successively as a young wife; as the charming divorcée with whom Anthony has his first sexual experiences; as a callous exploiter of his affections, manipulating him into his unwilling seduction of Joan Thursley; as the ageing mistress of Gerry Watchett, desperately trying to hold on to her lover's waning affection; and finally as a morphine addict, living in the utmost poverty and squalor. And, as if to emphasize the deficiencies of hedonism as a way of life, her career is paralleled by that of Beppo Bowles, a Wildean aesthete with homosexual proclivities, whom the passage of time treats just as unkindly. As he becomes progressively balder and more corpulent, his sexual relationships deteriorate into mere commercial transactions, in which affection plays no part, and he ends up miserable and alone, unable to find any consolation in the values by which he has lived his life.

If Mary and Beppo are enslaved by the attractions of the flesh, Brian and Mark are equally the victims of their denial of the demands of the physical world. Yet Huxley also seeks to show that freedom from such obsessions is not, by itself, enough; even a sane and balanced life can lead to disaster, if it is informed by an inadequate positive ideal. And it is with this in mind that he introduces the Communist, Ekki Giesebrecht—the man with whom Helen falls in love after leaving Anthony. Ekki is portrayed as being brave, generous, and resourceful, but at the same time as a man who is irrevocably compromised by his commitment to an ideology which Huxley sees as being one of cruelty and violence. For all his positive qualities, his idealism is seen as misplaced, and in the end he dies, cruelly, violently, and pointlessly, at the hands of the fascists.

What, then, is Huxley's positive idea? What alternatives does he offer to counterbalance his portrayal of so many unsatisfactory, wasted lives? Huxley clearly felt that in the context of the sombre world he had created the positives offered by Calamy and Rampion were insufficient, and that something more persuasive, more explicit was required. Rather than presenting the example of someone who, like Rampion, is able to live a full and harmonious existence in the midst of a chaotic and unsatisfactory world, he chooses to show how even the most unregenerate of individuals can change the patterns of their behaviour, and discover a right way of living.

The process of regeneration, however, is by no means simple. Anthony Beavis, the character who is eventually converted to what Huxley sees as a desirable way of life is, even by the standards of behaviour encountered in *Eyeless in Gaza*, conspicuously unregenerate. In addition to being one of those typically Huxleian figures who, like Chelifer or Quarles, attempt to avoid involvement by living only with the intellect, he also displays numerous other undesirable traits. At school he shows himself to be both a coward and a hypocrite, playing down his genuine friendship with Brian Foxe in order to maintain the good opinion of his school-fellows. Being characteristically self-conscious, however, he is not unaware of this, and at times he finds himself hating his friend for having

> . . . the courage of convictions which Anthony felt should also be *his* convictions—which, indeed, would be his convictions, if only he could bring himself to have the courage of them.
> (p. 82)

The same thing happens at university: once again, Anthony evades his commitments to his real friends in order to gratify his snobbery by mixing with the aristocratic circle of Gerry Watchett. Later on, he becomes the direct cause of Brian's suicide when, at Mary Amberley's instigation, he seduces his fiancée. And so it goes on: Anthony displays an inexhaustible capacity for making excuses, both to himself and to others, which will enable him to avoid commitments and responsibilities. Even in his love affairs he shrinks from emotional involvement, deliberately keeping them at a casual, purely physical level.

Nevertheless, it is while he is engaged in just such an affair that the event takes place which finally shatters his complacency, and sets in train the long sequence of events which enable him to break free from his life-long habits of hypocrisy and irresponsibility. Somewhat improbably, a dog falls out of an aeroplane onto the roof of the villa where he and his mistress are making love, drenching them both in blood. Seeing her standing before him, shuddering with horror, Anthony realizes, almost for the first time, that there is someone else there; his protective carapace has finally cracked, and he sees that there is another person in front of him—another person with their own demands and needs. She, however, hearing only the flippant remark with which he tries to pass the incident off, realizes what is equally true—that there is nothing there—and it is out of the dissolution of their relationship at the very moment when Anthony realizes what such a relationship ought to involve that his search for something which will give his life meaning begins.

At the time it seems to Anthony that his whole life has dissolved, leaving him with nothing, and in despair he accepts Mark's invitation to accompany him to Mexico to take part in an armed uprising. Not, it should be added, out of political conviction, but in order to see if he can find some kind of reality beyond the pointless, civilized existence he has been leading. Mark does not try to justify the cause for which they will be fighting: he seems rather to share the belief which Huxley put forward in *Do What You Will*—that revolution is 'a stimulus to present living'. '"Revolution for revolution's sake, then?"' asks Anthony, and Staithes replies:

> 'No, for mine. For the sake of every man who takes part in the thing. For every man who can get as much fun out of it as I can.' (p. 413)

But it proves to be a false trail. Although Rampion, with his belief in living life for its own sake, and his Lawrentian conviction that reality is obscured by the veneer of civilization, might have approved, the Mexican expedition turns out to be a disaster. The only 'fun' Mark gets is that of seeing Anthony make a fool of himself, which can hardly be seen as sufficient recompense for his losing a leg; while Anthony only discovers what he had suspected all along—that he is a physical as well as a moral coward. His humiliation by the drunken Mexican in the hotel at Tapatlán is the low point of the whole novel.

Yet it is only shortly afterwards that light appears, not in the shape of revolution for fun, or through the discovery, in the land of *The Plumed Serpent*, of some primeval Lawrentian blood-consciousness, but in the person of Miller, the pacifist doctor. It is Miller who shows Anthony the direction he should take, and gives him the impetus to explore it. This direction, however, is not simply towards the achievement of personal fulfilment, but rather towards the creation of a world where the opportunities for such fulfilment are greater. Unlike Calamy, whose solution is to withdraw from the world, or Rampion, who is content simply to *be* within it, Miller is the first of Huxley's guru figures who sees the need for the creation of a new and different world. For Miller the reform of oneself and of the world are inseparable, and through his example Anthony becomes actively involved in the pacifist movement, whilst at the same time embarking on a programme of re-educating himself both morally and physically, observing as he does so that

> States and Nations don't exist as such. There are only people. Sets of people living in certain areas, having certain allegiances. Nations won't change their national policies unless and until people change their private policies. All governments, even Hitler's, even Stalin's, even Mussolini's, are representative. Today's national behaviour—a large scale projection of today's individual behaviour. (p. 228)

The solution which Anthony pursues is to involve himself in 'right action' as a pacifist, while at the same time learning 'the proper use of self' through exercising discipline over both mind and body, and it is very much a reflection of Huxley's own preoccupations at the time. Whereas Rampion was a portrait of Lawrence, Beavis is very much Huxley himself, displaying in exaggerated form what Huxley felt to be his own personal weaknesses, and also finding comfort in the same kind of alternatives as he himself was exploring at the time he was writing *Eyeless in Gaza*.

It remains to be seen how far the alternatives proposed in *Eyeless in Gaza* provided Huxley with a lasting solution to his own personal difficulties, but in the context of the novel it is clear that they provide Anthony with the answer. As he becomes involved in changing every aspect of his life his old fears and compulsions begin to lose their hold over him. Abandoning the casual promiscuity which had always been his substitute for love, he leads a celibate existence whilst attempting to re-establish his relationship with Helen on a better, less selfish basis. At the same time, he begins to overcome both his moral and his physical cowardice. His acute discomfort in the face of other people's suffering disappears, and instead of the revulsion he had previously felt at Mary Amberley's bedside, or while listening to Beppo's self-pitying outbursts, he learns compassion. At the end of the novel it appears that even his physical fear has been exorcized. Despite having received ominous threats of physical violence, he sets off to address a pacifist meeting feeling only a serene sensation of confidence:

> ... he thought of what was in store for him. Whatever it might be, he knew now that all would be well.

Weak, self-conscious, over-intellectual, emotionally impoverished, Anthony is in most respects a typically Huxleian figure—a character very much in the mould of Denis Stone, Gumbril, Chelifer, Walter Bidlake, and Philip Quarles. Yet there is also an important difference: unlike any of his precursors, Anthony shows himself to be capable of changing.

During the composition of *Eyeless in Gaza* Huxley became actively involved in the work of the Peace Pledge Union, and also underwent instruction in the techniques of physical re-education pioneered by the Australian therapist, F. M. Alexander;[1] it would seem that his main purpose in portraying Anthony as engaged in almost identical activities was to suggest that the solutions which he had found applicable to his own problems were in fact relevant to everyone. Anthony's conversion is intended as an example to the reader, and although its presentation is obviously integral to the novel's artistic success, it is clear that Huxley is more interested in his central character's relevance to the real world than in artistic considerations.

Nonetheless, the real world, at least as portrayed in *Eyeless in Gaza*, may well seem somewhat unfamiliar to the majority of readers. While, in both *Point Counter Point* and *Eyeless in Gaza*, Huxley may be said to have adopted a 'realistic' approach, as distinct from the comic format of his earlier novels, there can be no doubt that his particular brand of realism is decidedly idiosyncratic.

So far as Huxley was concerned, the representation of reality was not a simple matter: as he saw it, most novelists' aspiration to realism was compromised by the inevitable discrepancy that exists between life and its artistic representation. Even the most thoroughgoing representational novel cannot include *everything*, and to the extent that it makes omissions, it also distorts and falsifies. The problem with Art, suggests Philip Quarles, in *Point Counter Point*, is that

> ... it's apt to be too true. Unadulterated, like distilled water. When truth is nothing but the truth, it's unnatural, it's an abstraction that resembles nothing in the real world. In nature there are always so many other irrelevant things mixed up with the essential truth. That's why art moves you—precisely because it's unadulterated with all the irrelevancies of real life. Real orgies are never so exciting as pornographic books. In a volume by Pierre Louys all the girls are young and their figures perfect; there's no fatigue or boredom, no sudden recollections of unpaid bills or business letters unanswered, to interrupt the raptures. Art gives you the sensation, the thought, the feeling quite pure—chemically pure... (p. 10)

And it is in this purity, in Huxley's view, that the distortion, the falsity lies.

It is a point which is developed at greater length in *Eyeless in Gaza*, where Mark Staithes complains of what he calls 'the profound untruthfulness of even the best imaginative literature'. It is not an untruthfulness which stems from the distortion of what *is* presented, but from the distorting effect of the omissions on which literature inevitably relies:

> Almost total neglect of those small physiological events that decide whether day-to-day living shall have a pleasant or unpleasant tone. Excretion, for example, with its power to make or mar the day. Digestion. And, for the heroines of novel and drama, menstruation. Then the small illnesses—catarrh, rheumatism, headache, eyestrain. The chronic physical disabilities... And conversely the sudden accessions, from unknown visceral and muscular sources, of more than ordinary health. No mention, next of the part placed by mere sensations in producing happiness. Hot bath, for example, taste of bacon, feel of fur, smell of freesias. In life, an empty cigarette-case may cause more distress than the absence of a lover; never in books. (pp. 520–1)

While it might be argued that the inclusion of such details would give a disproportionate emphasis to the routine and inessential, Staithes goes on to suggest that literature refuses to deal with things that *are* important, and that by doing so it gives a false picture of the reality it purports to represent:

> Lying by omission turns into positive lying. The implications of literature are that human beings are controlled, if not by reason, at least by comprehensible, well-organized, avowable sentiments. Whereas the facts are quite different. Sometimes the sentiments come in, sometimes they don't. All for love, or the world well lost; but love may be the title of nobility given to an inordinate liking for a particular person's smell or texture, a lunatic desire for the repetition of a sensation produced by some particular dexterity. Or consider those cases (seldom published, but how numerous, as anyone in a position to know can tell!), those cases of the eminent statesmen, churchmen, lawyers, captains of industry—seemingly so sane, demonstrably so intelligent, publicly so high-principled; but, in private, under irresistible compulsion towards brandy, towards young men, towards little girls in trains, towards exhibitionism, towards gambling or hoarding, towards bullying, towards being whipped, towards all the innumerable, crazy perversions of the lust for money and power and position on the one hand, for sexual pleasure on the other. Mere tics and tropisms, lunatic and unavowable cravings—these play as much part in human life as the organized and recognized sentiments. And imaginative literature suppresses the fact. Propagates an enormous lie about the nature of men and women. (p. 521)

What Huxley seems to believe (there is no indication that in this instance Staithes is anything other than the author's mouthpiece), is that the omission of trivial physiological details, of seemingly irrelevant thoughts and actions, of unavowable sentiments and motivations, creates the unnatural impression that life has shape and meaning. A novel may purport to represent reality, but in fact it imposes an artificial order on its raw material. The demands of the plot, considerations of aesthetic unity, the author's own prejudices and preoccupations—all these dictate what is included and left out, and create, in the end, a misleading impression of what reality is actually like. Perhaps part of the appeal of the avowedly representational novel lies in just that: with the irrelevant details whittled away, the characters appeal to lead tighter, more meaningful, more exciting lives than people do in real life—yet the illusion that life is like that is still maintained. Even the most complex novel represents a simplification, and that simplification is attractive in itself.

Huxley's fundamental objection to such literature, however, is that it is escapist. In *Do What You Will*, he suggested that

> ... it is the fear of the labyrinthine flux and complexity of phenomena that has driven men to philosophy, to science, to theology—fear of a complex reality driving them to invent a simpler, more manageable, and therefore consoling fiction. (pp. 119–20)

He himself, however, clearly believed that imaginative literature ought to be more than a consolation. Rather than imposing a specious, comforting order on reality, he believed that the Novel should illustrate ways in which real life itself might be given order and meaning.

In order to realize this aim various strategies were possible. As we shall see, Huxley experimented not only with realism, but also with fantasy and satire, rather as if he felt that, since representational fiction inevitably romanticizes reality, it would be more honest to turn to a medium which deliberately and avowedly distorts reality. In fantasy and satire, after all, the rules are different: both approach the truth by another route. Another alternative might have been an extreme form of naturalism: while, at the time of writing, his criticisms of representational fiction had some justification, subsequent novelists have gone on to experiment with the inclusion of just the kinds of detail he refers to. Concentrating on small areas of experience, or short stretches of time, novelists since then *have* sought to include everything: by accommodating their writing to the pace of life itself, by abandoning literature's pretensions to impose order on experience, they have tried to reproduce reality exactly as it is experienced. But for Huxley such an approach would have been impossible; while he was critical of literature for the way it falsified reality, he himself had other aims in writing than simple representational authenticity. Unwilling to make the sacrifices which the most extreme naturalism demands, he sought some kind of compromise which would allow him to remedy the deficiencies of orthodox imaginative fiction whilst continuing to be guided by artistic considerations.

In both *Point Counter Point* and *Eyeless in Gaza*, therefore, while going to considerable lengths to include the kind of details which literature normally leaves out, Huxley nevertheless fits them into an overall scheme which remains ordered and selective. While aspiring to represent reality more faithfully than ever before, he continues to employ a fairly traditional approach. For all their narrative complexity, neither *Point Counter Point* nor *Eyeless in Gaza* are in any sense technically revolutionary, and it is from the inherent contradiction between what would seem to have been Huxley's essentially radical aims and the orthodox methods he adopted in order to realize them, that most of his problems stem.

Thus, while in both novels Huxley presents his material in an ordered and schematic manner, he at the same time consistently seeks to dispel the impression that life operates in accordance with an orderly pattern of cause and effect. Both *Point Counter Point* and *Eyeless in Gaza* are full of wholly arbitrary incident: in *Point Counter Point* the more sensational occurrences just *happen*—mere co-incidence, together with a passing whim of Spandrell's, lead to Webley's murder, while the Quarles' child dies for no reason at all. Similarly, in *Eyeless in Gaza*, although there is perhaps more of an overall sense of direction, it is an accident that touches off the train of events that leads to Anthony's conversion. If the dog had not fallen onto the roof where he and Helen were making love, he might well have continued to live as he had always done, without questioning the premises of his way of life. *This*, Huxley seems to be saying, is what life is really like—full of incidents which, although they may affect us, have neither cause nor purpose.

The problem with this approach, however, is that while in real life it is possible to see the arbitrary, gratuitous occurrences that take place as indicative of an uncaring and meaningless universe, there is no disguising the fact that in a novel such occurrences are consciously willed by the author. As a result, their inclusion tends to detract from rather than heighten the impression of verisimilitude. Even if one privately believes that life has no pattern or meaning, it is hard to avoid feeling that the author who consciously introduces arbitrary and meaningless incident into the narrative is doing so in order to persuade the reader of his own belief in the meaninglessness of existence. Even the least orderly novel has some kind of pattern imposed by the author's selectivity, by the decision to include one thing rather than another, and while in real life meaninglessly sensational things do happen (people do get killed by escaped gorillas—indeed, for all one knows, dogs may fall out of aeroplanes on top of people making love on rooftops in the south of France), they are nonetheless rare, and in the context of a novel, their inclusion is likely to involve a disproportionate degree of emphasis. The inclusion, in what purports to be a representation of reality, of events which are not only outside the reader's experience, but are outside the realms of the reader's *likely* experience, are liable at the very least to prompt speculation as to the reason for their inclusion. And in Huxley's case the reasons are fairly obvious: in both novels purposeless events are included, on purpose, to show that there is no purpose. They are deliberately put in to illustrate the role of the accidental. There is an inescapable contradiction involved.

However, it is not just through the inclusion of arbitrary and meaningless events that Huxley seeks to create an impression of truth to life; he also goes out of his way to describe the 'small physiological events' which make up much of our experience of reality. His characters get drunk, feel sick, have hangovers; the most trivial details of their lives are shown; their actions often have no motivation other than the desire to kill time. It is as though Huxley is deliberately trying to avoid making his characters larger than life.

With this in mind, Huxley also seeks to demythologize the 'comprehensible, well-organized, avowable sentiments' which too often dictate the actions of characters in books. Even where his characters appear to be motivated by such sentiments, Huxley almost invariably stresses their ambiguous nature. Walter's unrequited love for Lucy is shorn of the pathos which might normally attach to it by the emphasis which is put on the unreal, romanticized nature of his feelings. The gulf between his adolescent idealization of Lucy, and the reality of her taste for being sexually humiliated is too great to allow us to see Walter's love as anything but the product of a more complex psychological need to avoid facing up to reality. Illidge's revolutionary idealism turns out to be simply a means of compensating for his cowardice and feelings of social inadequacy. Mark Staithes' courage is merely a by-product of his pig-headed obstinacy. Even what might seem the most comprehensible and avowable of sentiments—grief for the dead—is unsympathetically portrayed: John Beavis's sorrow after the death of his wife is shown as being almost pathologically self-indulgent. When we see him fumbling among his dead wife's clothing, we are in the presence, not of noble of justifiable emotions, but rather of 'mere tics and tropisms, lunatic and unavowable cravings'. The most laudable human qualities may well have a seamy underside; the qualities of gentleness and decency which attract Helen to Hugh Ledwidge are shown as having their origin in the 'squalidly tender little Eden of enemas and spankings' (p. 79) which Hugh is occupying when his school-fellows find him masturbating. Hugh grows up to prefer his onanistic fantasies to the reality of human contact, and it becomes apparent that the reason he is able to behave with gentleness and decency is because his real life is lived elsewhere.

But while all this may be taken to constitute a corrective to what Huxley saw as more normal fictional practice, this does not necessarily make his version of reality any more complete or less distorted than those of the writers whose defects he sought to remedy. Peter Bowering suggests that Huxley's preoccupation with squalid behaviour and repulsive physical detail serves a specific purpose:

> In his essay on Swift, Huxley notes that, considered as comments on reality, Gulliver and Prometheus, for all their astonishing difference, have a common origin—'the refusal on the part of their authors to accept the physical reality of the world'. Intense disgust with physiological phenomena is always associated, in Huxley, with a refusal to face reality. Almost all the characters in [*Eyeless in Gaza*] are guilty in their respective ways.
>
> (*Aldous Huxley: A Study of the Major Novels*, p. 127)

The trouble with this, however, is that Huxley's own 'disgust with physiological phenomena' is the equal of that of any of his characters. One of the most distinctive features of both *Point Counter Point* and *Eyeless in Gaza* is the revulsion from physical reality which informs them. Even when, under the influence of Lawrence, he was most insistent on the importance of the physical world, his instincts betray him. Deep down, Huxley shared Swift's morbid horror of the flesh, and it is because of this that he so consistently stresses the sordid aspects of both the physical world and of human motivation.

However, this is not to criticize Huxley, as Huxley criticized Swift, for his morbid outlook: Huxley's weakness lies in the way his outlook is expressed. While Swift's jaundiced attitude never interfered with his capacities as a satirist (an insistence on physical squalor being of positive assistance where the purpose is to undermine human pretensions), in Huxley's case his instincts are at odds with his intentions. For neither *Point Counter Point* nor *Eyeless in Gaza* are more than incidentally satirical: rather than setting out, as a satirist might do, to paint a distorted picture of society in the hope of exposing its underlying contradictions, Huxley presents his vision as being a truthful, realistic representation. Where Swift's insistence on the most squalid aspects of human behaviour is avowedly biased and polemical, Huxley purports to be offering an objective account of reality.

But although the pretence 'that human beings are controlled, if not by reason, at least by comprehensible, well-organized, avowable instincts' involves a distortion of reality, Huxley's almost exclusive insistence on the other side of the coin, on the 'lunatic and unavowable cravings' merely substitutes one distortion of reality for another. By concentrating almost exclusively on the more unpleasant aspects of experience, Huxley inevitably fails to tell what he described as the 'Whole Truth'. In fact, Huxley's bent is essentially that of a satirist: he sets out to offer a corrective to orthodox fictional practice, and to expose and deflate commonly held assumptions, both of which intentions might have been more easily realized in a satiric context; it is only his adoption of naturalistic representational techniques that seduces him into investing his basically negative and destructive vision with the guise of objectivity.

In his anxiety not to romanticize reality, Huxley in fact selects and orders his material just as rigorously as any of the novelists whom he implicitly criticizes: it is simply the principles by which he orders and makes his selections that are different. But it is not only his choice of detail and incident that is selective; what is even more schematic is his characterization. Both *Point Counter Point* and *Eyeless in Gaza,* in common with *Those Barren Leaves,* have a message to convey: Rampion, Miller, and Beavis, like Calamy, all indicate alternatives to normal human behaviour which Huxley believed were worth exploring. But whereas one of the weaknesses of *Those Barren Leaves* was the failure of the comically presented behaviour of most of the characters to offer substantiating evidence for Calamy's arguments, in the two later novels Huxley goes to the other extreme, quite obviously presenting his characters in a manner calculated to bear out the views expressed by the characters who act as his spokesmen.

Thus we find that in *Point Counter Point,* where the moral touchstone is the capacity for a full and harmonious response to life, almost everyone is in some way lacking in that capacity. Walter and Marjorie, Burlap and Beatrice, Philip and Elinor, Sidney Quarles, Spandrell, Illidge: it is practically a casebook of human inadequacy. Yet the trouble is not so much that Huxley's characters are individually unconvincing—all the above are perfectly believable. The difficulty is more that the realistic impression which they may give individually is compromised by the brazen way in which Huxley tailors each character to fit into an overall scheme whose function is to illustrate the views of Rampion.

Rampion, the advocate of the total and healthy human response to reality, describes the world as 'an asylum of perverts', and this, on the face of the evidence which is presented, might seem a reasonable enough point of view. Yet in the context of a work which, however biased its selection of detail may in fact be, is avowedly naturalistic in its conception, Rampion's opinions would seem to be illustrated a little too neatly. Just as the picture of a chaotic and meaningless world which Huxley strives to create is rendered unconvincing by the deliberate nature of his introduction of arbitrary incident into the narrative, so his portrayal of humanity as basically perverted and degenerate loses much of its force through its being so evidently designed to bear out a particular point of view.

The inherently contradictory nature of Huxley's approach to characterization becomes even more apparent in those cases where an individual, in addition to illustrating, by his inadequacies, a particular view of human nature, is also committed to a philosophy or ideology with which Huxley happens to disagree. Spandrell, for example, is clearly designed to illustrate not just a particular kind of human inadequacy, but also the limitations of Baudelairean romanticism. His actions are dictated not just by innate weakness, but also by erroneous beliefs. Spandrell's beliefs are the almost exact antithesis of Rampion's, and for this reason he is continually being contrasted with him. Spandrell's boasting about the way in which he corrupts innocent young girls is set against the description of Rampion's healthy and mature relationship with his wife. Where Rampion looks for meaning and reality in the world around him, Spandrell is continually searching for some transcendent and non-human source of value—absolute good, absolute evil, absolute beauty—and this contrast is crystallized in the scene where Spandrell tries to convince Rampion of the existence of God by playing him a record of a late Beethoven string quartet. More than anyone else, Spandrell is there to show that Rampion is right; the contrasts between the two men are *always* to Spandrell's disadvantage; Rampion *always* exposes Spandrell's decadence as the posturing it is. The final irony is that Spandrell is killed by Webley's thugs just as he has finished playing Rampion the Beethoven quartet: he died in the knowledge that Rampion is still unconvinced even by what he had thought to be an infallible proof of his point of view. It is a contrast which is deliberate, ironic, but above all, polemical.

But while Spandrell represents a very difinite point of view, it remains a highly idiosyncratic and individualistic one. In the case of Illidge, on the other hand, we find a character who is committed to a real-life ideology. Illidge is a Communist, and it is possible, by examining Huxley's handling of a recognizable set of beliefs, to judge just how far his objectivity extends. In fact, Illidge is yet another typically Huxleian character—unsure of himself, self-conscious, easily embarrassed—although, unlike

Denis, Gumbril, or Walter Bidlake, he is given to boasting and self-assertion as means of compensating for his feelings of inadequacy. (But then, also unlike Denis, Gumbril, and Walter Bidlake, he didn't go to a public school.) However, he is none the less convincing for that.

Significantly, with the exception of a few brief references to his childhood experiences, Illidge is hardly ever allowed to speak for himself. His views are almost invariably presented, usually ironically, through the eyes of others. Spandrell, for example, describes with sardonic amusement Illidge's 'inconsistency' in supporting his mother out of his own salary:

> ... it's disgustingly bourgeois! Theoretically he sees no distinction between his mother and any other aged female. He knows that, in a properly organized society, she'd be put into the lethal chamber, because of her arthritis. In spite of which he sends her I don't know how much a week to enable her to drag on a useless existence. I twitted him about it the other day. He blushed and was terribly upset, as though he'd been caught cheating at cards. So, to restore his prestige, he had to change the subject and begin talking about political murder and its advantages with the most wonderfully calm, detached, scientific ferocity. (p. 214)

Illidge would appear to have turned to Communism as a means of compensating for his own personal inadequacies. Because he is a coward, as his conduct during and after Webley's murder so clearly demonstrates, he tries to make up for it by advocating violence. The only difficulty is that, for all his psychological credibility, his compensatory beliefs appear to bear a closer resemblance to the political philosophy of Genghis Khan than to that expounded in the Communist Manifesto. Indeed, if one is to judge by the passage where Huxley appears to be advancing the rather curious argument that Communism has been rendered obsolete by the discoveries of Einstein, it would seem that one insuperable obstacle to his successful depiction of Communist ideas is that he completely failed to understand them. Illidge's advocacy of wholesale terrorism and the systematic liquidation of class enemies amounts to little more than the crudest kind of caricature. In a different context this might not have mattered, but it is clear from the way in which Illidge is characterized that Huxley is not attempting a Peacockian burlesque, where both character and ideas are treated purely comically, but to offer a serious critique of the philosophy which he espouses.

This contradiction between realistic characterization and the caricatured presentation of beliefs becomes even more acute in *Eyeless in Gaza*. Whereas Rampion represents not so much a set of ideas as a desirable way of life, which is principally contrasted to the unsatisfactory life-styles of others, the much more explicitly presented beliefs of Miller and Beavis are set in the context of what purports to be a serious debate between rival philosophies. As a result, Huxley's characterization becomes even more schematic than before: in *Eyeless in Gaza* the weaknesses which mar the presentation of Illidge and Spandrell are endemic.

One of the main problems is that Huxley consistently confuses the issue by making a rather simplistic equation between the merits of a particular philosophy or ideology and the personal qualities of its advocates. For Huxley, the cowardice, stupidity, or unsavoury sexual proclivities of a single individual often seem to constitute sufficient grounds for dismissing their point of view. But while it may well be true that one way of judging the validity of particular beliefs is by looking at the kind of people who hold them, Huxley never offers the kind of cross-section of the adherents of a given viewpoint which might make such an approach viable. Instead, he generalizes on the basis of individual cases; characters who hold a particular point of view eventually come to *represent* it—and this, in its turn, tends to detract from the psychological credibility of their portrayal. However believable the personal shortcomings of an individual character may seem, they become that much less convincing when it becomes obvious that their main function is to discredit that character's opinions. While critics may see *Eyeless in Gaza* as a 'novel of ideas', its pretensions to offer any kind of genuine debate are compromised by the fact that the major conditioning factor in Huxley's treatment of conflicting opinions and beliefs is his crude manipulation of character in order to support a specific point of view.

Thus Communism once more comes under fire for being

merely a compensatory belief. Helen becomes a Communist under the influence of Ekki, and maintains her loyalty to the cause after he dies partly as a continued expression of her love for him, and partly because the advocacy of violence offers some kind of outlet for the bitterness which she feels. Once again, she is psychologically credible, but as in the case of Illidge, there is the same tension between the realism with which she is characterized and the caricatured nature of the beliefs she is supposed to hold. Once again, she is hardly ever allowed to speak for herself: her views are usually presented through the highly critical medium of Anthony's diary, and appear to consist of a similar obsession with the liquidation of class enemies. However, there turns out to be a reason why such a nice girl should hold such unattractive opinions: it is misplaced romantic idealism which is responsible. When Ekki is making plans to go to Basel in order to meet a celebrated German revolutionary, we are told that

> In the course of these last months, the name of this most resourceful and courageous of all the German comrades engaged in the dissemination of Communist propaganda and censored news had become, for Helen, at once familiar and fabulous, like the name of a personage in literature or mythology. That Ludwig Mach should be at Basel seemed almost as improbable as that Odysseus should be there, or Odin, or the Scarlet Pimpernel. (pp. 591–2)

As for Ekki, there is at least no question of inconsistency in the manner in which he is presented: his characterization is just as wooden and unconvincing as the portrayal of his beliefs. Practically his first words to Helen are '"You are a wictim . . . a wictim of capitalist society."' (p. 310)—the function of the 'w' being to show that he is German, a fact which is further brought to our attention by his clicking his heels when he bows. On his subsequent appearances, the same heavy-handedness is in evidence: his Teutonic slowness and seriousness are continually emphasized, while his speeches consist of little more than indifferently observed Communist jargon. All in all, the absurdity of his portrayal only serves to further undermine the credibility of Helen's presentation, by making it glaringly obvious that both are there for a purpose.

Hedonism has its representative in Mary Amberley. She, too, is perfectly credible: it seems quite plausible that someone as irresponsible, amoral, and self-indulgent as she is should end up as she does. In fact the scenes from her later life, where she is portrayed as being wholly at the mercy first of all of her sexual appetites, then of morphine addiction, have a particularly ghastly kind of authenticity. Nevertheless, her degradation is quite clearly described for a reason—in order to expose the limitations of a particular attitude to life. Although, taken in isolation, the details of her steady decline are convincing enough, the fact that what happens to her is obviously intended to serve as a counterpoint to Anthony's discovery of a better way of life inevitably creates the impression that there is a certain amount of overkill involved. Mary is *always* irresponsible, *always* self-indulgent, *always* lacking in consideration for others; while hedonism, as a philosophy of life, may have its limitations, Mary's life-style has a great many more. In fact, the point that hedonism fails to take into account the facts of illness, senility, and death is made a good deal more effectively in *Those Barren Leaves*. There is a chilling understatement about Cardan's reflections on death, about the description of the brief moments when the merits of his whole way of life seem to be cast in doubt, which is ultimately far more frightening than the relentless portrayal of Mary's long, drawn-out degeneration.

Over-insistence also mars the portrayal of both Beppo and Mark Staithes. Beppo is an aesthete, whose love of beauty is repeatedly contrasted with his gross physical appearance, but these contrasts, together with Huxley's continual distasteful harping on Beppo's homosexuality, become increasingly mechanical, and end up by defeating their own purpose. After all, why shouldn't an aesthete be bald and fat? Why shouldn't an aesthete be a homosexual? Huxley insists on the 'contradictions' involved until they no longer seem contradictory. And the presentation of Mark becomes equally tiresome—he is given to the same self-conscious insistence on the 'reality' of what is ordinary and boring which made Chelifer so irritating. Just as Chelifer lived in a seedy boarding house and worked for *The Rabbit Fancier's Gazette*, so Staithes lives in a house whose hideousness '. . . was so complete, so absolutely unrelieved, that it could only have been intentional' (p. 311), and makes his living by running a perfume factory (professing himself to be delighted by the advertisements for his product, which, because they mention bad breath and body odour, force people 'to be fully, *verbally* conscious of their own and other people's disgustingness' (p. 245).

However, Mark is not simply the proponent of this rather preposterous brand of Manichaeism, he is also an advocate of violent revolution—a role in which, it ought to be said, he is even less credible than Helen or Ekki. While the plot dictates that he should be instrumental in getting Anthony to Mexico so that he can meet Miller, it is difficult to believe that someone trusted by a seasoned Mexican revolutionary to play a crucial role in an armed uprising would risk jeopardizing the undertaking by inviting someone as incompetent as Anthony to accompany him.

In fact, Mark is a revolutionary for philosophical rather than political reasons: the main reason he goes to Mexico is in order to confront the ultimate realities of violence and death. Unfortunately, however, his search for something which will make life more meaningful ends in disaster; espousing violence, he meets an ironically appropriate fate, losing his leg, albeit in an accident. But his is not the only fate which is ironically appropriate: Ekki, another advocate of violence, dies violently at the hands of the Nazis, while both Mary and Beppo, who are obsessed by sexual desire, become prey to increasing sexual frustration as they become older and less attractive. There is a relentless uniformity in way in which the implications of the rival life-styles and philosopies in *Eyeless in Gaza* are worked out, which only serves to emphasize how far the development of character is subordinate to the primary purpose of demonstrating the correctness of Miller and Anthony. Even Anthony himself is no exception: before he sees the light, as if to stress how much he is in need of reform, Huxley ensures that he *invariably* behaves in the weakest and most despicable way whenever the opportunity to do presents itself. Huxley never allows himself the luxury of the slightest detail of characterization which might prove inconsistent with his overall purpose.

Nevertheless, Huxley's conscious manipulation of characterization and narrative in order to prove his point is unable to disguise a further major weakness—namely, the poverty of the alternatives he suggests. Neither Rampion nor Beavis, for all their awareness of how one ought to live, seem able to communicate that awareness to anyone else. Rampion's ideal of harmony and balance, of living life to the full by exploring one's total potential as a human being, never seems even remotely accessible to anyone else. The balance which he advocates is, as he himself admits, 'damnably difficult' to maintain, and when one looks at the people by whom he is surrounded it seems, for anyone else, frankly impossible. Because of the thorough-going way in which Huxley chooses to illustrate Rampion's contention that the world is 'an asylum of perverts', nearly all the characters appear to be far too inadequate to hope to aspire to Rampion's ideals. Although both Spandrell and Philip Quarles seem to feel an obscure kind of happiness in Rampion's presence, neither shows the slightest sign of changing as a result. Desirable though Rampion's outlook and behaviour may be, the final implication of *Point Counter Point* would seem to be that Rampion's solutions are only viable if one has the good fortune to *be* Rampion. Given the almost unrelieved squalor and gloom of the rest of the novel, it is not much of a consolation.

However, the alternatives which Miller presents to Anthony Beavis in *Eyeless in Gaza* are far more avowedly intended as a solution, not only to the problems of the other characters, but also to those of the reader. While Rampion's ideal may seem vague and nebulous, Miller proposes concrete solutions. Put crudely, they are as follows: become an active pacifist; meditate; engage in critical examination of one's own motivation and behaviour; learn the Alexander technique. On the political level, it must be said that the case for pacifism is not so much argued as assumed; so far as Anthony is concerned, it would seem to be more the fact of his *involvement* that is beneficial, rather than the nature of what he is involved in—the major change which he has undergone is his abandonment of the role of a spectator, of someone who denies all responsibility for his actions. But the most important part of Miller's message is not its political content (one can advocate pacifism and still be immoral, miserable, irresponsible), so much as its insistence on the kind of desirable personal behaviour which should accompany political commitment. And there is a strong case to be made out for his contention that the majority of individuals in the Western world lead essentially unhealthy lives, largely as a result of their inability or unwillingness to exercise sufficient control over either mind or body; Miller's advocacy of techniques of psycho-physical self-discipline is not something with which it is easy to quarrel. The difficulty that arises, however, is not so much that the techniques which Miller advocates are undesirable, as that their benefits manifest themselves too gradually, subtly, and impalpably for it to be easy represent them *dramatically* in a convincing manner.

Thus, in the case of Anthony's conversion, while a dramatic change in his personality would clearly seem implausible, some kind of drama is necessary in order to show the reader that the change has, in fact, occurred. It is a contradiction which Huxley never succeeds in resolving. Most of the information concerning the changes which Anthony undergoes is conveyed through the rather prosaic medium of his diary, but when Huxley does try to dramatize various stages in the process of his conversation, the results are less than satisfactory. A traumatic shock is clearly required in order to shatter Anthony's complacency, but the grotesque incident where the dog falls from an aeroplane seems improbable rather than traumatic; the final epiphany, when Anthony has a vision of cones of light meeting in the darkness is distinctly unimpressive; and the first meeting with Miller, which sets Anthony on the road to self-discovery, is frankly ludicrous. Seeking help after Mark's accident, Anthony encounters a stranger who turns out to be a doctor. Lucky enough to meet a doctor in the middle of the Mexican desert, one may think—but Anthony's luck does not end there: within minutes of the meeting the stranger is interrogating him about the state of his bowels, recommending that he get married, criticizing his posture, and suggesting that he cut down his intake of milk and eggs. Compared with the vagueness of the alternatives explored or represented by Calamy and Rampion, it is certainly explicit enough, but it is also (to put it mildly) rather *sudden*.

Considering that *Eyeless in Gaza* is primarily concerned with an individual's conversion to a different way of life, it is a serious weakness that the depiction of the conversion is neither dramatically effective nor particularly convincing. For all that Huxley's positive values are stated more explicitly than in any of his previous novels, their relevance to the majority of his characters seems as limited as ever. The world of *Eyeless in Gaza* is even more of an asylum than that portrayed in *Point Counter Point*, its inmates even more hopelessly unregenerate. Although Anthony succeeds in reforming himself, the aberrations of those who surround him seem far too numerous for the solutions which Miller proposes to stand much chance of offering an effective antidote to them. In fact there is scarcely any attempt to relate Miller's beliefs to the situation of anyone other than Anthony: with the single exception of the argument between Miller and Mark Staithes as to whether it is better to treat people as equals or to try to dominate them, there is no direct presentation of a confrontation between Miller's ideas and those of anyone else. Although we are explicitly *told* of Beppo's interest in what Anthony has to say, and while Helen appears at the end to be moving towards some kind of reconciliation with him, which will presumably involve her abandoning Communism, in both cases the effect is unconvincing. Honourable though Huxley's intentions are, his attempt to make *Eyeless in Gaza* the vehicle for his suggestions as to what should be done in order to regenerate both the individual and society is ultimately unsuccessful. And no amount of authorial manipulation of the presentation of what are seen as less desirable ideals or life-styles can compensate for that.

Is Huxley's didacticism, then, the root of the problem? It would be tempting to attribute the deficiencies of *Point Counter Point* and *Eyeless in Gaza* to the fact that Huxley's ostensibly realistic treatment of his material is actually subordinate to his didactic purpose: didacticism, after all, is widely regarded as Huxley's besetting weakness, particularly in his later fiction, and it might seem that the implication of the foregoing criticism is that Huxley's shortcomings are the inevitable consequence of his attempt to use the Novel as a vehicle for a specific message. But in fact the explanation is not so simple: it is not so much Huxley's didactic intent that is the problem, as its incompatibility, *in these particular novels*, with the realistic approach adopted. In the different context of *Brave New World* and *After*

Many A Summer, as we shall see, Huxley's didacticism is far less of a liability.

The issue is further complicated, perhaps unnecessarily, by a widespread critical tendency to regard didacticism as *ipso facto* inadmissible in a novel. Even a critic such as Leavis, whose standards of judgement are far from being purely aesthetic ones, suggests that

> ... not much is said about a work of art in calling it didactic —unless one is meaning to judge it adversely. In that case one is judging that the intention to communicate an attitude hasn't become sufficiently more than an intention; hasn't, that is, justified itself as art in the realized concreteness that speaks for itself and *enacts* its moral significance.[2]

Nevertheless, leaving aside for the moment the question of how far Huxley's didactic intentions may be said to be satisfactorily realized or enacted, it should be stressed that didacticism, far from being a fault *per se*, in fact has a long and respectable history so far as the Novel is concerned. As has already been suggested, a didactic intent is integral to the purposes of nearly all the major English novelists. Richardson, Fielding, Jane Austen, George Eliot, Dickens—not one of them can be said to have been guided solely by the dictates of representational authenticity or aesthetic unity; all of them consciously set out to uphold the desirability of certain forms of behaviour. Richardson's portrayal of the relationship between Lovelace and Clarissa is clearly designed to inculcate or reinforce particular attitudes towards questions of sexual morality; Jane Austen continually implies clearly defined standards of behaviour—the episode in *Emma*, for example, where Emma is rude to Miss Bates, serves, among other things, as a lesson in what Jane Austen takes to constitute decent standards of courtesy; the work of both Eliot and Dickens is full of the most explicit moralizing. Examples could be multiplied *ad infinitum*, but the real point is that didacticism, rather than being some alien, indigestible element imported by Huxley into the Novel, is an important feature of the work of the greatest of his predecessors.

Huxley's problems stem, not from the inadmissibility of didacticism, but in the nature of his didactic intent—in the kind of things he was didactic *about*. As was suggested earlier, the standards of behaviour which he sees as desirable almost invariably imply the necessity of a radical change in society; whereas all the novelists mentioned above broadly accepted that their society was worthy of representation, and that it contained within itself sources of value to which the reader's attention might profitably be drawn, Huxley did not. The reason he was unable to enact or realize his didactic intentions, at least in the context of a realistic representation of society, was that he believed that society ought to be different. To represent society as it was was to represent only undesirable behaviour—since the alternatives he envisaged did not yet exist, they had to be embodied in something external to the world he described, such as the speculations of Calamy; in an idealized character, such as Rampion; or in an explicit programme for reform, like Miller's.

Unlike Huxley, the novelists we have mentioned are rarely concerned to make explicit suggestions as to what ought to be done; in the context of a broad acceptance of society it is possible for their didactic intentions to be enacted in an implicit injunction to the individual to give rein to his or her good impulses. To take *Middlemarch* as an example once again, we find that while Dorothea is a figure to be admired, even emulated, she is far from being the exponent of a philosophy by which everyone is recommended to live. While one of the main concerns of the novel is with the ethics of behaviour within marriage, there is no attempt to offer any *alternatives* to marriage. The unhappy relationships between Lydgate and Rosamond, between Dorothea and Casaubon are not made the excuse for an indictment of marriage as an institution, or for a plea for divorce law reform, or for an exposition of the merits of free love and communal living. George Eliot is concerned primarily to show that society can function more or less as it is, given sufficient goodwill on the part of its individual members. Although she does not ignore evil and suffering, she consistently emphasizes the possibility of choosing better courses of action rather than worse. Redemption is always possible: Fred Vincey is saved from going to the bad by Mary Garth and Farebrother; Lydgate's suffering is to some extent mitigated by the good offices of Dorothea; even Bulstrode is partially redeemed by his wife's conduct. And to this extent it can be said that George Eliot's didactic intentions are enacted; in answer to the question, how should one behave? she can point to Mary, to Farebrother, to Dorothea, to Mrs Bulstrode, and say, like *this*.

Huxley, on the other hand, rejects society, and the premisses by which people normally live. As he saw it, a lot more than good will was required if there was to be any hope of solving the problems of the individual and of society. To present a picture of a world in which more than a few isolated individuals were moving in the right direction would have seemed to him simply unrealistic. It is because society's values are wrong that Huxley is obliged to make such an explicit statement of what he sees as the right values; it is because he sees humanity as being, for the most part, hopelessly unregenerate that most of his characters seem to be beyond the reach of the solutions which he proposes. Ultimately, it is not didacticism as such which is the problem, so much as the fact that his particular *kind* of didacticism, and the attitude to society which it implies, is not really compatible with the realistic approach which both *Point Counter Point* and *Eyeless in Gaza* employ. Where, as in *Brave New World* and *After Many A Summer*, he uses a different, non-realistic format as the vehicle for his didactic intentions the results, as we shall see, are far less unsatisfactory.

The real question that proposes itself is why Huxley's critics rate *Point Counter Point* and *Eyeless in Gaza* so highly. It has already been suggested that critics in fact have a preference for novels which combine realism with formal complexity, but it might be as well, at this point, to examine why it is that two works which have so few other virtues to recommend them should nevertheless be regarded as Huxley's major achievements. Once again, it is worth asking whether critics do not read works in a different *kind* of way—a way, which in this particular instance, prevents them from seeing the deficiencies which may seem apparent to the ordinary reader.

Comparing the approach of the reader who picks up a book in the expectation of being entertained, stimulated, even edified, with that of the critic who reads and re-reads a work for the purposes of critical analysis, it would seem that there are in fact two distinct processes at work: in the one case it is the immediate impression which makes the most impact, while in the other it is those qualities which become apparent after maturer (or at any rate more prolonged) consideration that are likely to seem most important. This being so, it is scarcely to be wondered at if certain works seem to lend themselves better to one process rather than the other. For example, lightness of touch, vigour of expression, simplicity and directness of conception and presentation, are qualities which are likely to be better appreciated on a first reading than in the course of sustained critical analysis. Similarly, qualities such as formal complexity, depth and variety of characterization, subtlety of thematic relations, which make their impact after repeated readings, may well escape more than superficial recognition at first.

This is not to suggest that critical study will *necessarily* distort the qualities of a work of the first kind: indeed, the examination and analysis of a deft and simple work may well serve to enhance one's appreciation of it. Nor is it my contention that one can *only* understand and respond to a rich and complex work after repeated readings. The point is rather that each approach has its own dangers. At a first reading one may well overvalue a work which is merely slick, while in the process of critical analysis it is equally possible to become so involved in the study of a work that its author's *attempts* to create something which is rich, deep, complex may be mistaken for the actual achievement of that aim. The latter, I would argue, is the trap into which most of Huxley's critics have fallen in their discussion of *Point Counter Point* and *Eyeless in Gaza*.

The trouble is, that by pondering over a complex work, the critic may become so familiar with its component parts that he or she may, quite unconsciously, begin to make connections between them which are simply not there—connections which, in their turn, may lead to the work being credited with a degree of structural unity which it does not in fact possess. One of the things which the critic is looking for is the capacity to distil unity out of diversity; the danger is that what he may find will be merely the semblance of such unity, the product of his own subjective thought processes.

Huxley's critics seem to be especially prone to find what they are looking for. Jerome Meckier, for example, taking as his text the title of *Point Counter Point*, seeks to show how Huxley instils order and unity into his work by employing the literary equivalent of the musical device of counterpoint. By juxtaposing seemingly unrelated elements, Meckier suggests, Huxley succeeds in bringing out the hidden contrasts and connections between them. Which is fair enough: this kind of 'counterpoint' is certainly one of the novel's basic structural principles. The trouble is that Meckier then seems to get carried away by his discovery, and begins to multiply his examples of parallels and thematic links until his illustrations reach the point of absurdity. Discussing the party at Lady Tantamount's, for instance, he suggests that

> Most of the egoistic characters in *Point Counter Point* inhabit their own eccentric worlds and seldom tolerate opinions and disciplines contrary to their own. Yet their relationships with other characters are brought out in ironic ways they are powerless to stifle. In one sequence, Webley, Illidge, and John Bidlake are the major male figures. One instantly realizes how unsuited these three are for conversation, yet all are soon to be ironically linked by death. Illidge will participate in Webley's murder, and old Bidlake is marked for stomach cancer. Just as Webley does not realize Illidge's significance, Old Bidlake never suspects Webley is a possible lover for his daughter, Elinor. The connections between these characters remains ironic and, by them, unperceived.
>
> (*Aldous Huxley: Satire and Structure*, p. 132)

But though this may have seemed plausible in the comforting privacy of the study, it is hard to imagine that any reader would seriously make the kind of 'connections' which Meckier posits. Reading the fourth chapter of *Point Counter Point*, does anyone *really* 'instantly realize' that the important thing about it is that 'the major male figures' are unsuited for conversation? And even if anyone did, would they still be holding that particular sequence consciously in mind right up to the point when the ironic implications it is supposed to have become apparent? Again, what possible evidence is there to suggest that Bidlake's ignorance of his daughter's relationship with Webley is even significant, let alone ironic? It is difficult to see what relevance this kind of specious theorizing has to anyone's actual *experience* of the novel.

But Meckier is by no means alone in trying to find connections and relationships where none exist. George Woodcock, in his discussion of *Eyeless in Gaza*, makes the suggestion that

> The brutal rapacity of Gerry Watchett is balanced by the gentle rapacity, disguised as love, of Mrs Foxe. To Hugh Ledwidge's museum-bound ethnology, which liberates him from actuality to become the author of a nauseating novel of spiritualized love, is opposed Miller's arduous field anthropology, a true science of man rooted in human experience, not in abstractions. (*Woodcock*, p. 204)

But while it is true that *Eyeless in Gaza* is full of contrasts between the true love which Anthony learns, and its various distortions and perversions, or between the true perception of reality which Miller teaches, and the self-delusion to which nearly everyone else is prone, this is only the broadest of structuring principles. Once again, it is hard to imagine any normal reader making a connection between Gerry Watchett and Mrs Foxe, or between Hugh Ledwidge and Miller (except insofar as everyone is implicitly compared with Miller, and found wanting). There is simply no indication that such parallels are intended.

In both cases this multiplication of non-existent connections is directly responsible for the over-valuation accorded to the works in question: the superimposition of an imaginary network of sophisticated thematic relationships serves to disguise what would otherwise seem to be glaring weaknesses. Looking for the qualities which they believe ought to be there, Huxley's critics fail to ask the basic question whether, for all their elaboration, *Point Counter Point* and *Eyeless in Gaza* actually *work*.

5

Brave New World and *After Many a Summer*: The Development of Fantastic Satire

If *Point Counter Point* and *Eyeless in Gaza* represent Huxley's attempt to remedy the 'lying by omission' which glamorizes reality by excluding the more sordid and mundane details of human experience, *Brave New World* and *After Many A Summer* would appear to constitute a response to a far more radical criticism of realistic fiction, namely, that the nature of society is such that merely to represent it is morally unjustifiable. In *Ends and Means*, as we have seen, he suggested that most literature, by depicting in a straightforward fashion human behaviour which was essentially undesirable, gave tacit approval to unacceptable social values, and it is a contention which he develops at greater length in *After Many A Summer*. Literature, argues Propter, who acts as a commentator on the grotesque events which take place in that novel, is used by most people as a drug:

> . . . people don't read literature in order to understand; they read it because they want to re-live the feelings and sensations which they found exciting in the past. Art can be a lot of things; but in actual practice most of it is merely the mental equivalent of alcohol and cantharides. (p. 160)

He then goes on to complain of

> . . . the wearisomeness, to an adult mind, of all those merely descriptive plays and novels which critics expected one to admire. All the innumerable, interminable anecdotes and romances and character-studies, but no general theory of anecdotes, no explanatory hypothesis of romance or character. Just a huge collection of facts about lust and greed, fear and ambition. duty and affection; just facts, and imaginary facts at

> that, with no co-ordinating philosophy superior to common sense and the local system of conventions, no principle of arrangement more rational than simple aesthetic expediency. (p. 225)

Literature does not edify, nor is it read for the purposes of edification. Worst of all, however, is the unthinking conventionality it displays. The problem with what Propter describes as 'so-called good literature' is that

> ... it accepted the conventional scale of values; it respected power and position; it admired success; it treated as though they were reasonable the mainly lunatic preoccupations of statesmen, lovers, business men, social climbers, parents. In a word, it took seriously the causes of suffering as well as the suffering. It helped to perpetuate misery by explicitly or implicitly approving the thoughts and feelings and practices which could not fail to result in misery. And this approval was bestowed in the most magnificent and persuasive language. So that even when a tragedy ended badly, the reader was hypnotized by the eloquence of the piece into imagining that it was all somehow noble and worth while. Which of course it wasn't. Because, if you considered them dispassionately, nothing could be more silly and squalid than the themes of *Phedre*, or *Othello*, or *Wuthering Heights*, or the *Agamemnon*. But the treatment of these themes had been in the highest degree sublime and thrilling, so that the reader or the spectator was left with the conviction that, in spite of the catastrophe, all was really well with the world, the all too human world, which had produced it. No, a good satire was much more deeply truthful and, of course, profitable than a good tragedy. The trouble was that so few good satires existed, because so few satirists were prepared to carry their criticism of human values far enough. (pp. 226–7)

And it is to satire that Huxley turns in both *Brave New World* and *After Many A Summer*, adopting as his mentor not Peacock, but Swift. Instead of trying to integrate a criticism of society and its values with a realistic depiction of them, he elects to attack them from the outset, and there can be little doubt that his critique gains considerably in force and cogency as a result.

While the ideas and attitudes presented with authorial approval are similar to those contained in *Point Counter Point* and *Eyeless in Gaza*, the satiric, fantastic approach adopted seems to render them far less of a liability. Underlying *Brave New World* is a vitalist, individualistic outlook, closely resembling the Lawrentian philosophy expounded in *Point Counter Point*; Miller, the guru figure in *Eyeglass in Gaza*, is clearly the ancestor of Propter in *After Many A Summer*: yet the limitations of the ideas, the moral positives asserted in the two satires play a far less important part in determining their overall artistic effectiveness. Whereas the philosophies of Rampion and Miller, offered as the only hope in a universe of perversity, insanity, and despair, appear hopelessly inadequate, the messages of *Brave New World* and *After Many A Summer* are far more successfully embodied in their respective narratives. In *Brave New World* the limitations of amorality and hedonism are exposed by the grotesque lengths they are carried to, so that there is scarcely any need for explicit comment; while in *After Many A Summer* the sheer blackness of the black comedy goes at least some way towards corroborating Propter's exceptionally bleak view of humanity.

Once Huxley abandons his attempts to offer a realistic portrayal of society, his vision of the world becomes considerably more persuasive. Accepting the world of the distant future, or the depiction of a millionaire's quest for eternal life as being the author's invention, the reader tacitly admits the author's right to lay down the rules for the worlds he creates. Instead of aspiring to portray a world which his readers also know, and are liable to see quite differently, Huxley presents his vision as a fantasy. While parallels with the real world are hinted at, it is left to the reader to draw them: instead of insisting that life is like *this*, and thus incurring the resistance of readers who feel pressurized into accepting an account of reality which they do not believe to be accurate, Huxley, through his use of the medium of fantasy, is able to imply his own views of what constitutes reality with a far greater chance of their being accepted—after all, if the reader detects parallels between the fantasy and reality, it merely shows that the connections are already present in the reader's mind.

Additionally, Huxley exploits the fact that the worlds he

creates are *different*, foreign to the reader's experience, to arouse curiosity as to their nature. The more bizarre the events or setting, the more eager the reader becomes to find some kind of ordering explanation, with the result that the explanations that *are* offered are all the more likely to be accepted. And while he overtly answers the reader's questions, Huxley is able covertly to comment on the real world, with the advantage that whereas in a realistic context his explanations, his commentary might be rejected out of hand, in the context of a fantasy the instinct of rejection is usually outweighed by the feeling of curiosity satisfied.

Both *Brave New World* and *After Many A Summer* also exhibit a logic and dramatic conviction which his earlier fiction lacks. Huxley's first, comic novels were essentially episodic in structure, presenting a succession of vignettes, rather than a coherent overall story, while the motivation of the characters was as often as not simply the necessity of acting in character. Given Huxley's lightness of touch and command of tone, however, this was hardly a defect. But in *Point Counter Point* and *Eyeless in Gaza*, which are larger in scale and more serious in intent, the absence of any real dramatic development becomes more of problem. *Point Counter Point*, as its title implies, is a novel composed of a number of interweaving narrative threads, but its weakness is that none of them actually seem to lead anywhere. Walter Bidlake, for example, begins the novel as Lucy's unrequited lover, has an affair with her, and is finally rejected by her; but throughout the entire work both their characters and the essential nature of their relationship remain unaffected. There is no real interaction between them, and hence no sense of dramatic development: both the characters and the relationship are static. And exactly the same applies elsewhere—Walter's relationship with Marjorie Carling is just as static and unchanging; the incompatibilities between Philip and Elinor Quarles are never dramatically resolved; even Spandrell's suicide is merely the termination of an entirely aimless existence. The device of counterpart fails to counteract the effects of the absence of dramatic interaction, while the introduction of sensational incidents, such as the murder of Webley, only serves to emphasize the aimlessly chaotic nature of the world Huxley creates—it is significant that Spandrell's main motive for killing Webley is boredom.

Similarly, despite the ostensible coherence and direction afforded to the plot of *Eyeless in Gaza* by the theme of Anthony's conversion, there is exactly the same failure to depict any real interaction between people, and the same compensatory reliance on arbitrary and sensational incidents, such as dogs falling out of aeroplanes, and the events consequent on Anthony's sudden and scarcely credible decision to participate in a Mexican revolution It is possible that Huxley, feeling that life does not develop dramatically, wished, in an excess of enthusiasm for ultra-realism, to avoid dramatic development as being unrealistic, but whatever the cause, the results are unsatisfactory. Both *Point Counter Point* and *Eyeless in Gaza*, for all their positive ideals, afford a far more eloquent testimony to Huxley's scepticism as to man's capacity for any kind of significant action in the world as he saw it, a scepticism compounded by the suspicion that any real communication between human beings was impossible. And while Huxley might perhaps have generated some sort of dramatic conflict by the depiction of heroic, if doomed attempts by individuals to act as though significant human action was possible, his realistic fiction in fact portrays a world where most of the characters appear to share their creator's pessimistic outlook.

In *Brave New World* and *After Many A Summer*, however, the case is very different; in a fantastic context Huxley is able to resolve many of the difficulties created by his confused understanding of the relations between the individual and society. Indeed, the principal theme of *Brave New World* is precisely the conflict between the individual and society—a society which, because it is his own invention, he is able to understand and hence portray far more clearly. Although his view of society remains a pessimistic one, the tale of Bernard, Helmholz, and the Savage's confrontation with and defeat by authority provides the kind of backbone for Huxley's satiric vision of the world of the future which is so conspicuously lacking in his realistic portrayals of the society of the present. Similarly, in *After Many A Summer*, the story of Jo Stoyte's preposterous quest for eternal life becomes the ideal vehicle for Huxley's depiction of the

worldly and materialistic preoccupations of his characters. Quite apart from which there is a genuine sense of dramatic excitement surrounding the discovery of the Earl of Gonister's journal, with its account of earlier, possibly successful experiments in prolonging life. In common with *Brave New World*, and in distinction from Huxley's other earlier novels, the narrative of *After Many A Summer* is characterized by a certain sense of direction.

Above all, however, in both *Brave New World* and *After Many A Summer*, Huxley not only recovers, but develops the cool, ironic, detached tone which was one of the most attractive features of his early fiction. In *Brave New World*, for example, there is evident from the very outset the characteristic liveliness which, in *Point Counter Point*, seemed to have been sacrificed in the interests of a more realistic approach. With the opening words of *Brave New World*—'A squat grey building of only thirty-four storeys. . .' Huxley begins playing an elaborate game with his readers, alternating the assumption that they are, of course, familiar with the kind of world implied by '*only* thirty-four storeys', with the provision of information clearly designed to satisfy his audience's appetite for details concerning a world with which they are unfamiliar: information, for example, about the absurd technological features of the world he has created, such as the feelies, scent organs, escalator squash, electromagnetic golf, and so forth. Indeed, there could scarcely be a stronger contrast than that between the wit and panache of the opening sequence of *Brave New World*, with its vivid presentation of an imaginary society, culminating in a sense of nightmarish confusion induced by the accelerating cross-cutting between the various narrative lines, and the resolutely drab naturalism of the first scene in *Point Counter Point*, which led Wyndham Lewis to complain, with some justification, that Huxley had adopted 'the very accent of the newspaper serial'. Nor does the contrast end there: throughout *Brave New World* maintains a level of inventiveness, excitement, and energy which his realistic fiction never approaches.

Of course, part of the attraction of fantasy is that it allows the author to entertain his audience with novelties and inventions which are beyond the scope of a realistic approach, but Huxley uses the extra freedom which fantasy gives him for more than mere entertainment purposes. In both *Brave New World* and *After Many A Summer*, but particularly in the former, Huxley consistently exploits the reader's curiosity by integrating into the passages where he satisfies that curiosity a commentary on the real world, the world in which both he and the reader live. Take for example the early scene, where a group of Delta (low intelligence) infants are being conditioned into a hatred of books and flowers by the use of aversion therapy. The babies are first encouraged to crawl towards an attractive looking display of brightly coloured books and flowers, but on reaching it are then terrified by a combination of loud noises and electric shocks (pp. 15–16). At first sight it is a scene of wanton cruelty, conditioning for conditioning's sake—the infliction of pain and terror on young children is likely to arouse feelings of the most violent antipathy, and Huxley gives a lurid description of just that. As a result, the reader becomes anxious to learn the reason for this apparently motiveless cruelty, to hear the answer to the student's question—'"Why go to the trouble of making it psychologically impossible for Deltas to like flowers?"' (Books, obviously enough, might have a subversive and deconditioning effect.) It is this skilfully aroused curiosity which Huxley manipulates in order to give maximum effect to the critique of the consumer society which then follows. As the D.H.C., the official who has staged the demonstration of infant conditioning, explains:

> If the children were made to scream at the sight of a rose, that was on grounds of high economic policy. Not so very long ago... Gammas, Deltas, even Epsilons, had been conditioned to like flowers—flowers in particular and wild nature in general. The idea was to make them want to be going out into the country at every available opportunity, and so compel them to consume transport.
>
> 'And didn't they consume transport?' asked the student.
>
> 'Quite a lot,' the D.H.C. replied. 'But nothing else.'
>
> (p. 16)

Because 'a love of nature keeps no factories busy' a policy decision was taken to 'abolish the love of nature, at any rate among the lower classes...' They are still encouraged to travel to the country, of course—transport must still be consumed—but only in order to play sports requiring the use of elaborate manufactured apparatus. Human beings are conditioned by the society which manufactures consumer goods into a preference for the artificial, the complicated, and the expensive over the simple, the natural, and the cheap.

The parallel with our own society is too obvious to be missed, but the fantastic context enables Huxley to present his views far more effectively than he could have done in a more realistic setting; by making the explanation which the reader's curiosity demands as grotesque, vivid, and horrifying as possible, Huxley manages to avoid the invidious earnestness which is always liable to attend overt explanations of a realistically presented world. Just as Swift used the mechanisms of the traveller's tale in *Gulliver's Travels* to secure the attention of his audience, so that he might communicate his own views about society, so Huxley, in *Brave New World* relies on the attractions of Science Fiction to obtain a hearing for the message he wishes to convey.

Within the fantastic context, Huxley is also able to achieve a far greater economy and forcefulness of expression. In both *Point Counter Point* and *Eyeless in Gaza* human folly and weakness are illustrated by the accumulation of a large number of individual examples of undesirable attitudes and behaviour. But as we have seen, the drawback of such an approach is that the preponderance of negatively presented characters creates an imbalance which is at odds with Huxley's pretensions to be offering an objective and realistic account of the world.

In *Brave New World*, however, Huxley avoids the multiplication of individual examples, instead achieving a far more striking effect by linking together the most incompatible attitudes and behaviour, and using the resultant incongruity to expose their mutual absurdity. In *Point Counter Point*, where it is clear that Huxley rejects not only the values and conventional morality of the older generation, but also the irresponsibility and amorality of the younger, this dual rejection creates a certain confusion: there are perhaps too many targets for Huxley to hope to be able to hit them all, and the multiplication of objects of attack (the pomposity of General Knoyle, the immaturity of Lord Tantamount, the stupidity and lechery of Sidney Quarles among the older generation; the cynical amorality of Spandrell and Lucy, the emotional shallowness of Philip Quarles, the feebleness of Walter Bidlake among the younger) only serves to create the impression of a vague and generally negative outlook, rather than of a sharp perception of the deficiency of a variety of life-styles on the author's part. In *Brave New World*, by contrast, simply by *identifying* the promiscuity and irresponsibility of the younger generation with conventional morality, Huxley succeeds in bringing into focus both the objects of his attack.

In *Brave New World* any form of sexual behaviour *other* than promiscuity is socially unacceptable, and by making promiscuity respectable, Huxley deprives it of its aura of daring and excitement, thereby exposing its emptiness as a way of life. At the same time convention, once it is seen to uphold values to which it is normally opposed, no longer appears to be some kind of absolute standard, but merely a reflection of the unthinking assumptions of the day. The appalling inanity of the conversation in the helicopter between Henry and Lenina, where both complacently parrot the sentiments they have been conditioned into accepting, or the triteness of the synthetic folk wisdom enshrined in the proverbs everyone uses ('a gramme is better than a damn', 'one cubic centimetre cures ten gloomy sentiments'), stand out because of the unfamiliarity of the underlying assumptions, but the real target is clearly the fatuity of the popular beliefs of Huxley's own day. Few readers are likely to be free of their own unthinking assumptions—assumptions which are not thought about because of their very familiarity: it is the *unfamiliarity* of the endlessly reiterated sentiments in *Brave New World* that highlights the extent to which people's beliefs are unthinking and conditioned. It would be hard for any reader to ignore the relevance to the present world of high technology, mass communications, and advertising of the depiction of a society where everyone's opinions are acquired during their sleep.

Huxley similarly exploits incongruities for satiric effect by linking technology and religion. By making the deity ('Our Ford') a motor manufacturer, Huxley satirizes the way in which technological and scientific progress is worshipped as an end in itself: in the society of the future the salient qualities of the machine—efficiency and productivity—have become the cardinal virtues of mankind. At the same time, religion is exposed as mere escapist ritual; the pomp and dignity normally associated with religious ceremonies are deflated by the ludicrous rites of Ford-worship, solemnized by such officials as the Arch Community-Songster of Canterbury.

Incongruity, too, is at the root of Huxley's portrayal of the relations between Lenina and the Savage, in which both the irresponsible hedonism of the former and the romantic illusions of the latter are ridiculed. The Savage's intense emotions, dressed up in grand Shakespearian language, are rendered farcical by the object of his love. For an object is precisely what Lenina is, the product of conditioning rather than a person in her own right. Yet by her very vacuousness she helps to expose what a great deal of romantic love is all about—the projection onto someone else of a private fantasy, rather than a genuine attempt to *know* them. Lenina shows up this element of projection so clearly because she is, so to speak, a blank screen. On the other hand, ridiculous though the Savage is made to look, the fact that he has real emotions at all, however mis-directed, highlights the blandness and shallowness of the relations which the citizens of Brave New World accept as normal.

Fantasy, then, is a medium which enables Huxley to convey what he sees as unpalatable truths about the society in which he lives, and to do so with the maximum vividness and clarity. Yet at the same time, because the fantasy world he creates is so nightmarish, horrible in a far more definite and concrete way than is the case with the worlds described in his realistic fiction, some form of genuine opposition to it becomes possible. In *Brave New World*, for the first time, we find individuals in conflict with their environment, and Huxley makes good use of the sympathy and sense of identification which the reader feels with their struggles.

This is particularly noticeable in the case of Bernard, who is the first character encountered by the reader to possess good healthy neuroses, resentments and feelings of inferiority in the midst of a world of mindless, well-adjusted happiness—the first character, in other words, with whom it is possible to identify. However, just as Swift does in *Gulliver's Travels*, Huxley exploits the reader's sympathies for satiric effect. Much as the reader experiences a jolt when, having loftily identified with Gulliver's contempt for the pretensions of the little men of Lilliput, he finds himself condemned in similar terms by the gigantic King of Brobdingnag, so Huxley, having first established Bernard as a sympathetic character by making him a cogent critic of the dreadful world he lives in, then makes the reader uncomfortably aware of the self-betrayal involved when he succumbs to the lures of worldly success. Like Illidge in *Point Counter Point*, Bernard is hostile to society primarily because he is unable to succeed in its terms. But whereas Illidge is essentially unsympathetic, seen from outside, and also an unsuccessful creation, due to Huxley's attempt to embody in him some sort of portrait of a *typical* revolutionary, Bernard works as a character simply by virtue of the sympathy he engenders. Rather than attempting to discredit a particular ideological attitude by a jaundiced portrayal of one of its adherents, Huxley sets out, in his characterization of Bernard, to make his readers ask themselves whether or not they, too, might not be deterred from opposing what they knew to be wrong by the same bribe of success which Bernard accepts. Illidge, in the end, is merely a pathetic figure, whereas Bernard, whose criticisms of society we are likely to share, forces us to ask whether we do not also share his weaknesses.

Similarly, with Helmholz and the Savage, the sympathy engendered by their opposition to a distasteful society highlights rather than disguises the inadequate nature of their resistance to it. What is emphasized is not so much the fact that they are defeated, with the Savage committing suicide and Helmholz being exiled, but the nature of their defeat. The Savage's hatred of society is rooted in a self-indulgent romanticism and an asceticism which is obsessional and masochistic; Helmholz's dissatisfaction stems from frustrated creative aspirations: neither are able to live the kind of life they want. But in the end their opposition dissolves, with both of them taking what is in fact the easiest way out—the Savage commits suicide, and Helmholz acquiesces in his exile with something like pleasurable anticipation. Yet in sympathizing with their opposition, we are once again forced to ask whether their weaknesses, their failures would not also be ours. In effect, Huxley presents a world which is the logical conclusion of what he sees as the direction in which our society is going—a direction in which he believes it ought not to go. And while we, of course, would agree that the world he presents is undesirable, it is perhaps Huxley's most significant achievement that in *Brave New World* he makes us examine more closely the nature of our opposition to and disagreement with the assumptions of that world.

Nevertheless, *Brave New World* has its weaknesses, too. The focus of Huxley's satire does on occasion become blurred: there are local miscalculations of effect, isolated passages which work against rather than with the general satiric tendency of the work as a whole. One example of this is surely Mustapha Mond's tirade against family life. In the context of *Brave New World* one would suppose that the family—a social institution which might be seen as having developed relatively naturally, rather than being artificially imposed, and which is conducive to real emotion, however unhealthy—would be likely to meet with Huxley's qualified approval. Certainly there is no evidence to suggest that at the time of writing Huxley saw it otherwise: indeed, both Rampion and Miller in *Point Counter Point* and *Eyeless in Gaza* appear to see marriage as one of the prerequisites for a harmonious existence. Yet, instead of reflecting adversely on the values of the world he represents, the force of Mond's rhetoric lends a persuasiveness to his attack on the family which can scarcely have been intended:

> And home was as squalid psychically as physically. Psychically, it was a rabbit hole, a midden, hot with the frictions of tightly packed life, reeking with emotion. What suffocating intimacies, what dangerous, insane, obscene relationships between the members of the family group! Manically, the mother brooded over her children (*her* children) . . . brooded over them like a cat over its kittens; but a cat that could talk, a cat that could say, 'My baby, my baby,' over and over again. 'My baby, and oh, oh, at my breast, the little hands, the hunger, and that unspeakable agonizing pleasure! Till at last my baby sleeps, my baby sleeps with a bubble of white milk at the corner of his mouth. My little baby sleeps. . .' (p. 29)

The trouble with this is that Huxley succeeds only too well in creating the effect which Mond obviously intends. He *does* conjure up a sense of repellent closeness, possessiveness, sentimentality—and it is at points like this that the basic thesis of *Brave New World*, that any kind of real feeling or experience is preferable to the blandness and sterility of the world of the future, carries least conviction. Instead of reinforcing the overall satiric tendencies of the work, Mond's remarks read more like a first draft of the critique of the traditional family which Huxley was later to make in *Island*.

A similar disparity between intention and effect is also evident in Huxley's depiction of the Indian reservation where the Savage lives. Having had such sentiments as 'cleanliness is next to fordliness' and 'civilization is sterilization' drummed into them from birth, the inhabitants of Brave New World are obsessed with hygiene, and it is surely in order to satirize this that Huxley portrays Lenina's horror and discomfiture when she encounters ordinary, natural peasants living an ordinary, natural existence. Unfortunately, however, Huxley spoils the effect by the vividness of his evocation of the filth and squalor of the reserve. Given his own obsession with the repulsiveness of the physical, Huxley's sympathies would seem to lie with Lenina rather than with peasant life, and the morbid fascination with which he describes the dirt and stink of the reservation eventually defeats its own satiric purpose. Lenina's revulsion appears understandable rather than ludicrous.

But these are incidental flaws. The main weakness of *Brave New World* lies, as Huxley himself suggested, in his failure to envisage any kind of alternative to the horrors of the world he portrays. In a later preface to the work, Huxley admitted that:

> The Savage is offered only two alternatives, an insane life in Utopia, or the life of a primitive in an Indian village, a life more human in some respects, but in others hardly less queer and abnormal. At the time the book was written this idea, that human beings are given free will in order to choose between insanity on the one hand and lunacy on the other, was one I found amusing and regarded as quite possibly true. For the sake, however, of dramatic effect, the Savage is often

permitted to speak more rationally than his upbringing among the practitioners of a religion that is half fertility cult and half *Penitente* ferocity would actually warrant. Even his acquaintance with Shakespeare would not in reality justify such utterances. And at the close, of course, he is made to retreat from sanity; his native *Penitente*-ism reasserts its authority and he ends in maniacal self-torture and despairing suicide. 'And so they died miserably ever after'—much to the reassurance of the amused, Pyrrhonic aesthete who was the author of the fable. (pp. vii–viii)

This, however, is a little disingenuous. The author of *Point Counter Point*, *Proper Studies*, *Do What You Will* and *Music at Night*, the works which immediately preceded *Brave New World*, was anything but the frivolous cynic, the 'amused, Pyrrhonic aesthete' whom Huxley blames for the shortcomings of his satire. The absence of any positive alternative in *Brave New World* is not so much due to Huxley's irresponsible attitude, as to the basic poverty of his ideas at the time, his inability, rather than his lack of desire, to conceive of positive alternatives. And this poverty is reflected by the fact that the major debate in the work, the argument between Mond and the Savage about human attitudes towards freedom and its attendant responsibilities, is almost entirely derived from the Grand Inquisitor episode in *The Brothers Karamazov*. However, the second-hand philosophical profundities of the debate only serve to emphasize the limitations of the 'freedom' sought by the three main characters, whose opposition to their society remains essentially selfish and individualistic. Because the aspirations of Bernard, Helmholz, and the Savage are only really concerned with their own personal freedom, none of them are able to offer an effective challenge to the cynical view of human nature which Mond puts forward. Nevertheless, on the evidence of Huxley's other writings of this period, it is hard to believe it was seriously his intention to leave Mond's opinions unchallenged because to do so would be amusing; the pessimism of *Brave New World* is not so much the result of cynicism, as a reflection of Huxley's own inability to resolve the contradictions between his conviction of the desirability of individual human freedom and his fear that nothing could stop the manipulation of human beings in the mass by forces beyond their control.]

It was only later that Huxley came to believe in the possibility of individual human action to combat the processes which were gradually turning people into the zombies of Brave New World, and in his later preface he goes on to outline what might have been a positive alternative to the despairing vision of his earlier satire:

> If I were now to rewrite the book, I would offer the Savage a third alternative. Between the utopian and primitive horns of his dilemma would lie the possibility of sanity—a possibility already actualized, to some extent, in a community of exiles and refugees from the Brave New World, living within the borders of the Reservation. In this community economics would be decentralist and Henry-Georgian, politics Kropotkinesque and co-operative. Science and technology would be used as though, like the Sabbath, they had been made for man, not (as at present and still more so in Brave New World) as though man were to be adapted and enslaved to them... Brought up among the primitives, the Savage (in this hypothetical new version of the book) would not be transported to Utopia until he had had an opportunity of learning something at first hand about the nature of a society composed of freely co-operating individuals devoted to the pursuit of sanity.
>
> (pp. vii–viii)

In other words, a society which would have shown that Brave New World is not inevitable. One of the reasons why Mond has the better of his argument with the Savage is because he is able to say, in effect, that human nature *is* like this, that because everyone has accepted their conditioning, that must be what they want—the presence within the book of a society where people can and do act differently would clearly have exposed the fallacy of his reasoning.

Whether the depiction of such a society (which sounds like a blueprint for *Island*) could in fact have been integrated into *Brave New World* is of course doubtful. Huxley suggested that the hypothetical revised version would have possessed 'an artistic and . . . philosophical completeness, which in its present form it evidently lacks', but it is hard to avoid feeling that his proposed revision might well have created more problems than it resolved. Nevertheless, Huxley's analysis of the flaws of *Brave New World* has much to recommend it: it is worth remembering that in Dostoevsky's case, while the idiosyncratic Christian positives of *The Brothers Karamazov* may often seem intrusive and hard to accept, it is their presence which gives depth and dimension to many of the work's other features. There is, for example, an aura of evil surrounding the Grand Inquisitor and his arguments, which is completely absent from the portrayal of Mustapha Mond's slick cynicism—simply because in the former case there is indicated some source of value which can help to inform the reader's judgements. The full dimension of the Grand Inquisitor's evil is revealed through its being perceived in relation to something else. Huxley's posited anarcho-pacifist commune would doubtless have been difficult to present artistically, but its presence, simply by suggesting the feasibility of realizing human potential, might well have given an added resonance to the depiction of the sterility of a society which denies it.

Nevertheless, an awareness of *Brave New World's* weaknesses should not be allowed to exclude an acknowledgement of its strengths: its defects are of ideas rather than artistry, the reflection of an imperfect understanding of society, not of innate artistic incapacity. And the deficiencies of Huxley's thinking, instead of being compounded by the artistic miscalculations of *Point Counter Point* and *Eyeless in Gaza*, are outweighed by the success with which he exploits the possibilities of the medium he adopts. In fact, the significance of Huxley's choice of form can hardly be overstressed. That the superiority of *Brave New World* to its predecessor, *Point Counter Point* is due to the form employed, rather than being a reflection of growing maturity and mastery of the writer's craft is borne out by the comparative failure of *Eyeless in Gaza*: on reverting to a more realistic mode all the shortcomings which disfigured *Point Counter Point* immediately re-appear. In *After Many A Summer*, by contrast, where Huxley returns to fantasy and satire once more, his writing regains the order, economy and clarity so conspicuously lacking in its predecessor.

After Many A Summer is set in the America of the 1930s—a

somewhat more familiar location than the World State of the distant future, yet one which, because of the way in which it is presented, seems no less bizarre. Seen first of all through the eyes of Jeremy Pordage, scholar and gentleman, America appears unendingly strange and alienating, continually providing shocks to his comfortable English sensibilities. While he is still puzzling over the problems of etiquette presented by his first meeting with a negro chauffeur, Jeremy is baffled by the sight of large numbers of young women who are apparently engaged in silent prayer—it is only later that he realizes that they are in fact chewing gum. No longer in a familiar environment, he loses his bearings, and becomes vulnerable to all sorts of discomfitures. His little jokes, to the girl in the telegraph office, to Propter, to Jo Stoyte, all fall disconcertingly flat; he is embarrassed by Virginia Maunciple, insulted by his employer, and patronized by Dr Obispo. Alternately fascinated and appalled by the world of apparent insanity into which he has suddenly been thrown, it is only his colossal complacency which enables him to preserve his equilibrium.

The chief organizing principle of Huxley's California appears to be the juxtaposition of the most violent possible contrasts. Leaving the station in Los Angeles, Jeremy passes hoardings which advertise hamburgers alongside the comforts of religion, and cosmetics next to funerals. Taken to view, in passing, a vast cemetery called the Beverley Pantheon, he finds it adorned with 'the sort of statues one would expect to see in the reception room of a high-class brothel in Rio de Janeiro' (p. 13). And, as they pass from Los Angeles into the classic Western scenery beyond, there comes into view what is to be the principal setting of the novel, Jo Stoyte's castle—'... doubly baronial. Gothic with a Gothicity raised, so to speak, to a higher power, more mediaeval than any building of the thirteenth century' (p. 16).

Once inside, the contrasts become still more arbitrary: in the great hall, the ascetic visions of El Greco confront the sensual delights of Rubens; there is a Vermeer in the lift; a chromium-plated portcullis is lifted to allow one to drive into the courtyard, while from the battlements it is possible to dive into the swimming pool. The whole amounts to an anthology of the worst possible taste, compiled with the greatest possible relish.

Now clearly, such details are by no means unrepresentative of certain aspects of the United States. Indeed, considering that Huxley is describing a country where in real life a giant statue of Christ with a revolving Crown-of-Thorns restaurant at the top has been projected, one might well feel that his imagination is characterized by a certain modesty. What gives Huxley's America its fantastic, caricatured aspect is simply the principle of selection he adopts. While garishness and vulgarity are inescapable parts of any visitor's experience of the country, they normally appear against a background of more mundane and merely ordinary elements. No longer aspiring to realism, however, Huxley omits these elements, leaving only the most striking and sharply contrasting details, thus creating an effect rather like that of a high contrast photograph, where black and white remain visible, but all the half tones in between have disappeared. The omission of the middle range of connecting elements renders the end product more striking and dramatic, but also, on occasions, incomprehensible, and in *After Many A Summer* it would seem that Huxley is aiming at both effects. Accurate enough in the details he does describe, he deliberately excludes everything that might unify and normalize the scenes he paints, thereby creating a world which Jeremy describes as being like

> . . . the mind of a lunatic. . . Or, rather, an idiot . . . because I suppose a lunatic's a person with a one-track mind. Whereas this is a no-track mind. No track because infinity-track. It's the mind of an idiot of genius (p. 153).

Through the organizing principle of contrast Huxley contrives not only to create a world which is at once recognizable and distorted, accurately observed yet bizarre, but also to ensure that the inter-relation of his characters is carried to a higher level than in any other novel. Nearly all the characters display the same kind of incongruities and contrasts as their environment, and these are heightened as they are interwoven with and reflected by those of their fellows. Jeremy, for instance, combines the elegance and refinement appropriate to his public school and Trinity background with unsavoury personal and sexual habits. He picks his scabs like an ape, a parallel which has added significance in the light of the novel's ending, and fondly recalls his squalid fortnightly encounters with two prostitutes in Maida Vale. It is his first meeting with Jo Stoyte, which serves to reveal the coarseness and vulgarity of his employer, who is himself an amalgam of incongruous contrasts. On the one hand he engages in sharp and underhand business transactions, while on the other he indulges in grossly sentimental benevolence towards sick children, the two combining when, having obtained illicit information from the City Engineer's department which enables him to undertake some hugely profitable property speculation, he pays off the corrupt official who supplied it by giving his child free treatment in his private hospital. He also alternates between aggressive happiness and timorous despair, depending on whether his love of money or his fear of death is uppermost; and while his bullying serves to reveal the character of others by showing the ways they respond to his brow-beating, his weakness makes him the helpless victim of the unscrupulous Obispo, who plays on his fear of death for his own ends. And most incongruous of all are his feelings for Virginia, which are described as being 'simultaneously those of the purest father love and the most violent eroticism' (p. 44).

Virginia, in fact, is in many ways the focus of the contrasts and incongruities of the other characters. As well as exposing the contradictory nature of Jo's emotions, she also serves to reveal the confusions in the mind of Pete Boone. Pete is a romantic figure, a veteran of the Spanish Civil War, but one whose idealism extends rather disconcertingly to sexual matters. Not for him the hard-boiled attitude of a Hemingway hero—the naive enthusiasm that took him to Spain prevents him from seeing Virginia in any kind of realistic light, even to the extent that he fails to realize that she is Jo's mistress. Once again Huxley satirizes romantic love by highlighting the contrast between the feelings of the lover and the nature of the person towards whom they are directed. Of course, Pete is also there for another purpose: like Illidge, Ekki, and Helen, he is intended to expose the fallacies of Communism, and, also like them, he is less than convincing as a character (it is hard to believe, for instance, that his astounding emotional immaturity could have survived the realities of fighting in Spain quite as unscathed as it seems to have done). However, in the fantastic context of *After Many*

A *Summer*, this instance of one of Huxley's characteristic biases is far less of a liability: we are not asked to suppose that Pete is an objective, yet at the same time typical portrait of a communist, but rather one of a galaxy of lunatics.

Virginia is also contradictory in Jeremy's eyes, although in his case the contradictions are aesthetic ones. He sees her more as part of the landscape, as yet another example of the disturbing stylistic contrasts in which the castle abounds:

> One has only to look at such a face to *know* God exists. The one incongruous feature in the present instance is the costume. A pre-Raphaelite expression demands pre-Raphaelite clothes: long sleeves, square yokes, yards and yards of liberty velveteen. When you see it, as I did today, in a combination with white shorts, a bandana, and a cowboy hat, you're disturbed, you're all put out (p. 188).

But if Virginia exposes the contradictions of others, still more does she illustrate the principle of contradiction in her own behaviour. A mixture of innocence and worldliness, she is, in her own uniquely vulgar way, extremely religious. Her feelings of piety have their incarnation in the remarkable statue of the Virgin Mary which stands in her boudoir:

> You drew back a pair of short white velvet curtains (everything in the room was white), and there, in a bower of artificial flowers, dressed in real silk clothes, with the cutest little gold crown on her head and six strings of seed pearls round her neck, stood Our Lady, brilliantly illuminated by an ingenious system of concealed electric bulbs. (p.176)

Her religion, however, contrasts sharply with her sexual habits, and the bedroom location of her idol provides ample opportunities for black comedy and extremely bad taste, which Huxley, to his credit, exploits to the full. In her bedroom, Virginia decides that Our Lady pardons her sexual lapses, providing they occur in a suitably Romantic context, with 'a boy saying lovely things to you, and a lot of kissing, and at the end of it, almost without your knowing it, almost as if it weren't happening to you, so that you never felt there was anything wrong, anything that Our Lady would really mind...' (p. 178).

Our Lady also appears to condone Virginia's lesbian experiences, and only seems really reproachful when Virginia inadvertently leaves the curtains of the shrine open and the lights on when Obispo first seduces her.

Still further contradictions in her behaviour are exposed by her succumbing to the blandishments of Obispo rather than to Pete, who possesses all the romantic illusions she supposes herself to share. Yet despite her distaste for Obispo's cynicism, she prefers him in the end because he is also 'a real good looker . . . rather in the style of Adolphe Menjou . . . it was those dark ones with oil in their hair that had always given her the biggest kick!' (p. 49).

But with Obispo the contradictions stop. He is not hampered by any illusions, and is quite clear both about what he wants, and what he proposes to do to get it. He exploits Jo's fear of death, first to disguise his affair with Virginia (by giving him tranquillizers which he thinks are doing him good, but are in fact keeping him asleep while Obispo proceeds with seducing his mistress), and then, when Jo does find out, to secure his acquiescence (since Jo cannot afford to alienate the one person who can hush up his shooting of Pete). Equally, he exploits Pete: not only does he seduce the object of his adoration, he actually gets her to play on that adoration in order to divert Jo's suspicions; and, of course, it is Pete rather than Obispo whom Jo ends up shooting. Jeremy, too, is another to suffer from Obispo's ability to impose his will on other people: the doctor coolly appropriates his precious copies of Andrea de Nerciat and de Sade in order to entertain Virginia with them, and reaps the benefits of Jeremy's historical researches in order to further his own scientific ones.

But it is his manipulation of Virginia, above all, that illustrates the power which Obispo's single-mindedness gives him over others. Not only does he seduce her, but he does so without making the slightest concession to her notions of how such a seduction should proceed:

> She would take him, and take him, what was more, on his own terms. No Romeo and Juliet acts, no nonsense about Love with a large L, none of that popular song claptrap with its skies of blue, dreams come true, heaven with you. Just

> sensuality for its own sake. . . Facts were facts; accept them as such. It was a fact, for example, that young girls in the pay of rich old men could be seduced without much difficulty. It was also a fact that rich old men, however successful at business, were generally so frightened, ignorant and stupid that they could be bamboozled by any intelligent person who chose to try . . . that was the fact about old men. The fact about love was that it consisted essentially of tumescence and detumescence. So why embroider the fact with unnecessary fictions? Why not be realistic? Why not treat the whole business scientifically? (p. 139)

Obispo is uncompromisingly committed to the destruction of illusions, the reduction of everything to the purely factual. Interestingly enough, however, it is a doctrine which also caters to his own personal tastes. It is a 'fact', for example, 'that he personally found an added pleasure in the imposition of his will upon the partner he had chosen' (p. 140), and because it is a fact, it has to be accepted (and, indeed, forced on others). Yet in the end Obispo's determination to bring everything down to the level of physical fact is merely dehumanizing: while his scepticism about human illusions is often justified, the end product when they are stripped away is often, especially in the case of what he sees as love, a reduction to the animal, even to the mechanical—above all, a degradation. Obispo's reflections on the nature of sexuality culminate in a description of it in the familiar Huxleian terms of revulsion:

> You took an ordinarily rational human being, a good hundred-per-cent American with a background, a position in society, a set of conventions, a code of ethics, a religion . . . you took this good citizen, with rights fully and formally guaranteed by the Constitution, you took her . . . and you proceeded, systematically and scientifically, to reduce this unique personality to a mere epileptic body, moaning and gibbering under the excruciations of pleasure for which you, the Claude Bernard of the subject, were responsible and of which you remained the enjoying, but always detached, always ironically amused, spectator. (pp. 140–1)

Obispo's is certainly one way of bringing order to the chaos.

of coming to terms with the mind of an idiot which is Jeremy's simile for the world which he and everyone else inhabits. Only by detaching oneself from the insanity, by becoming an 'ironically amused spectator', Obispo appears to think, can one maintain one's self-respect. It is an attitude in many ways akin to that of a satirist, only with the difference that Obispo does not confine himself to merely observing and exposing human weaknesses—as an actor in the drama, he also exploits them, preserving his detachment and self-respect at the expense of the domination and degradation of everyone else.

Nevertheless, the very nature of *After Many A Summer* is such that the existence of Obispo has to be counterbalanced by some kind of opposite, and it is the final contrast, between the amoral doctor and the one wholly good character, William Propter, which acts as an enclosing framework for this novel of contrasts and incongruities. Like Opispo, Propter sees through the illusions of others, and also remains detached, as anyone must who wishes to preserve their sanity in the midst of the lunatic world which the novel portrays. Yet although their single-mindedness gives them a similar strength (the more confused and contradictory characters like Jo and Jeremy continually feel at a disadvantage when talking to either), the contrast between them could hardly be more complete. Whereas the Machiavellian Obispo accepts the weaknesses of others as a 'fact' because he can use them to his own advantage, Propter is possessed by a vision of what human beings could be, and tries to encourage people to overcome their weaknesses. Instead of exploiting them, he appeals to their better nature, to their strengths, and tries to show them how to think for themselves, rather than in the terms of the conventional assumptions which condemn them to be weak and stupid. He is a saintly figure, trying to convince a usually sceptical audience of the reality of a spiritual dimension which alone can make sense of the illusions and insanities of the everyday world, while Obispo, by contrast, acts as a kind of Mephistopheles, offering the delights of this world, only at a price. Virginia buys concrete, factual, physical pleasure, but at the expense of her peace of mind. Jo buys off the threat of a murder charge for the shooting of Pete, but only at the expense of acquiescing in his own cuckoldry, to say nothing of having to pay his rival an extremely large sum of money. His dignity thus undermined, Jo is prepared in the end to accept Obispo's ultimate gift, that of eternal life, but only at the expense of the loss of his humanity. Obispo's satanic laughter at the very end, his final display of ironic amusement, is at the spectacle of a man so obsessed by the fear of death that he would rather travel back down the evolutionary scale and become an ape than die.

Yet for all their contrasting natures, Obispo and Propter are the only conflicting elements in the novel which are not directly juxtaposed; the confrontation between their ideas and attitudes remains an implicit one. Nonetheless, their essential opposition is made clear, as for example in the scenes where each offers his interpretation of the Molinos text which Jeremy discovers among the Hauberk papers: 'Ame a Dios como es en sí, y no como se lo dice y forma su imaginación.' For Obispo the statement is meaningless, since he sees all perception as subjective: even if one purges the mind of illusions, one will still see things from one's own point of view.

> 'Why, you can't even love a woman as she is in herself; and after all, there is some sort of objective physical basis for the phenomenon we call a female. A pretty nice basis in some cases. Whereas poor old Dios is only a spirit—in other words pure imagination. And here's this idiot, whoever he is, telling some other idiot that people mustn't love God as he is in their imagination.' (p. 54)

Propter, on the other hand, while he concedes that Molinos' statement is meaningless in materialistic terms, sees it as an indication of the possibility of transcending materialism, of penetrating beyond the world of illusions to some deeper kind of reality. While he is as aware as Obispo of the delusions which most human beings suffer from, he believes that there is a further delusion inherent in relying solely on a literal and self-consciously unromantic conception of reality. Just as Calamy, in *Those Barren Leaves*, criticizes Chelifer for his insistence on the ultimate reality of boring everyday existence, accusing him of being a 'sentimentalist reversed', so Propter sees an exclusive belief in the reality of 'facts' as yet another kind of self-deception. He believes that most human beings define as 'reality' only what they can understand within the terms of the language systems, perceptions, and habits of thought which they have been conditioned into adopting—that their reality is in fact an artificial construct, which excludes the possibility of any experience which lies outside the area it encloses. Like Obispo, he knows that his theory can only be validated by 'a practical try-out': just as the women Obispo seduces can only discover the real nature of the sensual ecstasy he promises them by sleeping with him, Propter's audience can only be convinced of the existence of an ultimate spiritual reality which lies beyond language by experiencing it themselves. As Propter points out:

> ... there is a way between the horns. The practical way. You can go and find out what it means for yourself, by first hand experience. Just as you can find out what El Greco's 'Crucifixion of St. Peter' looks like by taking the elevator and going up to the hall. (p. 166)

Unlike Obispo's experimental validation, however, Propter's is lacking in immediate appeal. Transcendental spiritual experience is not quite so easy to attain as sexual satisfaction, as he himself concedes—

> ... in this case, I'm afraid, there isn't any elevator. You have to go up on your own legs. And make no mistakes ... there's an awful lot of stairs. (ibid.)

Dramatically, the victor in this confrontation of opposing attitudes is Obispo. Far more than Propter, the doctor is a man of action, the more so for being handicapped by fewer moral scruples. Unlike Propter, he feels no need to replace the illusion the destroys with anything positive, and this lends to his utterances a dismissiveness, economy, and directness which renders them all the more striking. Though ostensibly a detached observer of the world, he is in fact very much at home in it, and because his attentions are entirely directed towards worldly success, he has more scope for effective worldly action than does Propter, whose goals are ultimately unworldly.

Yet in the end, despite the confrontation between their respective attitudes, there is no real contest between them, any more than there could be one to determine whether Pele was a better footballer than Sviatoslav Richter was a pianist—the spheres in which they operate are completely different. Although they both seek to influence others, Obispo and Propter do so on different levels. Because the novel necessarily depicts the struggle between them in a dramatic human context, Obispo, who operates within the terms of such a context, emerges as the winner: Pete's confused progress towards an awareness of what Propter is actually talking about is abruptly cut short by the bullet which Jo intends for Obispo; Jo, despite the obscure feelings of peace and happiness which his friendship with Propter gives him, ends up entirely at Obispo's mercy. Obispo fools everyone, Propter included, over the circumstances of Pete's death, and ends up the novel having, quite literally, the last laugh. Nevertheless, even though Propter would seem to be the loser on the plane of action, there is not the slightest question of Obispo's views offering any kind of serious challenge to those of his adversary. His outlook is clearly untenable, being selfish and deficient in compassion, and he is also plainly unaware of any possibilities that might lie beyond his own narrow and literal-minded conception of reality. The question that remains is how far Propter's inability to offer any effective dramatic opposition to Obispo is intentional, and how far it reflects Huxley's continued inability to embody positive ideas in a dramatic context.

There are in fact a variety of reasons for Propter's failure, both as an effective participant in the action of the novel, and considered as a dramatic creation. First of all, his comments on the world around him, while clearly relevant to what goes on, often seem out of place—largely because they require a different *kind* of attention on the part of the reader than does the rest of the narrative. The straightforward exposition of a particular theory, demanding a fairly high degree of concentration, which many of Propter's speeches consist of, is never really integrated with the ironically angled presentation of the rest of the novel—which is also much easier to read. It is rather as if Huxley were a painter attempting to integrate into an impressionist work, of which the outlines only become clear at a distance, elements of fine detail requiring the closest examination for their proper appreciation.

But apart from the stylistic incompatibility involved, the

straightforward presentation of Propter's ideas tends to make only too obvious both the weakness of his arguments, and also the way in which Huxley rigs such debate as there is in an attempt to disguise that weakness. Pete, for example, tries to find out what answers Propter's pacifism and mysticism have to such problems as fascist aggression—a not unreasonable question, giving the date of the book:

> 'Well, how do you want us to act? Do you want us to sit still and do nothing?'
>
> 'Not nothing,' said Mr Propter. 'Merely something appropriate.'
>
> 'But what is appropriate?'
>
> 'Not war, anyhow. Not violent revolution. Nor yet politics, to any considerable extent, I should guess.'
>
> 'Then what?'
>
> 'That's what we've got to discover. The main lines are clear enough. But there's still a lot of work to be done on the practical details.' (p. 114)

At this point, however, we are told that 'Pete was not listening'—which is probably just as well, since if he had been he might have wanted to know something about the main lines, at least, if not the practical details. And it is this absence of any kind of illustration that makes Propter's suggestions seem so inadequate; he clearly believes that there are possible alternatives to the insane, normal behaviour that surrounds him, but he never at any point gives more than the vaguest hints as to what they might be.

Perhaps the main difficulty is that the spiritual enlightenment which Propter regards as so important is something which is essentially incommunicable. Not even the most vivid language can represent the reality which underlies 'the first-hand experience' of mystical awareness. Propter is doomed to failure not simply because people are more interested in re-living 'the feelings and sensations which they found exciting in the past' than in understanding reality, but because mystical experience is rarely attained. The only way in which Propter's message can be grasped is through first-hand experience, but since so few people have had such experience, the likelihood of his making himself understood either by the characters in the novel, or by its readers, is very small. An experience which is incommunicable cannot be understood; nor, if one has never had it, can it be re-lived.

Also, because the message involved is, once again, essentially individualistic, concerned with private and solitary solutions to life's contradictions, its relevance seems as limited as ever. In a world as nightmarish as that of *After Many A Summer* the possibilities of the individual obtaining enlightenment seem minimal. While admittedly Propter also works, with his projected community of transients, towards the creation of an environment where sanity might be possible (an alternative not dissimilar to that which was proposed in the preface to *Brave New World*), his efforts in that direction are so sketchily portrayed as to make hardly any impact. The possibilities for happiness in the world which Propter hopes might one day be created are scarcely even mentioned. And without such happiness being hinted at, all that is shown is the hard work, the struggles, the difficulties which Propter faces, not the rewards his actions might bring.

This joyless asceticism is reinforced by Propter's views on sexuality. Asked by Pete what constitutes 'normal' sexual behaviour—'not statistically normal, of course, but normal in the absolute sense in which perfect vision or unimpaired digestion may be called normal' (p. 228)—Propter replies that there is no such thing. All sexuality, in his view, is tainted by desires and motivations which tend to perpetuate wickedness and insanity. Celibacy, in fact, would seem to be the only form of behaviour which he would accept as correct. It is hardly a solution which, if universally adopted, would offer much hope for the future.

Nevertheless, Propter's analysis of the world around him is generally better than the remedies he suggests for its problems. His understanding of human behaviour is often acute. When he confronts Hansen, Jo's estate manager, over his appalling treatment of the migrant fruit-pickers who work in his orchards, he is at the same time aware that Hansen is 'a very decent, kindly man: one who would be shocked and indignant if he saw you hurting a dog; one who would fly to the protection of a maltreated woman or a crying child' (p. 91). Yet when Propter points out to him the contradiction between the conventional decency of his private instincts and the inhumanity of his conduct in his work, he only succeeds in making him angry. Angry, Propter reflects, with the anger

> ... of the well-meaning but stupid man who is compelled against his will to ask himself indiscreet questions about what he has been doing as a matter of course. He doesn't want to ask these questions, because he knows that if he does he will be forced either to go on with what he is doing, but with the cynic's awareness that he is doing wrong, or else, if he doesn't want to be a cynic, to change the entire pattern of his life so as to bring his desire to do right into harmony with the real facts as revealed in the course of self-interrogation. To most people any radical change is even more odious than cynicism. The only way between the horns of the dilemma is to persist at all costs in the ignorance which permits one to go on doing wrong in the comforting belief that by doing so one is accomplishing one's duty. (pp. 92–3)

Despite his ineffectuality, and the vagueness of the alternatives he suggests, Propter, by his very presence, gives an added perspective to the action of the novel. *After Many A Summer* is a chronicle of fear, greed, lust, hatred, and stupidity which, without Propter's commentary, it would be easy to read simply with sardonic amusement. But it is not Huxley's purpose to present a merely negative and destructive satire: to do so would almost be to make Obispo the author's spokesman. Propter, through the sadness and compassion with which he observes the behaviour of others, adds another dimension to the work, providing a framework within which it is clear that Obispo, too, is satirized.

After Many A Summer is by no means irretrievably damaged by the problems which surround the presentation of a figure such as Propter. Freed by the novel's fantastic character from the demands which he felt realism imposed, Huxley has no compunction about depicting a sequence of events which in a naturalistic context would doubtless seem improbably orderly, and the result is one of his strongest plots. Around his story of the unearthing of the Hauberk papers, and of their implications for Jo Stoyte's quest for eternal life Huxley creates a structure in which the interrelation of character and incident gives point and artistic inevitability to almost everything that happens. Even the most sensational occurrences fit into the novel's tight pattern. Where the killing of Webley in *Point Counter Point*, for example, seemed largely gratuitous, Pete's death is the outcome of a far more convincing combination of circumstances. That Jo Stoyte should kill the wrong person seems the most logical possible conclusion after the scene in the lift, where his insensate animal rage is grotesquely contrasted with the calm geometry and artistic perfection of the Vermeer which hangs there.

And out of this tightly organized narrative there emerge satiric strokes even more effective than those of *Brave New World*. It would be hard to imagine a bleaker comment on man's inability to come to terms with the inevitability of death than the final revelation that even the fate of the fifth Earl of Gonister has its attractions for Jo Stoyte. As a symbol of the futility of the aspiration to eternal life it surpasses even Swift's Struldbruggs, for while the 'reality' of immortality is depicted equally repulsively, Huxley provides an added twist by showing that the fear of death can overcome even that repulsion.

The basic principle of violent contrast, the transparent inadequacy of the way in which nearly all the characters live ultimately has the effect of turning one away from the unacceptable conclusions of Obispo, and back to those of Propter. Such is the strength of plot, structure and symbol in *After Many A Summer* that the work is able not only to carry a figure so dangerous to artistic unity as Propter is, but even to direct the reader's attention to what he says—if the content is less than adequate, that is no reflection on the presentation.

Nevertheless, the distinctive quality of *Brave New World* and *After Many A Summer* does not appear to have met with a great deal of critical recognition. For the most part, Huxley's critics have tended either to regard the two works as peripheral to his more significant achievements, or else to stress their essential similarity to the rest of his output. Keith May, for example, despite going to great pains to identify the formal character of *Brave New World* ('taking account of the main-sub-categories we should call *Brave New World* satirical utopian . . . science fiction [*Aldous Huxley*, p. 99]), concludes that 'in any general appraisal of Huxley's work (it) should be viewed primarily as we view any of the other novels. It is not an oddity, but takes its place in the line of development of Huxley's art and thought' (p. 116). At no point does he suggest that *Brave New World* is a different *kind* of novel, or that its distinctive qualities are directly related to Huxley's choice of form. Similarly, Peter Bowering sees nothing remarkable about *After Many A Summer*, commenting on its 'lack of interest in form, which characterizes all Huxley's later work', and describing it as a return to 'the country-house party formula of the early novels' (*Aldous Huxley: A Study of the Major Novels*, p. 142).

Other critics go further. D. S. Savage, in *The Withered Branch* (London, 1950) refers only in passing to 'the novelette called *Brave New World*—a satirical projection into the future of the way of life implicit in a deliberate hedonism, which need not concern us... (p. 142.) Jerome Meckier brackets *After Many A Summer* with *The Genius and the Goddess*, remarking that 'neither ... improve with re-reading' (*Aldous Huxley: Satire and Structure*, p. 160). And George Woodcock, as we have seen, takes *Brave New World* to constitute a 'special exception' to the general growth in 'complexity and quality' which he believes to be evident between *Crome Yellow* and *Eyeless in Gaza*. *After Many A Summer* is dismissed as 'inferior to his earlier novels' (*Dawn and the Darkest Hour*, p. 221), and receives barely more than three pages' discussion.

This general playing down of the significance of the two novels can be seen in part as the obverse of the critical predilection for complexity which has already been suggested as a possible reason for the consistent over-valuation accorded to *Point Counter Point* and *Eyeless in Gaza*. Neither *Brave New World* nor *After Many A Summer* are particularly complex works—their most distinctive qualities are their liveliness and immediacy, a directness which is perhaps more evident on a first reading than after lengthy critical scrutiny—and none of Huxley's critics really does justice to these. (It is significant that Meckier complains of *After Many A Summer* failing to improve on re-reading: one is tempted to wonder just how many re-readings were involved before the critic forgot the work's initial impact).

More generally, however, there can be sensed a certain critical predisposition in favour of representational fiction over fantasy and satire. It is rather as though the fact that most of the greatest novels are predominantly realistic has led critics to suppose that realism is *inherently* superior to any other mode—that because there are few examples of other kinds of fiction which measure up to the achievements of Eliot, Flaubert, Tolstoy, James, such non-representational genres must necessarily be less significant. Of course, there are exceptions—satiric fantasies such as *Gulliver's Travels*, hybrid blends of almost every possible genre, such as *Moby Dick*—works whose qualities demand recognition; but it is hard to avoid feeling that any writer below such levels who elects to write in other than a representational mode risks being regarded as having opted out, as having settled for something easier, rather as a composer might be who wrote only dance music, not essaying the larger forms.

And this, perhaps, is the real issue—the implication that the exercise of pure imagination is an easy matter compared to the labour involved in achieving representational authenticity, the puritanical contention that once the challenge of representing what *is* is disregarded by the novelist, the writing of fiction becomes easier, and hence, by questionable logic, inferior. But this prejudice against certain types of imaginative fiction on the grounds of their presumed easiness is not a new one: it is already implicit in Johnson's criticism of *Gulliver's Travels*, to the effect that 'when once you have thought of big men and little men, it is very easy to do all the rest',[1] and it is scarcely more reasonable now than it was then. Of course, there is something in both fantasy and satire which lends itself to the merely mechanical working out of a scanty store of ideas. The *Brave New World* theme of the conformist society of the future challenged by seekers after individual freedom is a familiar one to readers of Science Fiction—but whereas even the most literary (and, indeed, literate) imitators of Huxley, such as L. P. Hartley, in *Facial Justice*, or Ira Levin, in *This Perfect Day* seem to be describing the imaginary society of the future for little more than its own sake, Huxley, in common with Swift, succeeds in making the initial act of imagination—the thinking of the little men and the big men, as it were, the starting point for talking about society. Huxley uses the free rein which the idea of the world of the future, of the quest for eternal life gives to his imagination not self-indulgently, but intelligently, for a purpose. *Brave New World* and *After Many A Summer* may be easy to read, but it is hardly logical to suppose that they were therefore easy to write, and still less so to imagine that their qualities of wit and readability exclude an essential seriousness of intention.

Once again, the trap Huxley's critic appear to have fallen into is the familiar one of paying too much attention to what fiction ought to be, and not enough to what it is, of concentrating on what Huxley ought to have attempted to write and ignoring what he actually succeeded in writing. In *Brave New World* and *After Many A Summer* Huxley had just as much to say about the society in which he lived as he did in *Point Counter Point* and *Eyeless in Gaza,* and in the particular form of fantastic satire which he evolved he found a far more effective vehicle for saying it—one better suited to his talents, to the nature of the message he wished to convey, and one which made possible far greater clarity, economy, forcefulness of expression, and wit than he had hitherto achieved. It is when these kind of qualities come to be ignored that the critic begins to part company with the audience for whom Huxley's fiction was designed.

6

Huxley's Later Fiction: *Time Must Have a Stop*, *Ape and Essence* and *The Genius and the Goddess*

The outbreak of the Second World War, bringing with it what Huxley saw as the twin evils of armed aggression and violent resistance, only served to confirm him in the beliefs already expressed in *After Many A Summer*. In Huxley's eyes, the war was still further proof of the fact that conventional philosophies, morality, and social behaviour could only lead to disaster; while the peace that followed, marked as it was by the emergence of the threat of nuclear destruction, did little to alter his pessimism about the future of mankind. Nevertheless, despite the scale of the events involved—a war which engulfed whole societies, the development of a weapon which might destroy the entire planet —Huxley continued to believe that the only hope for humanity lay at the level of individual behaviour. What happened in the world at large was simply the logical conclusion of the unthinking acceptance, on the individual level, of conventional assumptions, and of patterns of behaviour which were ultimately undesirable. If individuals (so he reasoned), persisted in selfish, unthinking, and irrational behaviour, it was no wonder that the societies to which they belonged were characterized by selfishness and irrationality on a much larger scale. It was this conviction which Huxley sought to embody in his later fiction: his next novel, *Time Must Have A Stop*, and the succeeding novelettes, *Ape and Essence* and *The Genius and the Goddess* all represent attempts to find the kind of fictional vehicle which would be most suitable for the expression of his beliefs.

Time Must Have a Stop (1945) can be seen as a return, in many ways, to the methods which Huxley had adopted in *Eyeless in Gaza*. For all that it contains a number of passages which purport to represent the posthumous experiences of one of the characters, its approach is primarily realistic, and the narrative centres, as it does in the earlier novel, on the conversion of the main character (Sebastian), by the example of an ideally good man (Rontini). Huxley himself regarded *Time Must Have A Stop* as his most successful work, and certainly, as compared with *Eyeless in Gaza*, it does display some important advances. Rontini, for example, is a far more convincing creation than Miller: his mildness and humility contrast favourably with the latter's brashness, and, while his beliefs are made quite explicit, there is no parallel to the absurd scene in *Eyeless in Gaza* where Miller confronts Anthony in the middle of the Mexican desert and proceeds to hold forth on the virtues of a sufficiency of roughage in the diet. In addition, Rontini is perhaps the most dramatically effective of Huxley's gurus: the sequence of events whereby he becomes involved with Sebastian has a kind of logic and inevitability which is absent from *Eyeless in Gaza*, and Sebastian's conversion accordingly seems less stage-managed than that of Anthony.

It is perhaps a reflection of Huxley's satisfaction with the handling of the central conversion theme that his treatment of the subordinate characters becomes less schematic. While the minor characters continue to fulfil the function of illustrating a variety of limited and unsatisfactory life-styles, there is an almost Dickensian vitality in Huxley's portrayal of Fred Poulshot's dreariness and self-centred gloom, or of Mrs Gamble's callous eccentricity: a vitality which *Eyeless in Gaza* conspicuously lacks. Characters like Fred Poulshot, Mrs Gamble, and Daisy Ockham do not *simply* illustrate Huxley's theories of human behaviour—they also have their own independent artistic validation, which in its turn helps to disguise the extent to which they are part of an overall illustrative scheme.

On the other hand, *Time Must Have A Stop* also has certain weaknesses which are perhaps closer to those of *After Many A Summer*. There are, for example, certain difficulties surrounding the description of Eustace's experiences after death: while they are clearly *relevant*, inasmuch as they illustrate Huxley's contention that human beings have a basic impulse to resist enlightenment, the manner of their presentation is rather at odds with that of the rest of the novel. Just as he does in *After Many*

A Summer, Huxley introduces material which, though good in itself, demands a different *kind* of attention than that required by the rest of the work. While the description of what happens to Eustace after his death possesses an odd plausibility, the curious tone which Huxley necessarily has to adopt, particularly in those passages where he attempts to articulate Eustace's first glimmerings of posthumous consciousness, has the effect of dissociating them from the more straightforwardly presented main body of the narrative. This is not to say that the posthumous sequences are not an essential part of the work: not only do Eustace's experiences serve to illustrate and support what Rontini is trying to say, they are also integral to one of the funniest scenes in the novel—the seance, where Huxley appears to be suggesting that the chief obstacle to communication with the spirit world is not the fact that it does not exist, but rather the stupidity of those who try to contact it. What is lacking is not the ability to render such unusual material convincingly, as an overall style or tone of voice which might comprehend and unify the description of different kinds of experience.

This failure to integrate different styles and approaches is also evident in the epilogue, which portrays an older Sebastian reflecting on his conversion, and on events subsequent to the main action of the novel. Unfortunately, Sebastian's reflections amount to little more than random jottings, and while it might be argued that that is what they are supposed to be, their inconsequential nature makes the epilogue a rather unsatisfactory conclusion, particularly bearing in mind the tightness with which the main narrative is constructed.

However, the central weakness of *Time Must Have A Stop* is one which it shares with *Eyeless in Gaza*: returning to the essentially realistic approach of the earlier novel, Huxley once again comes up against the same problem of a basic incompatibility between realism and his particular kind of didacticism. In contrast to *Brave New World* and *After Many A Summer* the action of *Time Must Have A Stop* takes place in a familiar setting; its London and Florence are recognizably part of the world of the reader's own experience in a way in which Jo Stoyte's California is not, and this in its turn tends to work against the reader's acceptance of certain features which might have been seen as virtues in a fantastic context. The tightness of construction to which we have referred, for example, would seem to be at odds with the illusion of reality which Huxley successfully creates from the outset, with his vivid evocation of a foggy evening on Haverstock Hill. Because the world he creates is so recognizably that of the reader, his success in subordinating almost every aspect of the narrative to his didactic purpose is virtually self-defeating: the plot is in fact far better constructed than that of *Eyeless in Gaza*, but this only serves to make the element of intention all the more glaring. To an even greater extent than in the earlier novel, Huxley's reality conspires to make sense, to illustrate a thesis, in a way in which the reader's own experience of reality does not. A kind of vicious circle is created, in which the narrative virtues are transformed into vices by the realistic approach adopted.

Thus, for example, the very logicality of the sequence of events which leads Sebastian into a network of lies and deceit from which only Rontini can rescue him becomes almost a liability once the reader is awakened to the element of contrivance involved. The psychological realism with which Sebastian's behaviour is portrayed is ultimately compromised by the fact that the consequences of his initial misplaced desire to possess an evening suit are so clearly designed to illustrate the proposition that small iniquities inevitably lead to greater. And this element of design is still further emphasized by Rontini's explicit comments when Sebastian, suspected of theft, but in fact guilty of lying, comes to him for help. Rontini suggests that Sebastian, when he does wrong, should consider

> . . . a genealogy . . . a family tree of the offence. Who or what were its parents, ancestors, collaterals. What are likely to be its descendants—in my own life and other people's? It's surprising how far a little honest research will take one. Down into the rat-holes of one's own character. Back into past history. Out into the world around one. Forward into possible consequences. It makes one realize that nothing one does is unimportant, and nothing wholly private. (p. 238)

Rontini, in fact, explicitly invites us to examine the construction of the chain of events which put Sebastian into such a difficult situation, and in doing so once more draws attention to the neatness with which it all fits together. Sebastian is not simply guilty of deception—his lies lead to the unjust punishment of the peasant girl, who is suspected of stealing the drawing which he has actually sold; they are indirectly responsible for the retaliatory poisoning of Mrs Gamble's dog; and they ultimately result in Rontini's arrest and torture by the fascists. (If Sebastian hadn't wanted an evening suit, he wouldn't have sold the drawing; if he hadn't sold the drawing, Rontini wouldn't have had to force the dealer to give it back; if Sebastian hadn't boasted of his father's socialist connections, the dealer wouldn't have been able to denounce Rontini to the fascists.) Given that Sebastian's initial offence is no more than simple adolescent vanity, it all seems a bit extreme.

What happens to Sebastian is in the nature of a parable, but in a realistic context it seems overdone, serving only to alert us to the element of intention involved. This, in its turn, undermines the novel in other ways: even in the case of Eustace, who is a far more sympathetic character than Huxley would have dared to include in *Eyeless in Gaza*, there is apparent the same element of calculation in the stress which is laid on his imperfections. Eustace is an unashamed sensualist, addicted to the joys of the flesh, but in trying to demonstrate how far he is in fact at the mercy of his physical desires Huxley nearly always seems to exaggerate just a little too much. Describing Eustace's enjoyment of cigars, for example, Huxley compares him to a baby:

> . . . nuzzling with blind concupiscence for the nipple, seizing it at last between the soft prehensile flaps of its little mouth, and working away, working away in a noiseless frenzy of enjoyment. (p. 51)

Because Eustace is *not* wholly unsympathetic, Huxley seems to feel obliged to go out of his way to emphasize the fact that he is nevertheless basically unregenerate.

Of course, there is also another factor at work—the same revulsion from the physical which is a recurrent feature of Huxley's novels from *Antic Hay* onwards—and this is still more in evidence in the description of Sebastian's sexual experiences, which form a convenient counterpoint to Rontini's lecturing on the subject of transcendent, divine love. Following his nightmarish sexual initiation by a prostitute, Sebastian is seduced by Mrs Thwale, who introduces him to

> ... that almost surgical research of the essential shamelessness ... those spells of silent, introverted frenzy, those long-drawn agonies, under his timid and almost horrified caresses, of a despairing insatiability. (p. 223)

Above all, however, Huxley seems concerned to stress the separateness and alienation of his characters. Real communication seems to be impossible: nearly everyone appears to be isolated, locked within the worlds created by their own subjective perceptions; any awareness of the existence of other people who may see the world differently only serves to heighten the sense of alienation. Sebastian, for example, sees himself as an adult, but is at the same time painfully aware that everyone else treats him like an adorable child:

> To be seventeen, to have a mind which one felt to be agelessly adult, and to look like a Della Robbia angel of thirteen—it was an absurd and humiliating fate... (p. 2)

As a result, people respond to Sebastian on the basis of a perception of him which bears no relation to his own experience of himself: Daisy Ockham, for example, loves him, but only because he reminds her of her son.

For his own part, Sebastian tends to find the contrast between reality and his subjective perceptions a disconcerting one. On meeting Mrs Thwale, he is reminded of Mary Esdaile, the imaginary object of his innocent sexual fantasies, but soon finds that the reality of sleeping with her is far removed from the world of his imagination. Whereas his dreams had always been gentle, comforting affairs, the actual sensation of making love to another person proves to be almost alarming: '... the yet more rapturous experience of being totally out of bounds, the ecstasy of an absolute alienation'. (p. 223)

But while Sebastian is at any rate aware of the existence of other people, there are other characters on whom it never seems to impinge at all. Both Fred Poulshot and Mrs Gamble are far too self-absorbed to pay attention to anyone other than themselves;

while Sebastian's father's bitterness and puritanism succeeds in alienating him from his wife, his brother, and his son. At the end of the book he is described as 'a self-stunted dwarf who had succeeded in consummating his own spiritual abortion' (pp. 302–3). It would be difficult to go further in the direction of alienation than that. Even the affable Eustace is ultimately alone: his love of company is merely another addiction, like his love of food, drink, art, sex, and tobacco—a consolation, a substitute for real experience.

The world of *Time Must Have A Stop* is one where even the good are alienated, imprisoned by the limitations of their perceptions, unable to understand the true nature of the world in which they live. Reflecting on the lives of his relatives at the end of the novel, Sebastian acknowledges their 'absolutely sterling goodness', but sees it as 'limited by an impenetrable ignorance of the end and purpose of existence'. It is not enough to be good in the conventional, socially accepted sense of the word. Still thinking of his relatives, Sebastian goes on to suggest that

> Without Susan and Kenneth and Aunt Alice and all their kind, society would fall to pieces. With them it was perpetually attempting suicide. They were the pillars, but they were also the dynamite; simultaneously the beams and the dry-rot. It was thanks to their goodness that the system worked as smoothly as it did; and thanks to their limitations that the system was fundamentally insane—so insane that Susan's three charming babies would almost certainly grow up to become cannon fodder, plane fodder, fodder for any one of the thousand bigger and better military gadgets with which bright young engineers like Kenneth would by that time have enriched the world. (p. 273)

Mere passive goodness, which unthinkingly accepts the state of affairs obtaining at the time, is seen as being almost as pernicious as active evil: both are part of the same imperfect world. What is required is a different kind of goodness, and it is this which Huxley tries to embody in the character of Rontini.

However, just as in *Eyeless in Gaza*, there is the same fundamental problem of reconciling the presentation of positive alternatives with the intensely pessimistic portrayal of the world which they are designed to affect. Although Rontini's goodness is more convincing than that of Miller, it still seems hopelessly limited, unlikely to have much effect either on a society which is basically insane, or on the individuals (most of whom seem beyond redemption) who compose it. Morally, Rontini is clearly beyond reproach. Equally clearly, he exerts a good influence on Sebastian: it is due to him that Sebastian learns the self-knowledge necessary to remedy his numerous defects—at the end, even Sebastian's father grudgingly admits that knowing Rontini seems to have done his son some good. Yet it remains unclear just *what* Sebastian has learnt, or indeed, whether it has any relevance to anyone else. There is even less attempt made to show the actual *process* of conversion than in *Eyeless in Gaza*, and it is this failure to give any indication of how the kind of changes which Huxley envisages work that proves crippling. Rontini clearly represents an alternative, but its nature is so vague that in the end it is hard to tell exactly what it is that he is supposed to be offering. Faced with the horrors of fascism and impending war, Rontini seems hardly less impotent than the rest of Huxley's characters. His inner peace makes him no more able to oppose evil actively; indeed, so far as the fascists are concerned, he seems to connive almost wilfully in his own arrest, in an act of pointless self-martyrdom. If he has helped Sebastian to become wiser and more self-aware, there is no indication that Sebastian is capable of using what he has learnt to assist anyone else. Even though his relationship with Rontini seems more convincing than that between Miller and Anthony, or Propter and Pete Boone, it remains, like them, an isolated example, rather than a source of hope.

The question that remains is whether Huxley's failure to make the alternatives which Rontini represents seem convincing is simply a matter of insufficient artistry, or whether it in fact reflects the inadequacy of the alternatives themselves. Huxley's basic contention seems to be that the only hope for humanity lies in the actions of a 'tiny theocentric minority'—to whom, one imagines, Rontini, along with Propter and Miller, belongs—and in *Time Must Have A Stop* the clear implication is that all actions, whether honourable or dishonourable, which are not motivated by an essentially 'theocentric' attitude are likely to prove disastrous in the long run. The best intentions, Huxley seems to be saying, can cause just as much harm as the worst. Thus, in one of Eustace's posthumous visions, British brutality in Calcutta is equated with the torturing and murder of Jim Poulshot by the Japanese: Eustace merely laughs at the justification of a baton charge on an unruly crowd on the grounds that things would be a lot worse 'if the Japs were to get to Calcutta' (p. 228). Huxley's position is an idealistic one: there can be no distinctions between degrees of evil, since all evils, however slight, inevitably lead to greater evil, and there can hence be no justification of the use of undesirable means to achieve a desirable end; no end that can be achieved by such means is desirable. But this begs a number of important questions: is it actually true that the use of violence to maintain civic order in time of war is *just as bad* as the gratuitous sadism which prompts the torture and murder of wounded prisoners? Is the argument that 'it would be a damned sight worse if the Japs were to get to Calcutta' *self-evidently* laughable? Huxley believed that violence bred violence, and that to resist violence by violent means was simply to perpetuate the evil that all sane people wished to put an end to, and it was for this reason that he suggested, in 1941, that the continuation of the war until the Germans were defeated would be just as catastrophic as a victory on their terms (*Letters*, p. 470). Once again the question poses itself: is that *really* a justifiable position?

Huxley's problem is that his point of view is not necessarily one which the reader is prepared to accept. In the context of the nightmarish fantasy—world of *After Many A Summer* Huxley's contention that almost all human behaviour was equally misguided seemed not implausible, but in the more realistic context of *Time Must Have A Stop* the debatable nature of his thesis becomes more of a stumbling block. Seeing the world solely in terms of an ideal, and conceiving only of idealized solutions, Huxley refuses to distinguish between different forms of behaviour which fall short of the ideal in any way; the difference between *After Many A Summer* and *Time Must Have A Stop* is that in the latter work Huxley invites the reader to accept as realistic his picture of the world as a place in which such distinctions are meaningless. Yet if the reader does not accept this to be the case, he or she is that much more likely to reject Huxley's view of the world as unrealistic, and hence to find Rontini's solutions to the problems of that world unconvincing. Though Huxley's intention is clearly a polemical one, the realistic approach which he adopts is one which only the converted are likely to find acceptable.

Most readers, therefore, are likely to find Huxley's (and Rontini's) arguments unsatisfactory, deficient not only in execution, but also in conception. Rontini constantly harps on the necessity of achieving personal harmony before doing anything else:

> ... there's only one corner of the universe you can be sure of improving, and that's your own self...
>
> You've got to *be* good before you can *do* good—or at any rate do good without doing harm at the same time. Helping with one had and hurting with the other—that's what the ordinary reformer does.
>
> ... the wise man begins by transforming himself, so that he can help people without running the risk of being corrupted in the process. (pp. 82–3)

But in the context of *Time Must Have A Stop* his belief in the priority of self-improvement seems just as solipsistic as the outlook of the more obviously alienated characters. The limited help which he is able to give Sebastian offers no kind of counterbalance to the graphically portrayed horrors of the world in which he lives, and the ineffectiveness of his involvement in the action only serves to underline the weakness of the alternatives which he represents. As Huxley himself remarked,

> ... the negative is always enormously easier to express than the positive. Any fool can see motes in other people's eyes, even when his own are full of beams. But it takes a genius to describe; convincingly and interestingly, a character who is mote free, and a saint to describe at first hand, the nature of the light as it is when there are no motes or beams to interfere with its radiance and modify its purity. (*Letters*, p. 513)

Yet because he believed that only the saintly man could offer a viable alternative to the norms of a sick society, Huxley once more set himself the task of embodying his beliefs, as he had done in both *Eyeless in Gaza* and *After Many A Summer*, in the person of a man who could be seen as ideally good. In doing so, however, he succeeded only in demonstrating the limitations of such a strategy; while Rontini is a more successful dramatic creation than either Miller or Propter, inasmuch as he is actually seen to be *involved* in the action, it is paradoxically the very fact of that involvement which makes him appear so ineffectual.

Despite his professed satisfaction with *Time Must Have A Stop*, however, Huxley employs a very different approach in both the short novels which follow it. While he remained convinced that evil, on whatever scale it manifested itself, could only be resisted through the individual pursuit of goodness, this conviction is far less central to the construction of *Ape and Essence* and *The Genius and the Goddess* than is the case in *Time Must Have A Stop*. *Ape and Essence*, in fact, is a futuristic fantasy more in the manner of *Brave New World* than of the novel which Huxley regarded as his most successful.

Ape and Essence (1948) is set in the California of the future, some time after World War III, and its form, rather unusually, is that of a film scenario. Writing in 1949, Huxley described the trouble he had experienced in finding a vehicle suitable for the expression of what he wished to say:

> . . . there was no other form that would do. I tried at first to write it 'straight'; but the material simply wouldn't suffer itself to be expressed at length and in realistic, verisimilitudinous terms. The thing had to be short and fantastic, or else it could not be at all. So I chose the scenario form as that which best fulfilled the requirements. (*Letters*, p. 600)

At first sight there would seem to be no reason why the particular form he chose should not have proved ideal for Huxley's purposes. His experience of writing for the cinema[1] had given him ample opportunity to explore the possibilities of the scenario format, while, as we have seen, satiric fantasy had so far proved to be the most effective vehicle for his preoccupations. *Ape and Essence* is full of the ironic juxtapositions in which Huxley delighted, and with its rapid alternations between up-to-theminute cinematic effects and alliterative verse, between satire and overt moralizing, and between the depiction of a high-technology civilization and total barbarism, the diversity of its component parts would seem to bring it the closest of all Huxley's novels to satire in the classical sense of 'satura' or medley. Interestingly enough, it is possible to detect the influence of (of all people) Langland—not only in its use of alliterative verse techniques, but in the basic structure, where an introduction set in the 'real' world is then followed by Tallis's 'vision', which turns out to be a highly moralistic satire. In looking back to the example of one of the great mediaeval satirists, Huxley might be seen to be making perhaps his most interesting experiment in attempting to resolve his formal problems.

However, while this may be all very well in theory, it only goes to show that there is no such thing as a prescription for success. *Ape and Essence* is in fact one of Huxley's most disappointing works, its execution signally failing to match up to its imaginative conception. There are, of course, some effective satiric strokes, especially when Huxley is attacking the unthinking mentality which has made nuclear war possible: the Arch-Vicar's thesis that man's increasingly arrogant assault on nature can only be explained in terms of demonic possession, for example, is rather too plausible for comfort.

> As a man of science you're bound to accept the working hypothesis that explains the facts most plausibly. Well, what are the facts? The first is a fact of experience and observation—namely, that nobody wants to suffer, wants to be degraded, wants to be maimed and killed. The second is a fact of history—the fact that, at a certain epoch, the overwhelming majority of human beings accepted beliefs and adopted courses of action that could not possibly result in anything but universal suffering, general degradation and wholesale destruction. The only plausible explanation is that they were inspired or possessed by an alien consciousness that willed their undoing and willed it more strongly than they were able to will their own happiness and survival. (pp. 95–6)

Also, with his characteristic emphasis on individual responsibility, he paints a telling picture of the way in which ordinary people not only acquiesce in a state of affairs which makes their destruction likely, but actively work to assist the process:

> Take the scientists, for example. Good, well-meaning men, for the most part. But He (the Devil) got hold of them all the same—got hold of them at the point where they ceased to be human beings and became specialists. (p. 97)

In Huxley's view, it is not an inexorable fate which has brought humanity to the brink of disaster, but individual human complicity in stupid, evilly misguided courses of action. It is not simply wicked people who are responsible, but perfectly ordinary ones. And to illustrate this proposition, he describes the life-style of the average scientist working on the development of bacteriological weapons:

> To see that *all* shall die has been the task of some of those brilliant young D.Sc.'s now in the employ of your government. And not of your government only: of all the other elected or self-appointed organizers of the world's collective schizophrenia. Biologists, pathologists, physiologists—here they are, after a hard day at the lab, coming home to their families. A hug from the sweet little wife. A romp with the children. A quiet dinner with friends, followed by an evening of chamber music or intelligent conversation about politics and philosophy. Then bed at eleven and the familiar ecstasies of married love. And in the morning, after orange juice and Grapenuts, off they go again to their job of discovering how yet greater numbers of families precisely like their own can be infected with a yet deadlier strain of *bacillus mallei*.
>
> (pp. 31–2)

If Huxley's illustrations of the individual's capacity for doing good are seldom convincing, he has a much sharper eye for the corresponding capacity for irresponsibility and doing evil.

Unfortunately, however, the positive qualities of *Ape and Essence* tend to be overshadowed by its weaknesses: for every passage such as the above, one could point to a dozen which are both poorly conceived and clumsily executed. But even that is not the real problem: it is not Huxley's handling of detail which constitutes the main defect, so much as his overall failure to make the medium which he has chosen an effective vehicle for the expression of the message which he wished to convey.

Perhaps the first major weakness of *Ape and Essence* lies in the nature of the introduction. While, on the level of simple narrative mechanics, its function is to account for the survival of Tallis's somewhat uncinematic film script, its main purpose is clearly to lend support to Huxley's central contention that what happens at the macrocosmic level of international politics is merely a reflection of what goes on at the individual, microcosmic level—that the behaviour of societies is no more than an extension of the private behaviour of the individuals who compose them. Whereas the main action takes place in post-World War III California, the setting of the introduction is contemporary, and Huxley's evident intention is to depict individual behaviour in such a way as to make the outbreak of nuclear war in the intervening period seem plausible. He describes the machinations of Hollywood, the sexual anxieties of Briggs, the prejudice and ignorance of Mr Coulton, the empty garrulousness of his wife, and the gullibility and vanity of their granddaughter, yet once again the impression created is that reality is being manipulated to prove a point. Rather than adding up to an indictment of the society to which they belong, the weaknesses of the characters whom Huxley describes simply seem to furnish yet another illustration of his idiosyncratic processes of selection.

In any event, Huxley's frame of reference is so local, so small-scale, that the events of the introduction make little impact. The behaviour we are shown is for the most part so petty that its relevance to the subsequent outbreak of nuclear war seems far from self-evident. And when Huxley does make an attempt to emphasize the relevance of the introduction, the device he employs seems decidedly clumsy. Gandhi, we are truculently informed in the very first line, has just been assassinated, but Huxley's attempt to make this the symbol of the triumph of insanity over good sense appears somewhat forced:

> The headlines I had seen that morning were parables; the event they recorded, an allegory and a prophecy. In that symbolic act, we who so longed for peace had rejected the only possible means to peace and had issued a warning to all who,

> in the future, might advocate any courses but those which lead inevitably to war. (p. 7)

Such is the significance which Gandhi's death had for Huxley, and which he wished it to convey to his readers—but unfortunately, symbolic or allegoric significance cannot be achieved simply on the author's say-so. Huxley fails to put the events of the introduction in the kind of perspective necessary to make them seem relevant: the connections between Gandhi's death and the general lack of awareness displayed by the characters, or between their mundane, sordid behaviour and the subsequent holocaust never become apparent.

The scenario itself, however, presents other problems. In choosing this particular format, Huxley was deliberately adopting an approach likely to create very decided expectations on the part of the reader. By casting the main action of *Ape and Essence* in the form of a film script, he could scarcely have imposed a stronger imperative on the reader to visualize what takes place, to imagine the dialogue actually being spoken. While the process of reading is obviously very different from that of watching a film, the reader is nevertheless being invited to make at least some effort to imagine the action in a cinematic context. And it is here that the difficulties begin. Clearly, one sees from the outset, this is to be no ordinary film. But while there may be a certain surrealistic charm in the vision of baboon housewives frying sausages, the whole apes and scientists routine soon becomes extremely tiresome. (If one visualizes anything whilst reading the opening sequence, it is most likely to be a rapidly emptying cinema.) However, this can be dismissed as merely a misguided attempt on Huxley's part to liven up the credits, since the apes and scientists, mercifully, do not reappear. What really does violence to the reader's genre-created expectations is the narrator.

To begin with, the narrator's verbal style is, to say the least, off-putting. What Huxley asks us to imagine is something like the following being spoken as a voice-over:

> Into the satiety of this morning after [Alfred Poole has just had his first sexual experience] let loose a rodent conscience and the principles learnt at a Mother's knee—or not infre-

> quently across it (head downwards and with shirt tails well tucked up), in condign spankings, sadly and prayerfully administered, but remembered, ironically enough, as the pretext and accompaniment of innumerable erotic day-dreams, each duly followed by its remorse, and each remorse bringing with it the idea of punishment and all its attendant sensualities. And so on, indefinitely. Well, as I say, let loose those into this, and the result may easily be a religious conversion. But a conversion to what? Most ignorant of what he is most assured, our poor friend doesn't know. And here comes the last person he would expect to help him to discover. . .
>
> (p. 117)

As an account of Alfred's sexual psychology, this is clearly meant to be taken seriously, but in the light of Huxley's adoption of the vulgar jocularity of a Walt Disney animal film commentary—'. . . our poor friend doesn't know . . .'—it becomes rather difficult to do so. Rather than satirizing the knowing, patronizing tone of the conventional narrator, Huxley simply imitates it, with the result that he succeeds only in cheapening and making vulgar whatever he tries to say.

But it is not simply the combination of a cosy, low-brow style with continual references which imply a high level of culture that jars, seeming equally inappropriate either to a film script or a novel; the main problem is that the bizarre combination has the effect of giving undue prominence to what the narrator says. Of course, this is partly the fault of *what* he says, inasmuch as he is continually underlining the most obvious points. After the scene where Dr Poole walks behind Loola, mesmerized by the two prohibitory NOs sewn onto the seat of her trousers, the narrator informs us that

> It is the emblem, outward, visible, tangible, of her own inner consciousness. Principle at odds with concupiscence, his Mother and the Seventh Commandment superimposed upon his fancies and the facts of life. (p. 61)

This kind of commentary is unlikely to prove satisfactory in any context, but its banality is emphasized by the fact that the reader is asked to imagine it actually being spoken. Instead of integrating his moralistic commentary in such a way that the reader might be likely to absorb its precepts without being too aware of the fact, Huxley chooses an approach that guarantees a glaring prominence to his didactic intentions.

There is some overall improvement as the action develops, and the intrusions of the narrator become more infrequent, but even then, the working out of much of the story remains mechanical and uninspired. When the scientists on board the ship of the exploratory expedition vie with one another in giving their own specialist interpretations of the causes of the destruction of Los Angeles, it is clear that Huxley is once more harking back to the example of Peacock, but in comparison with his early fiction, his use of Peacockian comic techniques seems stale and predictable. And while it is hard to identify at exactly what point humour loses its freshness and ceases to amuse, the Chief's complaint that the vicious corporal punishment meted out in the schools is too lenient—a symptom of 'progressive education'—is a characteristic example of an ironic reversal which is simply too obvious to be funny. All too often in *Ape and Essence* Huxley seems simply to be resorting to old ideas and well-worn techniques, writing from force of habit, rather than through the impulse to say something new.

Perhaps part of the problem lies in his initial conception of the work. In a letter to Anita Loos (the author of *Gentlemen Prefer Blondes*), he suggested that he had it in mind to 'write something about the future':

> ... about, among other things, a post atomic-war society in which the chief effect of the gamma radiations has been to produce a race of men and women who don't make love all the year round, but have a brief mating season. The effect of this on politics, religion, ethics etc. would be something very interesting and amusing to work out. (*Letters*, p. 569)

But it is a conception which, however interesting and amusing it might be, is more akin to science fiction than to the satiric fantasy of which Huxley had already proved himself to be an able exponent. Unlike *Brave New World*, *Ape and Essence* relies on the positing of a future which is purely arbitrary, rather than on the extrapolation of tendencies which are already at work in society. Between the regimented society of *Brave New World* and the world of Huxley's own day all kinds of parallels could be drawn; by contrast, the future society of *Ape and Essence,* with its devil worship and its brief mating season, has no more relevance to contemporary reality than do the great majority of works of science fiction, whose appeal lies simply in the novelty of the basic idea—be it Martian invasion, intergalactic travel, rebellious robots, or whatever. Rather than furnishing a commentary on present-day society, *Ape and Essence,* with its baboons and its scientists, its trite psychology, and its preoccupation with sex and violence, would seem to be essentially a case of self-indulgence, with Huxley parading his obsessions for little more than their own sake. One can pardon George Orwell's asperity when he described the book as

> . . . awful . . . the more holy he gets, the more his books stink with sex. He cannot get off the subject of flagellating women. Possibly if he had the courage to come out and say so, that is the solution to the problem of war. If we took it out in a little private sadism, which after all doesn't do much harm, we wouldn't want to drop bombs etc.[2]

The solution which *Ape and Essence* proposes, however, is not private sadism, but rather (as one might expect) the individual pursuit of decency and sanity. Amid a world of cruelty and barbarism, of genetic mutations and universal superstition, the only ray of hope is provided by the love which grows up between Alfred and Loola. Even when things are about as bad as they can be, the individual, Huxley seems to suggest, can still aim at achieving peace and harmony in his or her own life. When Alfred tells Loola, who has been brought up to believe in the omnipotence of the devil, that it is possible to resist him, she asks him why he believes that. He replies:

> 'Because there's something stronger than he is.'
>
> 'Something stronger?' She shakes her head. 'That was what He was always fighting against—and He won.'
>
> 'Only because people helped Him to win. But they don't have to help Him. And remember, He can never win for good.'

'Why not?'

'Because He can never resist the temptation of carrying evil to the limit. And whenever evil is carried to the limit, it always destroys itself. After which the Order of Things comes to the surface again.'

'But that's far away in the future.'

'For the whole world, yes. But not for single individuals, not for you and me, for example. Whatever Belial may have done with the rest of the world, you and I can always work with the Order of Things, not against it.' (pp. 147–8)

Somewhere in the North, we are told, there is a colony of normal people, who make love all the year round. And while we are told nothing about their society beyond that, one presumes that they *are* working with the 'Order of Things', and against the worshippers of the devil. But although they may perhaps offer some kind of hope for the regeneration of humanity, in the context of the novel their community is no more than a place to escape to. It is on the possibilities of Alfred's relationship with Loola that Huxley places the emphasis.

Nevertheless, the gleam of hope which is offered is rather a faint one—as a positive, the achievement of a decent monogamous relationship between two people scarcely seems commensurate to the scale of the evils which Huxley describes. Indeed, at the end of the book, it still remains unclear as to whether Alfred and Loola will finally escape the burying party. It would seem that, from *Eyeless in Gaza* onwards, it is possible to observe a steady process at work whereby, as his portrayals of society grow progressively bleaker, the positive alternatives which Huxley offers become correspondingly more small-scale. Coming after Miller, who advocates involvement in a large-scale political movement; Propter, with his project of establishing small self-sufficient communities; and Rontini, who contents himself with doing good on a purely personal level, Alfred and Loola might seem to represent the logical conclusion—a couple who are concerned with no-one other than themselves.

In *The Genius and the Goddess*, however, where the focus is almost exclusively on a small group of people, the problem of disproportion between the individual potential for good and the evil of which society is shown to be capable does not arise. Although we learn that, some time after the mean events of the story have taken place, Henry Maartens becomes involved in the development of the atom bomb, and that his son is killed at Okinawa, these amount to no more than isolated references to the horrors of the outside world. For the most part, the action takes place strictly on the personal level.

The story of *The Genius and the Goddess* is related by two narrators, the first of whom quickly becomes an audience for the second, Rivers, whose reminiscenses make up the main body of the narrative. Rivers, in fact, embodies much of the wisdom and experience which had seemed so obtrusive a characteristic of figures such as Propter and Rontini but, since it is he who tells the story, his good qualities no longer seem so improbable or out of place. If he appears perhaps a little *too* wise, a little *too* knowing, or if the ambience of the two strong, mature men discussing the follies of their youth over a few stiff drinks seems somewhat off-putting, it is nevertheless *their* world, and particularly that of Rivers, which constitutes the novel. The conflict between an idealized character and a realistic setting disappears, as does the unevenness of texture which, in earlier works, reflected the difficulties which Huxley experienced in integrating expository or didactic passages into a third person narrative. Rivers' reflections are part of his narrative style, and as a result *The Genius and the Goddess* creates an impression of overall unity, which is further enhanced by Huxley's skilful handling of the numerous shifts between past and present—the action develops with a smoothness which contrasts favourably with the comparatively random time shifts of *Eyeless in Gaza*.

Rivers, as he describes the past events which helped to mould his character, speaks from the point of view of someone who has attained wisdom and inner peace. Whether he is talking of the distant past, when the events of the story took place, of the more recent death of his wife, or of the future which is embodied in his grandson, his manner is at the same time compassionate and dispassionate. He is what Huxley would term 'non-attached': capable of intense direct experience, yet at the same time able to maintain a perspective which makes it possible for him to see through and beyond the facts of that experience. And it is from this vantage point that he looks back to the time when he was considerably younger and more foolish. '"It's like a puppet play,"' he remarks, describing his youthful affaire with Katy Maartens, '"it's like Romeo and Juliet through the wrong end of the opera glasses"' (p. 45). Huxley had, in fact, originally intended to call the book *Through the Wrong End of the Opera Glasses*, and that is perhaps the central image of the work: it is from just this curious, remote perspective that Rivers looks back as he tries to ascertain the truth of what took place, and at the same time to prove his initial proposition that 'the trouble with fiction . . . is that it makes too much sense. Reality never makes sense' (p. 7).

Two main difficulties arise, however. One is that, in the course of Rivers' narrative, reality *does* make sense. Even the oddest events are part of a pattern, with explicable causes and observable effects. The bizarre sexual encounter between Katy and Rivers after the death of Katy's mother, with Henry Maartens apparently on the verge of death elsewhere in the house, is no freak of chance: it has the same inexorable logic and inevitability as does the car crash in which Katy and her daughter are killed. Horror is no longer gratuitous and arbitrary, as was the case with the death of Phil in *Point Counter Point*, or the falling dog in *Eyeless in Gaza*: it is the inevitable culmination of particular (and by no means random) sequences of events. In fact, nothing in *The Genius and the Goddess* is random: the work as a whole combines a quasi-Buddhist acceptance of Fate with an almost Calvinist belief in pre-destination. Although Huxley's characteristic tendency to dwell on the oddest and most seemingly inexplicable aspects of human experience is still very much in evidence, it now seems to conflict with what would appear to be a new-found belief that life has meaning and order.

However, the contradiction is not too damaging. Perhaps having Rivers contradict himself is as good a way as any of illustrating the paradox that even the oddest and most apparently pointless occurrences nevertheless have their own logic. What is a much more serious problem is the question of whether Rivers' approach is in fact suitable—whether it actually does justice to, or throws light on the events he describes. Following on his remarks about his affaire with Katy being like Romeo and Juliet seen through the wrong end of the opera glasses, Rivers continues:

> And Romeo once called himself John Rivers, and was in love, and had at least ten times more life and energy than at ordinary times. And the world he was living in—how totally transfigured! (p. 45)

How, one wonders, will Rivers, looking back to a past so remote, be able to recreate the immediacy of the transfiguring experience which alone can make sense of what he says, and give point to the generalizations he makes from it? The problem is to combine a vivid and convincing account of experience with what George Woodcock aptly, if scathingly, terms 'a blizzard of moralistic analysis' (*Dawn and the Darkest Hour*, p. 280).

The problem is not necessarily an insuperable one. In the earlier story, 'Two or Three Graces', which employs similar narrative methods, there is almost as much reflection and analysis on the narrator's part. But this is not in itself a fault: in 'Two or Three Graces' the analysis and generalizations are carried off by Huxley's lightness of touch, and by the fact that the narrator has a wit and elegance which Rivers conspicuously lacks. Moreover, the predominantly cool and analytical tone of the earlier story becomes the means of making all the more effective the few occasions when real feeling breaks through. When John Peddley's wife leaves him, for example, Peddley is suddenly transformed from being an archetypal bore—a walking illustration of the narrator's theory of bores—into a human being, capable of grief and bewilderment. The fact that for most of the story he is no more than a stereotype only serves to emphasize how greatly the blow has affected him, shattering the world of unthinking routine which made him such a bore in the first place, and forcing him to think and feel practically for the first time.

But such delicacy of touch is absent from *The Genius and the Goddess*. It is a more serious story, and the generalizations and analysis it contains are correspondingly more ponderous. Also, to make matters worse, Huxley attempts to mitigate the rather essay-like tone of Rivers' reflections by saddling him with a spurious colourfulness of expression, which consists largely of a propensity to seize on metaphors and work them to death:

The proof of the pudding is in the eating, not in the cook book. Pleasure received and given, virtue restored, Lazarus raised from the dead—the eating in this case was self-evidently good. So help yourself to the pudding and don't talk with your mouth full—it's bad manners and it prevents you from appreciating the ambrosial flavour. It was a piece of advice too good for me to be able to take. True, I didn't talk to her; she wouldn't let me. But I went on talking to myself—talking and talking until the ambrosia turned into wormwood or was contaminated by the horrible gamey taste of forbidden pleasure. (p. 104)

But however Huxley seeks to dress up Rivers' analyses, he fails to avoid a besetting feeling of remoteness: it would be hard to guess from the foregoing, for example, that Rivers' floundering metaphor is supposed to describe his feelings after becoming sexually involved with Katy.

Nor is this all: Huxley continually employs devices which are virtually guaranteed to distance what is described, and hence to reduce its emotional impact. As Rivers himself remarks, returning to a familiar Huxleian theme, the emotion conveyed by a description is dependent on its manner and style:

'Oedipus, for example, or Lear, or even Jesus and Gandhi—you could make a roaring farce out of any of them. It's just a question of describing your characters from the outside, without sympathy and in violent but unpoetical language. In real life farce exists only for spectators, never for the actors.' (p. 100)

Huxley's treatment is not farcical, however—more clinical. Though Rivers may *feel* compassion and sympathy, he seldom succeeds in conveying it, perhaps because of his tendency to describe everything in the most abstract possible terms. Wondering how best to do justice to the reality of his relations with Katy, he suggests that

'Maybe one could take a hint from the geometers. Describe the event in relation to three co-ordinates.' In the air before him Rivers traced with the stem of his pipe two lines at right angles to one another, then from the point of intersection, added a vertical that took his hand above the level of his head. 'Let one of these lines represent Katy, another the John Rivers of thirty years ago, and the third John Rivers as I am today. Now, within this frame of reference, what can we say about the night of April 23rd, 1922? Not the whole truth, of course. But a good deal more of the truth than can be conveyed in terms of any single fiction.' (pp. 89–90)

And this distancing goes on all the time: describing Ruth Maartens' emotions, the adolescent passion she had felt for the John Rivers of thirty years before, he remarks:

> 'How hard it is, without those still non-existent words, to discuss even so simple and obvious a case as Ruth's! The best one can do is flounder about in metaphors. A saturated solution of feelings, which can be crystallized either from the outside or the inside. Works and events that fall into the psycho-physical soup and make it clot into action-producing lumps of emotion and sentiment. Then come the glandular changes, and the appearance of those charming little zoological specimens which the child carries around with so much pride and embarassment. The thrill-solution is enriched by a new kind of sensibility that radiates from the nipples, through the skin and nerve-ends, into the soul, the sub-conscious, the superconscious, the spirit. And these new psycho-erectile elements of personality impart a kind of motion to the thrill-solution, cause it to flow in a specific direction—towards the still unmapped, undifferentiated region of love...' (p. 53)

This is Huxley at his worst, describing his characters as though they were so many insects in bottles. Yet it is not so much a deficiency of sympathy which prompts passages such as the above, as a continuing confusion of purpose: Huxley still appears to be wrestling with Calamy's dilemma—trying to ascertain the truth by examining it from every possible angle—while at the same time attempting to include all the facts whose absence from orthodox fiction he had deplored in *Eyeless in Gaza*. In trying to arrive at the whole truth, however—in trying to cram the maximum possible number of explanatory factors into his description—Huxley seems to lose sight of the subject he is discussing: his involved, over-analytical approach only serves to spawn further complications. Thus, when it comes to discussing Ruth's feelings (which, after all, turn out to have the direst possible consequences for everyone concerned), the remoteness caused by the sheer weight of analysis is still further intensified by the prefatory remarks with Huxley distances his description: '"I had the story from Beulah, to whom she had confided it. A tragic little story..."' (p. 54).

Clearly, it would be difficult to describe so ill-founded a passion as Ruth's in a manner which would be commensurate with the intensity of her feelings, but Rivers' wordy, patronizing descriptions, together with his abstract, detached manner, make his account not so much objective, as uninteresting. Even when dealing with the most keenly felt and intimate experience, Huxley seems unable to resist the temptation to distance it as much as possible. As Katy and Rivers embrace one another, we are told that

> '... even the living are utterly alone. Our only advantage over the dead woman up there in Chicago, over the dying man at the end of the house, consisted in the fact that we could be alone in company, could juxtapose our solitudes and pretend that we had fused them into a community. But these, of course, were not the thoughts I was thinking then. Then there was no room in my mind for anything but love and pity...'
> (p. 88)

Love and pity, then, were the uppermost emotions in Rivers' mind at the time which Huxley insisted was the most real, the most important—the time when the events actually took place, when the moment was present, not past. Yet despite this, Huxley describes those emotions in such a way as to make them seem almost illusory.

It is perhaps because of this pervading feeling of remoteness that Huxley resorts to a compensatory extravagance of language when he does attempt to evoke the reality of what actually happened. In *The Genius and the Goddess* he is aiming to do justice to the facts of direct experience, to convey their incandescent reality—their capacity, as Rivers suggests, to transfigure the world—as well as to show that it is possible to be detached from such experience. Thus, for example, we find Huxley, almost for the first time, describing sexual experience, not with his customary disgust, but with what would seem to be an attempt at tenderness and reverence. Unfortunately, however, the results are frequently exaggerated to the point of being embarassing. Katy, for example, is described in superhuman terms:

> 'Cut off from animal grace, Katy had been an impotent phantom. Restored to it, she was Hera and Demeter and Aphrodite gloriously rolled into one, with Aesculapius and the Grotto of Lourdes thrown in an a bonus. . .'
> (pp. 99–100)

As one might imagine, sexual relations with so remarkable a partner prove to be no ordinary experience, either:

> 'That night of the twenty-third of April we were in the Other World, she and I, in the dark, wordless heaven of nakedness and touch and fusion. And what revelations in that heaven, what pentecosts! The visitations of her caresses were like sudden angels, like doves descending.' (p. 93)

Conveniently enough, Huxley himself provides an explanation for this ludicrous disparity between laudable intention and disastrous effect, when he allows Rivers to discuss the contrast between the vividness and intensity of Ruth's feelings and the rottenness of the poetry which they inspire:

> 'What a gulf between *im*pression and *ex*pression! That's our ironic fate—to have Shakespearean feelings and (unless by some billion-to-one chance we happen to *be* Shakespeare) to talk about them like automobile salesmen, or teenagers, or college professors. We practise alchemy in reverse; touch the pure lyrics of experience, and they turn into the verbal equivalents of tripe and hogwash.' (pp. 35–6)

Yet although the language of *The Genius and the Goddess* is considerably closer to Ruth's than to that of Shakespeare, it also reflects the fact that Huxley was trying to do something different. Coming after the line of novels stretching from *Eyeless in Gaza* to *Ape and Essence*, where increasingly limited and individualistic alternatives are explored in progressively more nightmarish contexts, *The Genius and the Goddess* represents a dramatic change of direction. For the first time, Huxley seeks to communicate a joy in actual experience which might serve as an antidote to the dreariness and alienation he had so often described before. For all its flaws, *The Genius and the Goddess* is the first of Huxley's novels in which it is implied that alienation is *not* inevitable, and where his earlier, rather theoretical mysticism seems to give way to the conviction that there is such a thing as a tangible reality which is not merely subjective, and which the individual can experience without necessarily requiring the help of some improbably saintly guru figure.

Huxley's penultimate three novels are all failures, certainly; but it would be a mistake to see them as constituting the downward curve of the parabola which represents his artistic progress. When we look at the reasons for their failure, we find that *Time Must Have A Stop* suffers from the same incompatibility between approach and underlying intentions which was at the root of *Eyeless in Gaza*'s lack of success, while *Ape and Essence* suffers not only from Huxley's self-indulgence, but also from his failure to realize the implication of his use of the scenario format as a vehicle. In both cases there is also the complicating factor that it is difficult to convey a positive message with much conviction when one's outlook is essentially negative—especially given the nature of the message. But in *The Genius and the Goddess* the problems are very different: it too is a failure, only in this case its failure would seem rather to be a reflection of the difficulty which Huxley experienced in trying to adapt and alter his old habits of technique and expression in the service of an outlook which had radically changed. In itself, of course, that is no justification for failure: what is interesting about *The Genius and the Goddess* is simply the fact that it announces a change of direction. It is the cause and nature of that change that I propose to examine in the concluding chapter.

7
From *The Doors of Perception* to *Island*

Up until the composition of *The Genius and the Goddess*, the course of Huxley's development proceeds with a certain logic. His later commitment to a search for solutions to the problems of life in a society which he regarded as fundamentally insane is already implicit in his early fiction, with its attitude of ironic amusement at the spectacle of human folly. It is simply a question of detachment giving way to concern and involvement. The same basic preoccupations underlie nearly all his novels: his concern with the meaninglessness of existence in the face of the facts of suffering and death is first adumbrated in the relatively untroubled early comedies; the distaste for physical experience, which becomes an almost obsessive feature of the later fiction, is already evident in *Antic Hay*; and the alienation and loneliness of the individual is a theme which runs through all his work. Yet in *The Genius and the Goddess* we become aware of a change. Death and suffering are still there, but they no longer render life meaningless, or devalue its positive aspects. Physical experience is honoured, not rejected. And, almost for the first time, Huxley seems to be suggesting that real communication between human beings is possible after all.

The earliest evidence of this radical change of outlook, however, is to be found, not in *The Genius and the Goddess*, but in *The Doors of Perception* (1954), a non-fictional account of his experiences with the drug, mescalin. Here, almost for the first time, Huxley describes a positive experience with a vividness comparable to that of his earlier evocations of horror and suffering, and in doing so communicates a sense of warmth and optimism quite unlike the tone of anything that had gone before.

During the last ten years of his life, Huxley made use of various forms of psychedelic drug—mescalin, psilocybin, and LSD—on some eleven or twelve occasions, the last being on his deathbed. *The Doors of Perception* describes his first such experience, which took place in May 1953. It is a striking description: as the mescalin began to take effect, Huxley found himself ushered, not into a world of visions and hallucinations, but rather one of which the most salient characteristic was its appearance of uncompromising, almost supernatural, reality. Perception, rather than being a matter-of-fact registration of the outside world, became an ecstatic experience of the fact of that world's existence.

The first thing to catch Huxley's eye was a vase containing three flowers—a rose, a carnation, and an iris:

> At breakfast that morning I had been struck by the lively dissonance of its colours. But that was no longer the point. I was not looking now at an unusual flower arrangement. I was seeing what Adam had seen on the morning of his creation—the miracle, moment by moment, of naked existence.
>
> (p. 11)

It was an experience so intense as to leave no room for judgement or evaluation: asked if he found it agreeable, he replied: 'Neither agreeable nor disagreeable . . . it just *is*.' What he saw were unquestionably real objects in the outside world, but objects so wholly denuded of their normal range of associations as to appear with a freshness which bordered on the alien:

> . . . I was looking at my furniture, not as the utilitarian who has to sit on chairs, to write at desks and tables, and not as a camera-man or scientific recorder, but as the pure aesthete whose concern is only with forms and their relationships within the field of vision or the picture space. But as I looked, this purely aesthetic Cubist's-eye view gave place to what I can only describe as the sacramental vision of reality. I was back where I had been when I was looking at the flowers—back in a world where everything shone with the Inner Light, and was infinite in its significance. The legs, for example, of that chair—how miraculous their tubularity, how supernatural their polished smoothness! I spent several minutes—or was it several centuries?—not merely gazing at those bamboo legs, but actually *being* them—or rather being myself in them; or, to be still more accurate (for 'I' was not involved in the case,

> nor in a certain sense were 'they') being my Not-self in the Not-self which was the chair. (pp. 15–16)

And this is perhaps the most significant feature of the experience—not the transfigured aspect of the outside world, but the fact that Huxley was no longer experiencing himself as an individual, as a centre of consciousness organizing the objective world around him in accordance with his own conceptions. Instead, he was Not-self—simply an existence among, and on a par with other existences, whether animate or inanimate. From being an observer of the world, he had become an integral part of it, too absorbed in the experience of being to be aware of himself as a separate entity. Thus, looking at a chair in the garden, he saw that

> Where the shadows fell on the canvas upholstery, stripes of a deep but glowing indigo alternated with stripes of an incandescence so intensely bright that it was hard to believe that they could be made of anything but blue fire. For what seemed an immensely long time I gazed without knowing, even without wishing to know, what it was that confronted me. At any other time I would have seen a chair barred with alternate light and shade. Today the percept had swallowed up the concept. I was so completely absorbed in looking, so thunderstruck by what I actually saw, that I could not be aware of anything else. Garden furniture, laths, sunlight, shadow—these were no more than names and notions, mere verbalizations, for utilitarian or scientific purposes, after the event. The event was this succession of azure furnace-doors separated by gulfs of unfathomable gentian. It was inexpressibly wonderful, wonderful to the point, almost, of being terrifying. (pp. 41–2)

Huxley compares this sense of terror to being on the verge of madness, and he explains it in the following terms:

> Confronted by a chair which looked like the Last Judgement—or, to be more accurate, by a Last Judgement which, after a long time and with considerable difficulty, I recognized as a chair—I found myself all at once on the brink of panic. This, I suddenly felt, was going too far. Too far, even though the

> going was into intenser beauty, deeper significance. The fear, as I analyse it in retrospect, was of being overwhelmed, of disintegrating under a pressure of reality greater than a mind accustomed to living most of the time in a cosy world of symbols could possibly bear. (p. 43)

Nevertheless, despite its frightening aspect, it was an experience, not of the horror and alienation which had obsessed him for so long, but of involvement, a sense of being part of a world of infinite wonder and glory. The question is, how far can Huxley's experiences be regarded as real? And, further to that, how far can be be considered justified in attributing visionary or religious significance to them? Huxley, after all, accepts perceptions which many might regard as illusory, unreal—mere hallucinations—as being at least as real as the perceptions characteristic of everyday existence. Significantly, he prefers the term 'psychedelic' (meaning mind- or consciousness-revealing) to hallucinogen as a description of the drug he took. Perhaps the best thing, given the different constructions which could be put on his experiences, might be to examine the mechanics of the perceptions involved.

The notion that psychedelic experience is unreal or illusory is based on the assumption that one normally sees what is *there*, and that under the influence of psychedelic drugs one does not; in other words, that everyday perception is real—an objective registration of what exists or takes place in the outside world. This, however, is a view which the existing psychological and neurological evidence would seem to contradict. Rather than simply transferring the sensory information provided by the outside world directly to the brain, in an unadulterated form, it would appear that our sense perceptions in fact interpret and edit what is there in a complex and highly selective way. As Ulric Neisser puts it, in his basic textbook on cognitive psychology:

> . . . we have no direct, immediate access to the world, nor to any of its properties. The ancient theory of *eidola*, which supposed that faint copies of objects can enter the mind directly, must be rejected. Whatever we know about reality has been *mediated*, not only by the organs of sense but by

complex systems which interpret and reinterpret sensory information. (*Cognitive Psychology*, New York, 1967, p. 3)

In other words, what we take to be 'reality' is in fact a construct—a product of the interaction between our consciousness and the objective world which it interprets.

What psychedelic drugs do is modify the *way* in which the senses interpret the available sensory information provided by the objective world, and the consequence of this is a new construct—the product of the interaction between the objective world and a different set of interpretations. It is hard to see why this new construct should be seen as being any less valid than the old, customary one, since it would appear to constitute no more than a different mediation of objective reality. Whether, on the other hand, it is actually *more* valid than the construct created by normal, everyday perception, is open to debate. Certainly its freshness and strangeness might seem likely to alert one to aspects of reality which one's normal interpretative processes might lead one to ignore, which might have the effect of making the experience seem more 'real' than everyday consciousness, but from a rational point of view it would seem that psychedelic experience simply provides a different perspective on the objective world, no more and no less valid than that afforded by one's customary habits of perception. What it would seem likely to do, however, is provide a more concrete *overall* sense of reality—a two- rather than one-dimensional awareness of the outside world.

Nonetheless, Huxley's own contention was that mescalin and other psychedelics actually allow us to perceive *more* of the surrounding reality, rather than just modifying our interpretation of it.

> Reflecting on my experience, I find myself agreeing with the eminent Cambridge philosopher, Dr C. D. Broad, 'that we should do well to consider much more seriously than we have hitherto been inclined to do the type of theory which Bergson put forward in connexion with memory and sense perception. The suggestion is that the function of the brain and nervous system and sense organs is in the main *eliminative*. . . The function of the brain and nervous system is to protect us from

being overwhelmed and confused by this mass of largely useless and irrelevant knowledge, by shutting out most of what we should otherwise perceive or remember at any moment, and leaving only that very small and special selection which is likely to be practically useful.' (p. 16)

While it is possible to perceive more of reality than is strictly biologically useful, our normal experience is of 'a measly trickle of the kind of consciousness which will help us to stay alive on the surface of this particular planet'. And because it is our normal experience, it is easy to see it as the only reality, particularly in view of the fact that we are taught to rationalize our experience in the terms of language systems which have themselves been evolved to articulate that normal, reduced consciousness:

> To formulate and express the contents of this reduced awareness, man has invented and endlessly elaborated these symbol-systems and implicit philosophies which we call languages. Every individual is at once the beneficiary and the victim of the linguistic tradition into which he or she has been born—the beneficiary inasmuch as language gives access to the accumulated records of other people's experience, the victim in so far as it confirms him in the belief that reduced awareness is the only awareness and as it bedevils his sense of reality, so that he is all too apt to take his concepts for data, his words for actual things. That which, in the language of religion, is called 'this world' is the universe of reduced awareness, expressed and, as it were, petrified by language. The various 'other worlds', with which human beings erratically make contact are so many elements in the totality of the awareness belonging to Mind at Large. Most people, most of the time, know only what comes through the reducing valve and is consecrated as genuinely real by the local language. (pp. 16–17)

Huxley suggests the mescalin impairs the efficiency of the 'reducing valve', thus enabling us to perceive aspects of reality which the mind normally excludes. Those who take it are ushered into a world with which language systems are unequipped to cope—a world whose manifestations cannot be rationalized and explained:

> When the brain runs out of sugar, the under-nourished ego grows weak, can't be bothered to undertake the necessary chores, and loses all interest in those spatial and temporal relationships which mean so much to an organism bent on getting on in the world. As Mind at Large seeps past the no longer watertight valve, all kinds of biologically useless things start to happen. In some cases there may be extra-sensory perceptions. Other persons discover a world of visionary beauty. To others again is revealed the glory, the infinite value and meaningfulness of naked existence, of the given, unconceptualized event. In the final stage of ego-lessness there is an 'obscure knowledge' that All is in all—that All is actually each. (p. 19)

Which leads us to the basic controversy: granted that Huxley's experiences may be regarded as 'real', rather than illusory, what is their significance? The *kind* of experiences which he describes are clearly akin to what many people would regard as specifically 'religious' experience—the discovery that the world has meaning, that it possesses a visionary beauty beyond the range of normal experience, that it has an underlying unity. And it is this which most of Huxley's critics find hard to accept.

In fact, the claims which Huxley makes for psychedelic drugs are remarkably moderate. He considered psychedelic experience to be essentially an aid to religious insight and enlightenment, rather than an actual source of or substitute for it:

> I am not so foolish as to equate what happens under the influence of mescalin or of any other drug, prepared or in the future preparable, with the realization of the end and ultimate purpose of human life: Enlightenment, the Beatific Vision. All I am suggesting is that the mescalin experience is what Catholic theologians call 'a gratuitous grace', not necessary to salvation but potentially helpful and to be accepted thankfully, if made available. To be shaken out of the ruts of ordinary perception, to be shown for a few timeless hours the outer and the inner world, not as they appear to an animal obsessed with survival or to a human being obsessed with words and notions, but as they are apprehended, directly and unconditionally, by

Mind at Large—this is an experience of inestimable value to everyone... (p. 58)

Liberation from one's normal priorities, preoccupations, and habits of perception opens the way to an awareness of the richness, the sheer wonder of existence, and this may be an experience sufficiently profound as to permanently alter one's outlook on the world.

In *Heaven and Hell* (1956), which is the sequel to *The Doors of Perception*, Huxley does go on to argue that psychedelic experience bears marked similarities to the experiences described by mystics and religious visionaries in the past, but his stance is still far removed from the manic prophetic zeal of someone like Timothy Leary. Whereas Dr Leary would suggest that psychedelic drugs *are* a source of ultimate religious enlightenment (quite apart from enabling one to perform such remarkable feats as travelling back down one's own DNA chains to explore one's prehistoric origins), Huxley's claim is no more than that psychedelics are a welcome and unexpected aid to self-knowledge, and to the attainment of enlightenment—yet even that is a suggestion which many people would seem to find a disturbing one.

Much the most comprehensive critique of Huxley's discussion of psychedelics is provided, not by any of his critics, most of whom appear anxious to avoid the subject, but by the Oxford orientalist and religious scholar, R. C. Zaehner. Zaehner's chief quarrel with Huxley is that he fails to distinguish sufficiently between different *kinds* of mystical experience, and that by doing so he misunderstands the nature of such experience, with the result that his comparison between psychedelic and mystical awareness is a misleading one. Yet Zaehner's own definition of mysticism as being 'a unitive experience with someone or something other than oneself'[1] hardly seems to differ from Huxley's: in the end, their difference of opinion appears to be largely a question of semantics. For Huxley, the important thing about mysticism is the fact of *union*, the loss of self in a larger and more comprehensive unity, whereas for Zaehner it is the nature of the 'someone or something other than oneself' that matters. Whether or not one accepts Huxley's contention that all forms of mystical experience are essentially similar, it would seem that arguments concerning the *nature* of mysticism are likely to be inconclusive, simply because all verbal accounts of mystical experience are necessarily imprecise, being rendered in the terms of a language system evolved to articulate different areas of experience.

What is a much more interesting feature of Zaehner's critique, however, is what would seem to be his deep suspicion of anything which might be construed as making religious experience easier. While he charitably attributes Huxley's claims to 'enthusiastic exaggeration', he also believes that their effects have been pernicious. Huxley

> . . . was, simply by equating his own drug-induced experiences with the experiences of those who approach their goal by more conventional means, striking at the roots of all religion that makes any claim to be taken seriously.
>
> (*Mysticism Sacred and Profane*, p. xiv)

Huxley, however, considered that mystical (and psychedelic) awareness was an experience of a wholly different order than the feelings that normally arise from the observance of the moral code, or participation in the rituals of an organized religion (which is presumably the kind of religion which makes a claim 'to be taken seriously'). By equating psychedelic and mystical awareness, he was simply proposing the contradiction between different *kinds* of religious experience more clearly than ever before, inasmuch as, until the advent of psychedelic drugs, the type of experience which Huxley discusses would normally have been the consequence of practising the ascetic disciplines associated with a particular religion. Psychedelic experience, on the other hand, requires no such religious context.

The potential dissociation of mystical experience from a specifically religious context clearly worries Zaehner, himself a committed Roman Catholic—but what throws an even more interesting light on the nature of his conception of religious experience is his contention, not only that psychedelics do *not* induce mystical awareness, but that even if they *did*, their use would still be undesirable.

> In the past mystics, even in India, have been few and far

> between, and preternatural experiences of any sort have been well out of the reach of the average man; and no visible harm has been done by the small band of ecstatics who had, or thought they had, transcended good and evil... Obviously, if mescalin can produce the Beatific Vision here on earth,—a state that we had hitherto believed to have been the reward for much earnest striving after good,—the Christian emphasis on morality is not only all wrong but also a little naive. Mescalin presents us not only with a social problem,—for how on earth could a society composed exclusively of ecstatics possibly be run?—but also with a theological problem of great magnitude. (p. 13)

This, however, is simply fatuous—an almost wilful confusion of the issue. As we have seen, Huxley explicitly states that he does *not* equate psychedelic experience with 'the Beatific Vision', and while he does believe that such experience can have a profound effect on the subsequent life of those who undergo it, he nowhere suggests that it induces a permanent state of ecstasy. Indeed, as we shall see, *The Doors of Perception* includes a lengthy discussion of the problem of how the insights afforded by a state of mind where good and evil no longer appear to be meaningful distinctions are to be reconciled with one's everyday awareness and behaviour—a discussion which Zaehner chooses to ignore.

In fact, Zaehner's suspicion is not simply of psychedelic drugs, but of mystical perception as such. Unfair as it might seem, there never has been much indication that mystical enlightenment is 'the reward for much earnest striving after good'. Striving after good may produce a pleasant feeling of righteousness, together with a certain confidence of expectation with regard to whatever posthumous joys one's religion happens to promise, but it does not guarantee mystical enlightenment. Visionary experience has always been something gratuitous and arbitrary, the sudden revelation of a wholly different order of things; if any process of cause and effect is to be posited, it would seem that mystical experience is consequent on the inducement and exploration of abnormal physical and psychological states, rather than on earnest moral striving. Unlike organized religion, mysticism is not concerned with precepts and moral codes which are intended to be of universal application, so much as with a particular kind of individual experience which transcends all human codes and concepts.

However, Zaehner's mistrust of the very phenomenon of mysticism is more than simply a reflection of his adherence to an organized religion. His basic assumption, which he shares with those of Huxley's critics who choose to discuss the matter at all, is not so much that 'abnormal' experience is morally suspect, but rather that it is inevitably less real than ordinary, everyday perception. To attribute supreme reality to such experience, as Huxley does, is to fall victim to an illusion, and illusions are, of course, a symptom of insanity. Seizing on Huxley's own suggestion that 'a schizophrenic is like a man permanently under the influence of mescalin' (*The Doors of Perception*, p. 44) Zaehner promptly proceeds to tar psychedelic experience with the brush of madness. Nevertheless, although one of the chief purposes of research into psychedelic drugs has been the exploration of the affinities between psychedelic consciousness and schizophrenia, the extent of such affinities remains in dispute. R. D. Laing, for example, would appear to regard the two states of mind as being closely related; while Dr Humphrey Osmond, on the other hand, who first introduced Huxley to the use of psychedelics, seems concerned to stress the numerous differences between psychedelic and schizoid awareness.[2]

Yet while there is at least *some* evidence to suggest a connection with schizophrenia, there is none at all which would point to a relationship between psychedelic consciousness and manic-depressive psychosis. Nonetheless, it is with an example of this, rather than of schizophrenia, that Zaehner chooses to illustrate what he regards as the similarity between drug-induced perception and madness. Ironically, in view of his criticism of Huxley for his failure to distinguish between different *kinds* of mystical experience, Zaehner himself appears to ignore the very much greater distinctions which exist between types of mental disorder. Although schizophrenia, for example, involves a loss of the sense of self, while manic-depressive psychosis brings with it a heightened sense of its presence, Zaehner treats the two states as being not just similar, but *synonymous*:

> Oddly enough, Huxley realized the connection between the effects of mescalin and schizophrenia, yet he seems to have refused to face the fact that what he calls religion is simply another word for manic-depressive psychosis. (p. 88)

It is a remarkable piece of reasoning; but, in all fairness, it cannot be said that the illustration with which he chooses to support it lends much weight to his argument. While he gives a lengthy account of the experiences of a manic-depressive, they appear to bear singularly little resemblance to Huxley's own description of the effects of mescalin.

All that remains is the lingering effect of the repeated assertions of an association between drugs and madness. Chemical changes take place in the body when one ingests psychedelic drugs; they also take place (although whether as cause or effect remains uncertain), in cases of schizophrenia. What validity, then can be assigned to an experience which is merely the by-product of a change in one's body-chemistry? Huxley's answer would be that

> . . . in one way or another, all our experiences are chemically conditioned, and if we imagine that some of them are purely 'spiritual', purely 'intellectual', purely 'aesthetic', it is merely because we have never troubled to investigate the internal chemical environment at the moment of their occurrence. Furthermore, it is a matter of historical record that most contemplatives worked systematically to modify their body chemistry, with a view to creating the internal conditions favourable to spiritual insight. (*Heaven and Hell*, pp. 127–8)

Fasting, flagellation, sleep-deprivation, the breathing exercises of the yogis—all, Huxley suggests, are productive of chemical changes in the body, which are often strikingly similar to those caused by psychedelic drugs. Asceticism and self-mortification are essentially long and laborious methods of achieving a physical state, and hence a correlative mental condition, which can be more easily induced by the use of mescalin or LSD. To ignore the chemical component of certain types of experience, while questioning the validity of other, similar types of experience because of what is known of their chemical causation is inconsistent—an indication of preconceptions which are incompatible with any objective, rational discussion of the subject. Or, as William James put it, writing more than fifty years earlier:

> To plead the organic causation of a religious state of mind, then, in refutation of its claims to possess superior spiritual value, is quite illogical and arbitrary, unless one has already worked out in advance some psycho-physical theory connecting spiritual values in general with determinate sorts of physiological change. Otherwise none of our thoughts and feeling, not even our scientific doctrines, not even our disbeliefs, could retain any value as revelations of the truth, for every one of them without exception flows from the state of its possessor's body at the time...
>
> ... Let us play fair in this whole matter, and be quite candid with ourselves and with the facts. When we think certain states of mind superior to others, is it ever because of what we know concerning their organic antecedents? No! It is always for two entirely different reasons. It is either because we take an immediate delight in them; or else because we believe them to bring us good consequential fruits for life.
>
> (*The Varieties of Religious Experience,* New York, 1902, pp. 15–16)

In the end, there is no argument which will convince someone who believes that only certain experiences are 'natural', and hence of value to one's understanding of life, that there can be any real validity in the experiences consequent on something as 'artificial' as taking a pill. All one can really do is to short-circuit the whole discussion by the adoption of the kind of empiricist approach which James suggests. The important question is how far it is possible to detect a significant change of attitude in Huxley's last works, and how far such a change can be attributed to his experience of psychedelic drugs. We already know of the 'immediate delight' which their use occasioned him —what remains to be estimated is the extent to which his experiences also brought him 'good consequential fruits for life'.

As we have seen, Huxley had always been inclined to the view that the individual's perception of reality was inescapably subjective—a view which was never really counterbalanced by his strictly theoretical belief in the existence of an ultimate reality which lay beyond the world of subjective perceptions. Psychedelic experience, however, which introduced him to a world of sheer sensation, of naked and un-self-conscious perception, seems to have constituted for Huxley a practical confirmation of the existence of such a reality. And while such an experience, with its revelation of the partial and distorted nature of everyday perception, might have been expected to reinforce his conviction that the individual is condemned to perceive only a world of subjective illusion, its effect was, if anything, quite the reverse. *The Doors of Perception,* in fact, testifies to an altogether new sense of being part of the world, as opposed to being an isolated observer, unable to communicate with anyone else, and condemned by an analytical turn of mind to a partial and inadequate perception of reality. Writing in 1962, he gave some indication of how far his habitual feelings of loneliness and alienation had thereby been alleviated:

> In experiments with LSD and psilocybin subsequent to the mescalin experience described in *Doors of Perception,* I have known that sense of affectionate solidarity with the people around me, and with the universe at large—also the sense of the world's fundamental All Rightness, in spite of pain, death and bereavement. (*Letters,* pp. 938–9)

Which, given the almost obsessive concern with pain, death, and bereavement which characterizes most of Huxley's fiction, would seem to indicate a considerable change of attitude.

In *The Genius and the Goddess,* as we have seen, this change of attitude is reflected in Huxley's rather less than successful attempts to do justice to the more positive aspects of physical experience—in particular, sexuality; but it is in *Island,* where nearly all the old obsessions with pain, death, bereavement, alienation, and the negative aspects of sexuality are confronted and resolved, that the extent of the change is most apparent. For *The Doors of Perception* is not simply an account of an ecstatic new experience—it also reveals how Huxley was prompted by that experience to examine some of the basic contradictions in his thinking.

The basic proposition that underlies nearly all Huxley's later fiction is that without the employment of desirable means (i.e. the actions of enlightened and non-attached individuals) there can be no realization of desirable ends (such as the creation of a just and enlightened society); one must *be* good, before one can *do* good. The preoccupations of his 'good' characters are nearly always primarily individualistic, inasmuch as they are concerned to achieve the individual perfection which is seen as the pre-requisite without which effective action in the world is impossible, and Huxley's chief problem was always how to portray these characters acting on the world around them in a dramatic and convincing fashion. Because Calamy, Miller, Beavis, Propter, Rontini are so concerned with the mechanics of *being* good, the amount of good they actually *do* rarely seems to make much impact on the hopelessly imperfect worlds which they inhabit.

Of course, part of the difficulty was that, at the time of writing, Huxley's conception of the nature of perfection and enlightenment remained strictly theoretical. Because he had only the haziest notion of what the ideal his characters were so persistently striving to attain actually *was*, he found it difficult to relate it to anything else. In *The Doors of Perception*, however, Huxley is concerned with first-hand experience; he had, so he believed, been given a glimpse of some kind of ultimate reality—and that glimpse was sufficient to put all his views about enlightenment, about reality, about ends and means into an entirely new perspective. It is no co-incidence that in *The Doors of Perception* he actually discusses, for the first time, the relationship between individual enlightenment and individual action, rather than leaving it vague while at the same time pretending that it is self-evident—which is what he tends to do in most of his later fiction.

Thus, while Huxley's experience of mescalin was largely an ecstatic one, he nevertheless feels obliged to ask himself a number of pertinent questions:

> . . . if one always saw like this, one would never want to do anything else. Just looking, just being the divine Not-self of flower, of book, of chair, of flannel. That would be enough. But in that case what about other people? What about human relations? . . . How could one reconcile this timeless bliss of

> seeing as one ought to see with the temporal duties of doing what one ought to do and feeling as one ought to feel? (p. 26)

This is the problem so often skirted in his novels: the enlightenment about which Huxley's characters talk so vaguely may be all very well, but where does it actually fit in? Once one has seen reality as it really is, what does one do? Is the only correlative of enlightenment the rather limited and ineffectual actions of a Propter or a Rontini? 'How', Huxley goes on to ask

> . . . was this cleansed perception to be reconciled with a proper concern with human relations, with the necessary chores and duties, to say nothing of charity and practical compassion? . . . In the intervals between his revelations the mescalin taker is apt to feel that, though in one way everything is supremely as it should be, in another there is something wrong. His problem is essentially the same as that which confronts the quietist, the *arhat*. . . Mescalin can never solve that problem: it can only pose it, apocalyptically, for those to whom it had never before presented itself. The full and final solution can be found only by those who are prepared to implement the right kind of *Weltanschauung* by means of the right kind of behaviour and the right kind of constant and unstrained alertness. Over against the quietist stands the active-contemplative, the saint, the man who, in Eckhart's phrase, is ready to come down from the seventh heaven in order to bring a cup of water to his sick brother. Over against the *arhat*, retreating from appearance into an entirely transcendental Nirvana, stands the Boddhissatva, for whom Suchness and the world of contingencies is an occasion not only for transfiguring insight, but also for the most practical charity. . . (pp. 31–2)

As a rider, Huxley adds that the ethical value of pure contemplation should not therefore be underestimated:

> Half at least of all morality is negative and consists of keeping out of mischief. . . The one-sided contemplative leaves undone many things that he ought to do; but to make up for it he refrains from doing a host of things he ought not to do. . . Contemplatives are not likely to become gamblers, or pro-

> curers, or drunkards; they do not as a rule preach intolerance, or make war; do not find it necessary to rob, swindle, or grind the faces of the poor. (pp. 33–4)

Huxley by no means relinquishes his attachment to the ideal of contemplative virtue, but in *The Doors of Perception* he gives evidence of having become more aware both of its limitations and its negative aspect.

The Doors of Perception by no means represents a resolution of the contradictions in Huxley's thinking; nevertheless, the very fact of his recognizing them as contradictions and being prepared to confront them represents an advance. It is significant that his last novel, *Island*, constitutes an extended attempt to show human beings in action, realizing desirable social ends, rather than mainly concerning themselves with the resolution of purely individual problems. If *The Perennial Philosophy* reveals Huxley's commitment to Hinayana Buddhism, whose primary aim is withdrawal from the world, the effect of his psychedelic experiences seems to have been to incline him more towards Mahayana and Tantric Buddhism, which emphasize the importance of active attention to and involvement in the world. The society depicted in *Island*, whose whole spiritual life is rooted in Mahayana and Tantric Buddhism, is anything but an ascetic one: the religion of its inhabitants emphasizes, not withdrawal, but rather the joy and richness of life.

Huxley's development in the last years of his life would seem to illustrate his own contention that psychedelic experience, by producing momentous changes in one's perception of the world, could profoundly affect one's whole consciousness, which is normally based on the acceptance as natural and accurate of a very different, habitual set of perceptions. Psychedelic experience, he suggested, was, to use H. G. Wells' phrase, a 'Door in the Wall' through which one could pass from everyday reality into a different world. Yet it is by no means an escape:

> . . . the man who comes back through the Door in the Wall will never be quite the same as the man who went out. He will be wiser but less cocksure, happier but less self-satisfied, humbler in acknowledging his ignorance yet better equipped

> to understand the relationship of words to things, of systematic reasoning to the unfathomable Mystery which it tries, forever vainly, to comprehend. (p. 63)

Nevertheless, as he lamented, the insights which such experience could bring were deliberately ignored by a world which seemed to prefer to accept as valid only that account of the world furnished by routine habits of perception, and by the language systems evolved on the basis of such perception:

> . . . look at the history of mescalin research. Seventy years ago men of first-rate ability described the transcendental experiences which come to those who, in good health, under proper conditions, and in the right spirit, take the drug. How many philosophers, how many theologians, how many professional educators have had the curiosity to open this Door in the Wall? The answer, for all practical purposes, is None.
> (p. 60)

One can only imagine what he would have thought had he known that, after his death, nearly every country in the civilized world was to make opening the Door illegal.

Nearly all Huxley's critics have minimized the importance of his psychedelic experiences. George Woodcock, for example, seems primarily concerned to demonstrate how essentially unremarkable his experiences were:

> It is difficult to determine how much Huxley did in fact learn from his experiments; certainly *The Doors of Perception* reveals little more than the poverty of his natural equipment for metaphysical explorations. . . One is left . . . with the impression that Huxley's experiences may have been little different from those which others have enjoyed repeatedly without the stimulation of drugs.
> (*Dawn and the Darkest Hour*, p. 276)

Laurence Brander,[3] on the other hand, who actually goes so far as to devote a short chapter to *The Doors of Perception* and *Heaven and Hell*, reasons that because Huxley's experience of mescalin was different than he had expected it to be, his account of his experience is a case of 'confessing failure' (p. 190). Further reasoning that, because Huxley was a poor visualizer, he was ill-equipped to be a visionary, he concludes, all the evidence of *The Doors of Perception* notwithstanding, that Huxley's experience was 'thoroughly disheartening' (p. 194).

A commoner reaction still is to dismiss the experience as essentially escapist. Mescalin is a drug—and we all know about drugs. The equation between psychedelics and the *soma* of *Brave New World* is made with monotonous regularity: although Huxley could scarcely have made the distinction between their radically different properties clearer, the effort of paying attention to the details of what he actually wrote appears to have been too great, for example, for Frank Kermode, who remarks that, in *Island*,

> The *soma* which was once anathematized as a cheap escape from the ardours of reality is now essential to social health...
> ('Fiction Chronicle', *Partisan Review*, No. 3, 1962, p. 472)

John Atkins declares that

> ... like the animal life, life in the spirit is exclusively in the present, never past or future...

and he notes that

> ... a drug such as mescalin can help in the attainment of this condition. It should be used as a gratuitous grace, Huxley says in *Doors of Perception*. One is reminded of Lenina Crowne as she takes her soma, murmuring 'Was and will make me ill, I take a gramme and only am.'
> (*Aldous Huxley* (Revised edition), London, 1967, p. 176)

Or, as Milton Birnbaum puts it:

> A freedom induced by a drug extracted from mushrooms seems hardly different from the euphoria induced by *soma* in *Brave New World*.
> (*Aldous Huxley's Quest for Values*, Knoxville, Tennessee, 1971, p. 174)

Almost without exception, the critics appear tacitly to assume that Huxley's experiences were simply not 'real'. Birnbaum suggests that

> On the pilgrimage to reach the shrine of understanding the ultimate reality, he ended by embracing not reality, but an escape from it. The Jesting Pilate had become a narcotic-seeking Narcissus... (p. 41)

Or, in the rather more sober words of Jerome Meckier,

> ... few authorities on mysticism would accept mescalin ... as (one of the) genuine paths to the state of being traditionally reached only through mortification and non-attachment.
> (*Aldous Huxley: Satire and Structure*, p. 153)

One can only presume that by such an 'authority' he means someone like Professor Zaehner.

Despite the clarity and sanity of Huxley's discussion of psychedelic drugs, and the eloquence of his testimony as to their effects on him, the fact of that experience is uniformly devalued, ignored, or denied, with the result that the extent of the changes he underwent in the last years of his life are likewise minimized or neglected. Nonetheless, it would seem that Huxley's pre-occupation with the limited and inevitably subjective nature of individual perception was drastically modified by his experience of what it was *possible* for the individual to perceive. In both *The Doors of Perception* and in *Island* Huxley shows himself to be far more fully conscious of the possibilities of human awareness than ever before. While his eyes are still very much open to the weaknesses and limitations of human beings, as may be seen from his portrayal of Murugan and the Rani, his emphasis is no longer so exclusively on the negative characteristics of humanity. In *Island* it is noticeable that vitality is no longer the prerogative of those who are evil, stupid, unaware: imperfect awareness does not involve the debilitating cynicism of a Chelifer or a Quarles; full awareness is not attended by the remoteness of a Propter or a Rontini. Huxley's last novel advocates attention to and involvement in the world, rather than a vague and joyless asceticism. And while the realities of death, pain, and suffering are still acknowledged, they are no longer seen as the only realities.

Above all, *The Doors of Perception* and *Island* testify to a new-found sense of happiness in simply being alive in the world;

life is no longer seen as a struggle towards some vague and unattainable goal, but as something worth living for its own sake. Although Huxley continues to criticize society, his critique is no longer primarily grounded in dissatisfaction; instead of being aware only of the dreariness, the limitations of contemporary society, he is also alive to the human possibilities which society denies. And because his critique is no longer so querulously one-sided and obsessively negative, it gains in force; Huxley's sense of a 'fundamental All-Rightness', of the reality of humanity's potential for good as well as evil, balances his awareness of its limitations.

Huxley's critics, however, prefer to see the developments of his last years, not as something new, but merely as the logical conclusion of what went before; if his attitude has changed, it is no more than a sign of the mellowing brought about by old age. Because they refuse to acknowledge the significance of the changes which he underwent in the last few years of his life, their emphasis is on what is taken to be the valedictory quality of his later works, rather on the renewed vigour which his writing displays, or on the new ideas which it expresses. George Woodcock explains the new-found sense of joy and compassion which *Island* communicates as being an indication

> . . . that Huxley has come to terms with a great many things, partly through advancing age and partly through maturing philosophy. . . (Woodcock, p. 284)

His last novel is seen, not as the expression of a new outlook, but as the logical conclusion of his earlier, largely theoretical commitment to a very different, more ascetic kind of mysticism: 'the austerity of the aspiring mystic destroyed the austerity of the novelist. . .' (p. 285) And the fact that *Island* confronts and comes to terms with most of the obsessions of his earlier fiction is seen merely as

> . . . an ironic farewell to Huxley's past; there are many deliberate and playful echoes from the earlier novels, and personal ghosts are laid at last. (p. 281)

Because it is his last novel, Huxley's critics vie with one another in investing *Island* with a spurious finality: that it represents a new departure is disregarded as being incompatible with the judgement that it represents, to use the words of Jerome Meckier, 'his final, Herculean attempt at resolution and synthesis...' (Meckier, p. 208)

Yet to see *Island* in such terms is to ignore all the qualities which earned it (in the face of widespread critical disapproval) its very considerable popularity. It is a novel primarily designed to appeal to an eudience of its own time, to speak to the society of the 1960s, rather than to resolve a process of artistic development which had begun forty years earlier. In any event, Huxley's development was primarily dictated, not by artistic concerns, but by a continuous process of change which involved every aspect of his outlook and thinking; for Huxley, each new work was less a resolution of his development up to that point in time, than the beginning of an exploration of developments which were yet to come, and it is to this that *Island* owes much of its appeal. It is read for its ideas, for the freshness of much of its description of physical experience, for the fact that, unlike much of Huxley's later fiction, it communicates the feeling that he actively enjoyed writing it—but above all, for its relevance to the world in which its audience live. It is not the work of an old man.

However, before going on to examine the nature of Huxley's achievement in *Island* in greater detail, it might be as well to turn briefly to his remaining non-fictional works: *Adonis and the Alphabet*, a collection of essays; *Brave New World Revisited*, which considers the various threats to human freedom posed by a far more immediate future than that envisaged in his earlier novel; and *Literature and Science*, which examines the different ways in which the two disciplines approach and interpret reality.

Huxley is at his best in these works when dealing with certain specific preoccupations. In *Adonis and the Alphabet*, for example, he develops the contention, first adumbrated in *The Doors of Perception*, that the whole nature of our perception is conditioned by the language systems which we employ to articulate it. Once again, he reiterates his conviction that

In ordinary seeing we are hardly ever directly aware of our

> immediate impressions... Every perception is promptly conceptualized and generalized, so that we do not see the particular thing or event in its naked immediacy... (p. 73)

Far from being just a vehicle for thought, language conditions how and what one thinks:

> ...the age-old preoccupation of Western philosophers with the notion of substance was the natural consequence of their speaking a language, in which there were clearly distinguishable parts of speech, a verb 'to be', and sentences containing subjects and predicates... In Chinese there are no fixed parts of speech, sentences do not take the subject-predicate form, and there is no verb meaning 'to be'. Consequently, except under foreign influence, Chinese philosophers have never formulated the idea of 'substance', and never projected the word into the universe... Their concern has always been with the relationships between things, not with their 'essences'; with the 'how' of experience rather than the inferred 'what'. (pp. 188–9)

However, Huxley is not only concerned with the conditioning effect of the *nature* of the language system one employs, but also with the conscious abuse of language. In *Science, Liberty and Peace* he had already discussed the way in which advertisers and media-men used language, not to encourage understanding, but as a means of by-passing it, and in *Brave New World Revisited* he pursues this theme. While 'the survival of democracy depends on the ability of large numbers of people to make realistic choices in the light of adequate information' (p. 73), commercial advertising has been so successful in encouraging people to make unrealistic choices on the basis of irrational assumptions that those who are involved in the processes of democratic government nearly always succumb to the temptation of marketing themselves in a similar fashion. Politicians have become concerned with the projection of an 'image', rather than with demonstrating their capacity to act effectively on the basis of a rational analysis of the problems with which they are supposed to deal, for, as Huxley suggests,

> The methods now being used to merchandise the political

candidate as though he were a deodorant, positively guarantee the electorate against ever hearing the truth about anything. (p. 84)

Huxley's preoccupation with demographic and ecological problems is also very much in evidence. He found it hard to see how mankind could have any future at all, so long as finite resources continued to be squandered by an ever-increasing world population, and in *Adonis and the Alphabet* he launches a violent attack on the Toynbeean view of history, and on all those who are so absorbed in the drama of human conflict that they forget the existence of the stage on which it is played out. Consulting the index at the end of Toynbee's *A Study of History*, Huxley notes that whereas 'Popilius Laena gets five mentions and Porphyry of Batamaea two . . . the word you would expect to find between these names, *Population*, its conspicuous by its absence' (p. 211). The nearest one gets to 'famine' in the index is 'a blank space between Muhammad Falak-al-Din and Gaius Fannius' (p. 212). It says little for a society's priorities that its historians should be so preoccupied with the Great Men of the past as to ignore such elementary considerations as how the bulk of the population was fed. 'Agriculture', we are told, is 'not referred to in Mr Toynbee's index, though Agrigentum gets two mentions and Agis IV, King of Sparta, no less than forty-seven' (p. 213).

But while this is a point well taken, Huxley, too, has his blind spots. Although his recognition of the conditioning effects of language on perception, or of the very real dangers of ecological disaster show him to be in many respects ahead of his time, his clear-sightedness in specific areas is unable to disguise a continuing obtuseness about the mechanics of social organization. Thus, while *Brave New World Revisited* (1959) contains a far clearer exposition of what Huxley conceived of as the main threats to human freedom than does the thematically similar *Ends and Means*, it nevertheless shares many of the limitations of the earlier work. *Brave New World Revisited* is structured so that each chapter deals with a separate threat to freedom, and with each successive chapter his inability to distinguish between different *kinds* of threat becomes more and more apparent. The various dangers he describes include external pressures on society, such as the exhaustion of natural resources; the problems arising from the increasing size of societies as the population increases; and a variety of different instruments and techniques which might be used for the purposes of social control—such as propaganda, drugs, brainwashing and hypnosis. (Indeed, the discussion of these instruments and techniques occupies the bulk of the work.) But there is no discussion at all of the *kind* of society which will use, or refrain from using such methods. With the exception of one brief chapter which suggests that increased centralization, on the grounds of greater efficiency, would be detrimental to individual freedom, the question of social organization is completely ignored.

Huxley's own conception of the nature of freedom is suggested in *Adonis and the Alphabet*, and it is very much an individualistic freedom which is proposed:

> . . . freedom from the unanalyzed postulates in terms of which we do our second-hand experiencing, freedom from our conventional thoughts and sentiments, freedom from our stereotyped notions about inner and outer reality. (p. 33)

What it amounts to, is a radically conceived freedom of thought, but what remains unclear is the question of how such freedom is to be realized. It would depend, apparently, on the institution of some form of education in freedom—but the practical details are passed over:

> The problem of incorporating a decent education in the non-verbal humanities into the current curriculum is a task for professional educators and administrators. What is needed at the present stage is research—intensive, extensive, and long-drawn research. Some Foundation with a few scores of millions to get rid of should finance a ten or fifteen-year plan of observation and experiment. (pp. 37–8)

And that is Huxley's besetting problem: however full of ideas he might be, he rarely appears to have any idea of how they might be implemented.

By 'a decent education in the non-verbal humanities' Huxley means the acquisition of a proper awareness of the nature of one's mind and body, and the achievement of harmony and balance between them—the kind of thing, in fact, advocated by every guru-figure in his novels from *Eyeless in Gaza* onwards. Yet, even if practicable, Huxley himself concedes that such an education might still have its limitations. Even were it to be integrated into the curriculum of schools and colleges, he concedes that

> . . . the disintegrative effects of the kind of civilization, under which our technology compels us to live, may completely cancel out the constructive effects of even the best and completest system of formal education. (p. 38)

But the implications of this, that the evils of society may be an obstacle too great for even the sanest and most well-balanced individual to overcome, are scarcely considered. While one might suppose that a society capable of undoing the beneficial effects of even the best education must be in need of radical change, Huxley's suggestion is rather the reverse: that it might be unsettling to have too many people who were aware of the defects of their society. In *Brave New World Revisited* he suggests that

> Too searching a scrutiny by too many of the common folk of what is said by their pastors and masters might prove to be profoundly subversive. In its present form, the social order depends for its continued existence on the acceptance, without too many embarrassing questions, of the propaganda put forth by those in authority and the propaganda hallowed by the local traditions. The problem, once more, is to find the happy mean. Individuals must be suggestible enough to be willing and able to make their society work, but not so suggestible as to fall helplessly under the spell of professional mind-manipulators. Similarly, they should be taught enough about propaganda analysis to preserve them from an uncritical belief in sheer nonsense, but not so much as to make them reject outright the not always rational outpourings of the well-meaning guardians of tradition. (pp. 148–9)

Huxley's ideal of freedom, it would seem, is only for the chosen few; too much awareness on the part of too many individuals would represent a threat to the status quo.

What then do we learn from Huxley's later non-fiction? Primarily, it confirms the impression that, however perceptive he might be about problems in the abstract, he had no concrete sense of how the society they affected actually *worked*: while he might be aware of the threat posed by demographic and ecological problems, he had little concept of how society might be organized to deal with it; if he grasped the way in which language systems influence the way we think, he had less idea of how social systems affect the way we live. In *Adonis and the Alphabet* he makes what is surely a significant remark: discussing Communism, he suggests that

> For the Communists, all the ills of the world have one cause, namely capitalists, and all capitalists and their middle-class supporters are sub-human enemies of mankind... (p. 44)

Capital*ists* not capital*ism*: as he sees it, a communist objects, not to a system of social organization, but simply to a collection of evil individuals—to those who are 'sub-human enemies of mankind'. Even when confronted with an ideology which, perhaps more than any other, is concerned with the structure and workings of society as a whole, Huxley is incapable of seeing it in any other than wholly individualistic terms.

Considering that one of the major concerns of *Island* is with the organization and mechanics of an ideal society, this is a significant weakness, and it is interesting to compare *Island* with the later non-fiction, particularly in light of the emphasis which Huxley's critics place on the non-fictional characteristics of his last novel. 'A blueprint', an outline—more of an essay than a novel: this would seem to be the received critical opinion of *Island*. Jerome Meckier sees the 'essay-like *Island*' as representing the final breakdown of 'the distinction between Huxley's novels and his essays' (Meckier, p. 159). George Woodcock describes it as 'an unwieldy manifesto', and declares that it cannot 'really count as an example of the art of fiction' (Woodcock, p. 266). And, according to Peter Bowering, '... it is the one major novel to which the criticism of "a lengthy essay with added entertainments" might fairly be applied' (Bowering, p. 15). Yet for all that, if one compares *Island* with *Adonis and the Alphabet* or

Brave New World Revisited—works which were actually *intended* as essays—it is impossible to ignore the extent of the differences between them. Whereas in the non-fiction nearly all the characteristic weaknesses of Huxley's thinking are in evidence, in *Island* he is forced, by the very fact of having to imagine a social context for the freedom he proposes, and for the realization of the awareness he had glimpsed, into a far deeper and more extensive consideration of the implications of his views. *Island* is simply better—both more coherent and more stimulating—than any of the essays contained in *Adonis and the Alphabet* or *Brave New World Revisited*; for all its 'essay-like' elements, it remains a work of fiction offering, not a blueprint of an ideal society, but a vision.

The novel begins with an evocation of all the most familiar Huxleian nightmares. Lying injured on a clifftop in Pala, the island where he has been shipwrecked, the journalist Will Farnaby thinks back over his past life, recalling the death of his wife. Ostensibly an accident, the fact that it occurred less than an hour after he had told her that their marriage was at an end makes him feel just as responsible for it as did Anthony Beavis for the suicide of Brian Foxe in *Eyeless in Gaza*, and his guilt is compounded by the recollection of having betrayed his wife by having an affair with another, more sexually attractive woman. The spectre of Walter's relations with Marjorie Carling in *Point Counter Point* is raised, as Will wrestles with his memories of the contradiction between his desire for one woman, and his feelings of duty and responsibility towards another. This, in its turn, gives way to the recollection of the familiar feeling of sexual alienation, as he recalls making love in his mistress's flat, with their ecstasies were lent a quality of surrealistic ghastliness by being alternately illuminated in crimson and green by the neon light of a gin advertisement on the other side of the street. And finally, with morbid jealousy, he forces himself to remember that he had lost his mistress's affections—that '. . . her strawberry-pink alcove sheltered another guest, and its owner's body was shuddering ecstatically under somebody else's caresses' (p. 10).

Nor, as his thoughts turn to the more immediate past, are his memories any more pleasant. Trying to scale the cliff the previous night, he had been frightened by a snake and had fallen badly, injuring his leg; his memories are of death narrowly avoided, of horror, fear, and pain. Despite the grotesque chorus of mynah birds, with their incessant cries of 'Attention' and 'Here and now, boys', Will remains trapped in his own private, self-created hell of bad memories, incapable of paying attention to the here and now.

Here then, encapsulated, are all the most characteristic pre-occupations of Huxley's fiction from *Those Barren Leaves* onwards. Will is obsessed by lust and jealousy, fear and guilt, pain and death—by all the painful realities which had previously driven Huxley to embrace the austere mysticism voiced by such figures as Propter and Rontini. Yet in *Island* the answer to Will's anguished introspection is provided, not by another of Huxley's guru figures, but by a ten-year-old child.

The second chapter opens with the entry on the scene of Mary Sarojini, who, once she has established that Will is not dangerous, and that he is genuinely hurt, sends her younger brother off to fetch help. In the meantime, after giving Will food, she questions him about his arrival, and he describes the horrors of the previous night—the horror of death, the horror of snakes, the horror of falling. Her reaction, as she sees him beginning to tremble at the recollection, is to force him to re-live his horror. As though it were the most natural thing in the world, she makes him go through it again, until he re-creates it so vividly in the present that it no longer has the power to horrify as a memory. By living *through* the experience, by paying attention to it, Will is enabled to see it in proportion, instead of in the magnified, distorted light of uncontrollable fascination. The shipwreck, the climb, the snakes, the fall—all have done their worst, and that worst is over. The therapy concluded, Mary Sarojini asks Will what now seems to be an obvious question:

> 'So what's all the fuss about?' the child inquired.
>
> There was no malice or irony in her tone, not the slightest implication of blame. She was just asking a simple, straightforward question that called for a simple straightforward answer. Yes, what *was* all the fuss about? The snake hadn't bitten him; he hadn't broken his neck. And anyhow it had all happened yesterday. (p. 17)

In his relief, Will bursts out laughing, and both Mary Sarojini and the mynah bird perched on her shoulder join in. Where the first chapter, centred on memory and introspection, ended with Will giving way to a violent and uncontrollable fit of trembling, the second, with its insistence on paying attention to the present, and to the outside world, ends with the sound of laughter echoing through the forest glade 'so that the whole universe seemed to be fairly splitting its sides over the enormous joke of existence' (p. 18).

It is an episode which epitomizes the Palanese attitude to life: while they do not deny the unpleasant facts of experience, they try to see them as clearly and as much in proportion as they can. In the words of the old Raja, the co-founder of the society to which Will is introduced:

> One third, more or less, of all the sorrow that the person I think I am must endure is unavoidable. It is the sorrow inherent in the human condition, the price we must pay for being sentient and self-conscious organisms, aspirants to liberation, but subject to the laws of nature and under orders to keep on marching, through irreversible time, through a world wholly indifferent to our well-being, towards decrepitude and the certainty of death. The remaining two thirds of all sorrow is home-made and, so far as the universe is concerned, unnecessary. (p. 86)

So far as Will's experience is concerned, while his fright, his fall, his injury were inescapable facts, it is the way he dwelt on them which magnified them from being simple, manageable misfortunes to the proportions of full-blown, all-encompassing horror. Pain and suffering are accepted as being an inescapable part of human experience, but to concentrate on them exclusively, as Huxley had tended to do in his earlier novels, would be regarded by the Palanese as self-indulgent pessimism. While they accept the unavoidable one third of sorrow, they see their priority as being the elimination of the two thirds about which something can be done.

In effect, Pala is the realization of the ideal set out in Huxley's preface to *Brave New World*, of 'a society composed of freely co-operating individuals devoted to the pursuit of sanity', and while it incorporates many of the suggestions to be found in *Adonis and the Alphabet* and *Brave New World Revisited*, these gain in force and plausibility from their fictional context. What seems like empty speculation in the essays becomes far more concrete and convincing once Huxley is obliged to show how his ideas complement one another in an overall social context. Pala is also the embodiment of the speculations of the Arch-Vicar in *Ape and Essence* as to what might have been the alternative to all-out nuclear war: a combination, not of the worst, but of the best features of Western and Eastern culture—

> Eastern mysticism making sure that Western science should be properly used; the Eastern art of living refining Western energy; Western individualism tempering Eastern totalitarianism . . . it would have been the Kingdom of Heaven.
>
> (*Ape and Essence*, p. 138)

Thus Pala remains an agricultural society, using the resources of modern Western technology, but not letting themselves be used by them. While the Palanese will utilize electricity, improved plant breeding methods, and modern techniques for preserving food, they see a fully industrialized consumer society as something to be avoided at all costs. They exhibit a proper concern for ecology: resources are used according to need, not as fast as they can be exploited. (In fact, Pala's downfall is largely the result of an international oil company's conspiracy to get its hands on its oil reserves, which are merely used to supply local demand, rather than as a means of getting rich quickly.)

But a sensible use of resources and a regard for ecological considerations is only possible if society is not subject to the pressures of ever increasing need. As Dr Robert points out, the happy relationship between Palanese society and its natural environment is only made possible by a sane policy of population control. That everyone is properly fed, clothed, housed, and educated is because the size of their population allows them to live, as it were, within their means. Free and universally available contraception, together with the widespread practice of *maithuna*, a yogic technique of *coitus reservatus* which is also designed to heighten sexual awareness, enables the Palanese to keep the population level relatively stable, thus avoiding the poverty and starvation which afflict the rapidly rising populations of India, Ceylon, Central America, and the neighbouring dictatorship of Rendang.

On its own, however, population control is not enough; the ideal society must be not only limited in size, but also rational. That Palanese society *is* rational, unlike most of the societies to which it is contrasted, is due to the nature of its social arrangements. The Palanese, seeing rational behaviour as being dependent on psychological health, have set out to remove all the pressures which are likely to impair it. To begin with, the structure of the family has been radically modified: unlike the conventional Western family, whose members co-exist in an exclusive unit based on the imposition and acceptance of parental authority, the Palanese family is part of a much more open association of groups, which operate on the basis of co-operation and shared responsibility. Families are loosely linked together in groups of about twenty, which 'mutually adopt' one another. The incompatibilities and tensions which so often render family life intolerable are alleviated by allowing the free movement of individuals amongst the various family groups. Children, for example, are free to run away from home, whenever life there becomes too impossible.

> If a child feels unhappy in his first home, we do our best for him in fifteen or twenty second homes. Meanwhile the father and mother get some tactful therapy from the other members of their Mutual Adoption Club. In a few weeks the parents are fit to be with their children again, and the children are fit to be with their parents. (p. 93)

Because the Palanese see the family as a grouping based on biological accident, rather than as an inalterable unit of social structure, their attitudes towards such concepts as 'natural' affection, parental responsibility, filial duty are radically different from those of Western society. Their family is an open, rather than a closed institution, and it is this which enables them to avoid the horrors characteristic of family life elsewhere: Will's family history, with his brutish, alcoholic father, and a mother who had taken refuge in pious High Anglicanism; the oppressive mother-son relationship of the Rani and Murugan; or the rituals of the MacPhail family—

> . . . homilies before breakfast and at the midday dinner; there was the catechism on Sundays and learning the epistles by heart; and every evening, when the day's delinquencies had been added up and assessed, methodical whipping, with a whalebone riding switch on the bare buttocks, for all six children, girls as well as boys, in order of seniority. . . (p. 115)

—all would be unthinkable in Pala.

No less unconventional than Palanese domestic arrangements is the system of formal education, which is designed to ensure that the learning process is accompanied by a proper awareness of the nature of the mind and body doing the learning. As the Palanese Under-Secretary for Education puts it:

> A trained mind-body learns more quickly and more thoroughly than an untrained one. It's also more capable of relating facts to ideas and both of them to its ongoing life. (p. 208)

As an illustration of what can happen when the mind-body which does the learning is neglected in the interests of learning for its own sake, he cites the example of two Cambridge academics whom he had met on a visit to England:

> One of them was an atomic physicist, the other was a philosopher. Both extremely eminent. But one had a mental age, outside the laboratory, of about eleven and the other was a compulsive eater with a weight problem that he refused to face. Two extreme examples of what happens when you take a clever boy, give him fifteen years of the most intensive formal education and totally neglect to do anything for the mind-body which has to do the learning and the living. (ibid.)

It is results such as these which the Palanese seek to avoid. Will, recalling his own education, remarks that '". . . we never got to know things, we only got to know words"' (p. 240). In Pala, by contrast, equal importance is attached to both the capacity for receptivity and that for analysis:

> . . . one can always substitute a bad ready-made notion for the

> best insights of receptivity. The question is, why should one want to make that kind of choice? Why shouldn't one choose to listen to both parties and harmonize their views? The analysing tradition-bound concept maker and the alertly passive insight-receiver—neither is infallible; but both together can do a reasonably good job. (pp. 218–19)

Thus, as one of the Palanese teachers whom Will meets observes:

> 'There are degrees of receptivity... Very little of it in a science lesson, for example. Science starts with observation; but the observation is always selective. You have to look at the world through a lattice of projected concepts. Then you take the *moksha*-medicine, and suddenly there are hardly any concepts. You don't select and immediately classify what you experience; you just take it in.' (p. 219)

Moksha is Pala's own form of psychedelic drug, and the insights it provides not only fulfil an important educative function, but are also integral to the spiritual life of the island. It is taken, as we are shown, as a sacrament during the ritual which marks the passage from childhood into adolescence, and also, later on, by Will himself, as a means of experiencing what the Palanese take to be the ultimate, underlying reality. Through the vividness and immediacy which it confers on perception, it serves to reinforce people's awareness of the surrounding world; in a different way, its message is essentially the same as that of the mynah birds which continually cry 'Attention'—both are reminders of the importance of a continual awareness. And it is this which makes the atmosphere of *Island* so different from that which obtains in most of the rest of his fiction: it is the only novel in which there is a sense that reality is joyfully embraced. Life, for all that it contains suffering and sorrow, is seen for once as *healthy*, and is presented as such: the Palanese ideal is 'the sacramentalizing of common life, so that every event may become a means whereby enlightenment can be realized...' (*Letters*, p. 929)

Nearly all the areas of experience which Huxley had once portrayed with horror, or disgust, or morbid fascination are presented in an altogether new light. Sexuality, for instance, no longer degrades or alienates, but is seen instead as a source of joy and a means of communication. The revulsion with which Will recalls his sexual relations with Babs is finally exorcized during his *moksha* experience, when he learns to accept the fact of his sexual attraction to Susila. At every turn it is stressed that sexuality only becomes indecent when it is distorted by an unhealthy attitude towards it. Murugan's disgust at the open sexuality of the Palanese is put in perspective by the furtiveness of his homosexual affair with the dictator of Rendang;[4] the cheapness of Will's cynical remark about Radha and Ranga sleeping together after Lakshmi's death is shown up by Susila's dignified reproof; and the real nature of Mr Bahu's desire for Radha is exposed by his attempt to bribe her into sleeping with him. Sexuality may become disgusting when tainted by secrecy, guilt, or commercial considerations, but only because they all imply a neglect of its real function, which is to enhance one's awareness of the existence both of oneself and of others.

This belated acceptance of sexuality's positive aspects is perhaps the most striking *volte-face* in *Island*, but it is by no means an isolated one. Physical reality in all its aspects becomes something to be rejoiced in: for example, grace at Vijaya's house consists of paying the closest possible attention to the taste and texture of one's first mouthful of food. At the market place, Will is struck by the life and bustle of the crowds, by the 'good gross odours' of food being prepared, and by 'the perfume, thin and sweet and ethereally pure, of the many coloured garlands on sale beside the fountain' (p. 242). The contrast with the claustrophobic urban settings of *Antic Hay* and *Point Counter Point*, and with his former emphasis on the filthiness and stink of humanity could hardly be more marked. His Swiftian revulsion from the flesh had at last disappeared.

There are still unpleasant experiences in life, of course, but their unpleasantness is seen in a far more realistic light. Death is still a reality—but a reality no longer distorted by hysteria and horrified fascination. Lakshmi's death, because it is presented in a calm, matter-of-fact manner, rather than with the maximized ghastliness of Huxley's earlier fiction, is infinitely more affecting and real than most of his other death scenes. His primary design is no longer to horrify, but rather to describe what *actually happens* when someone dies.

Lakshmi shows the extent to which the Palanese accept and prepare for the inevitability of death. There is far less of a sense of missed opportunities and wasted chances when someone dies if their life has been lived as fully and richly as possible, and when Lakshmi dies, it is in a manner very different from Will's Aunt Mary, whose courage and generosity were transformed by cancer into 'a bitterly querulous self-pity, an abject despair' (p. 254). Lakshmi dies, fully aware of the fact that she is dying, not without regrets for the end of a life well-spent, but nevertheless in a state of mind where sorrow and regret are inextricably mingled with happiness and acceptance. The scene was modelled, in fact, on the death of Huxley's first wife, Maria,[5] and just as that was an experience which enabled him to come to terms with the horror of death which he had felt ever since the deaths of his mother and his brother Trevenen, so Lakshmi's dying, marked as it is by calmness and reconciliation, serves to exorcize the morbid fascination with the subject which had haunted his earlier fiction. That human beings have bodies, that they eat, drink, make love, suffer pain, die, are inescapable facts —and Huxley's acceptance of them brings with it a sense of release. Reiterated throughout the book is the Buddhist insistence on both the fact of sorrow and the fact of the ending of sorrow, and it is the consciousness of the limited, finite nature of suffering and horror, of their being only part of a far richer texture of existence, that so sharply differentiates *Island* from its predecessors.

Island, then, depicting a society so constructed that genuine happiness is possible, is Huxley's Utopia. Yet it differs from most Utopias in two important respects. First of all, it is not simply a blueprint for a better world. While Huxley's main purpose is to describe such a world, his Utopian theme is given added resonance by being counterpointed by the changes which take place in the character who observes it. For Will is not just there, like most visitors to Utopia, to observe and record, to point out the superiority of the world as it might be to the world as it is; in seeing how the world might be changed, he too changes. His visit to Utopia enables him to come to terms with his past, and to shed the protective carapace of cynicism under which he had sheltered for so long from the realities of his own world. In Pala, Will learns respect for other human beings, rather than seeing them, as he had done in his nightmarish vision on Fleet Street, as so many maggots. He discovers that their good qualities are real, rather than illusions to be exposed by the superior reality of suffering and death. Above all, he finds that his conviction that everyone is fundamentally alone becomes an irrelevance once he realizes that experience need not necessarily be conceptualized and verbalized in purely subjective terms; when he finally takes the *moksha*, he realizes that between Susila and himself there *is* such a thing as communication. Where Calamy, in *Those Barren Leaves*, had puzzled over the infinite variety of possible ways of looking at reality, *Island* sets out to show that, for all their variety, they are simply aspects of a larger whole. Will is transformed from an outside observer of the random manifestations of reality into a participant in its richness and variety.

Unlike most Utopias, *Island* does not simply present a different world: it also shows how it can affect the individual within it. For the first time Huxley treats the possibility of sanity in a social context; his goal is no longer the elitist one of becoming one of the 'tiny theocentric minority' for whom sanity is alone possible, but rather the creation of a society where sanity might be possible for everyone. Alienation is resolved, not by an individualistic withdrawal into an isolation still more intense, but by becoming aware of the world in which one live, and above all, of the fact that it contains other people.

The other distinctive feature of *Island* is that it is a Utopia which can be seen to have developed as the result of specific choices and decisions. Whereas the origins of most Utopias are left extremely vague (Thomas More's is simply discovered; Edward Bellamy's, in *Looking Backward*, purports to be the logical development of American capitalism; H. G. Wells's, in *In the Days of the Comet*, supervenes as the result of the release of a vapour which changes human nature; even in *News from Nowhere* William Morris's account of the preceding revolution reads as a rather unconvincing interpolation), the genesis of Palanese society is described in an unusually concrete manner. While Huxley's conception of the combination of factors necessary for the creation of a sane society is in certain important respects incomplete, his attention to the philosophical assumptions which must underlie such a society, and the extent to which he avoids unthinkingly reproducing the features of the society to which he wishes to offer an alternative, make Pala more than just a sterile construct. *Island* is both one of the most thoroughly imagined, and most radical of Utopias.

Nevertheless, *Island* also has its weaknesses, of which perhaps the most serious is the evidence which it gives of Huxley's inability to envisage any political concomitant to the social reforms suggested. Given the radical modifications of spiritual, cultural, and even economic institutions which are proposed, one might have supposed that Huxley could have envisaged an accompanying system of government somewhat less primitive than enlightened despotism—particularly in view of the fact that it is precisely this system, with the power it gives to the appalling Murugan, which facilitates Pala's downfall. Huxley's continued adherence to pacifism, too, creates problems. As in all Huxley's novels, the possibilities for freedom which he outlines remain contingent on their being permitted by the rest of the world, and when Will inquires what help the psychological and spiritual maturity of the Palanese will be in the event of an invasion from Rendang, the reply he receives seems far from satisfactory: '"... being reconciled to one's fate, that's already a great achievement"' (p. 222). Given the enormous disparity between the quality of life in Rendang and Pala, such fatalism seems more like sheer irresponsibility.

Yet these criticisms are in themselves an indication of Huxley's success in achieving what was surely one of his main aims in writing *Island*—to stimulate argument, to force the reader into a consideration of the practicalities and implications of the Utopian society he depicts. Argument on the part of the reader is part of the reaction envisaged by any author who writes with the polemical intent evident in *Island*—for argument is a sign that, even if the reader has not been convinced, he or she has at least been prompted to *think*.

It is possible, of course, to point to technical weaknesses as well—to a certain clumsiness in the integration of exposition and action, to numerous infelicities of dialogue. The language in some of the discussions, for instance, is scarcely converted into credible everyday speech by the insertion of bald stage-directions:

> 'Psycho-physical means to a transcendental end,' said Vijaya, raising his voice against the grinding screech of the low gear into which he had just shifted, 'that, primarily, is what all these yogas are...' (p. 149)

With passages such as that, Huxley creates an effect, not so much of verisimilitude, as of unintentional comedy. Yet while one can only regret such lapses, Huxley's failures of execution remain incidental: they do not affect the reader's involvement in the consideration of his ideas, nor do they detract from the qualities which have made the novel deservedly popular.

Critical estimation of *Island*, however, remains low. In the opinion of Frank Kermode it is 'one of the worst novels ever written' (Kermode, p. 472), and represents a sad falling-off from 'the considerable achievement of *Point Counter Point*'. 'Esthetic estimate of the novel cannot rise very high; *Island* is not so much a novel as a mixture of most of the genres in which Huxley worked' is the verdict of Harold Watts.[6] Huxley 'wanted desperately for it to be admired,' suggests John Atkins, 'but the critics could not praise it—and in fact it is second-rate and tedious' (Atkins, p. xxxi). Once again, there are clearly two different kinds of reading at work, one of which involves a response to Huxley's polemical intent, while the other sees it as inadmissible. As Jerome Meckier puts it, *Island* 'is a novel only by courtesy of definition' (Meckier, p. 203), and it is the question of definition which appears to dictate the critics' reaction to the work.

One might debate at length the respective merits of the two approaches—whether it is best to respond to a work on its own terms, or in accordance with what one believes it ought to be like—but in the case of Huxley there can be little doubt as to which is the more helpful in assisting an understanding of his work. For, particularly in the case of *Island*, it is hard to feel much confidence in critical procedures which appear, on the whole, to be associated with the crassest possible incomprehension of what Huxley is actually doing.

How, for example, can one explain Frank Kermode's facile equation of *soma* and *moksha*, or William Barrett's contention that

> Brave New World turned upside down is Brave New World

> still. The Palanese, without conflicts and tensions, are as humanly insipid as the denizens of a world ruled by mass production. (*Atlantic Monthly*, April, 1962, p. 156)

—or, indeed, Milton Birnbaum's suggestion that Palanese education 'does not seem vastly different from the kind of Pavlovian conditioning which Huxley had scathingly attacked in *Brave New World*'? (Birnbaum, p. 96) Equally, one might well wonder what kind of critical attention can possibly lie behind Harold Watts' suggestion that

> The Rani's movement has, however, structurally embarrassing overtones because it contains echoes of a theosophy that is first cousin to Huxley's own 'Clear Light'... One wonders how, on the level of intellectual discrimination, 'perennial' philosophic sense is to be confidently winnowed from theosophic nonsense. (Watts, p. 145)

Considering that one of the principal themes of *Island* is the distinction between true and false spirituality, to say nothing of the fact that Huxley portrays the differences between the Palanese conception of spirituality and that of the Rani with a firmness bordering on caricature, one can only speculate as to the nature of the critical principles which make so basic a failure of understanding possible.

Of course, part of the critical misunderstanding of *Island* can be explained as being due to the application of narrowly aesthetic criteria to a work whose implications are considerably wider, but there would also seem to be other factors at work. What is perhaps more disturbing is the widespread tendency of Huxley's critics to use the guise of critical objectivity as a cloak for their own unsupported value judgements about Huxley's actual ideas. Jerome Meckier, for instance, suggests that

> If one recalls the smugness of certain Palanese—such as the eighteen-year-old Nurse Apu discussing the spiritual quality of orgasms—the destruction of Pala becomes less difficult to bear. A society in which the ability to practice advanced psychology extends to all the inhabitants including the children cannot be consistently appealing. One is tempted to equate Pala, despite its spiritual maturity, with a magnified

> Boy Scout Camp, just as *Brave New World* was an enlarged assembly line. The unflagging attention each person pays to his own mental and spiritual development while prescribing for that of all around him seems almost neurotic.
> (Meckier, p. 204)

This is by no means an isolated example of what amounts to simple prejudice masquerading as literary criticism, and when one examines the work of Huxley's critics in detail, it is hard to avoid the conclusion that in many cases what purport to be aesthetic judgements on his work are, in fact, no more than rationalizations of the critic's own discomfort at the radical nature of Huxley's ideas.

Yet there are alternatives to the narrow-mindedness, stupidity, and dishonesty of much of what passes for Huxley criticism. The suggestion that one should accept Huxley's novels on their own terms, without preconceptions as to what they ought to be like—or, in other words, that one should adopt the attitude of the average, informed reader—is by no means a new one. Wayne Booth, for example, in his review of *Island,*[7] also questions the relevance of the critical obsession with definitions of the novel:

> . . . it will be easy to show, once more, that he hasn't written a true novel since *Antic Hay*—or has he, in fact, *ever* written one? And that takes care of Huxley. Only here is *Island* still, calling itself a novel, and to refuse it the title hardly takes care of the critical task. (p. 631)

Instead of worrying over whether *Island* is a 'true' novel, a 'real' novel, or a 'traditional' novel, critics would do well to see it for what it is:

> Properly placed within that other, non-Leavisonian 'great tradition'—works like *Gulliver's Travels, Candide, Rasselas, Erewhon,* using fictional devices to provoke thought, *Island* can command full attention and respect. . . (ibid.)

The only problem, as we have seen, is that even those critics who acknowledge the influence of Peacock and Swift, or who talk of satire and the 'novel of ideas', seem unable to modify their approach accordingly. The unspoken acceptance of the supremacy of a particular *kind* of fiction continues to inform their discussion of Huxley's work, which suffers as a result.

Booth, on the other hand, stresses the importance of getting away from theoretical preconceptions, and back to the central experience of actually reading Huxley. *Island*, he says, took him 'through to the end, arguing with Huxley all the way'—and that is surely the essence of Huxley's appeal. After the brilliance of his early comedies, he went on to produce fiction which, while scarcely conforming to the traditions by which his critics set so much store, provides not only entertainment, but also a powerful stimulus to thought and argument—an intellectual art, perhaps, but an art nonetheless. And this, the author with whom one argues all the way, is very much the readers' rather than the critics' Huxley: not a writer who aspired to the 'splendid aesthetic unity' of the great fiction of the past; simply someone worth reading, worth arguing with, worth thinking about—above all, someone whose work deserves a better fate than being sacrificed on the altar of an inappropriate critical theory.

Notes

Chapter 1

1 Bernard Bergonzi, 'Life's Divisions—The Continuing Debate on Aldous Huxley', *Encounter*, July 1973, pp. 65–8.
2 Philip Thody, *Aldous Huxley: A Biographical Introduction*, London, 1973; Keith M. May, *Aldous Huxley*, London, 1972; Peter Firchow, *Aldous Huxley, Satirist and Novelist*, Minneapolis, 1972; George Woodcock, *Dawn and the Darkest Hour: A Study of Aldous Huxley*, London, 1972.
3 'E. M. Forster on his Life and his Books' – An interview recorded for television by David Jones, *The Listener*, 1 January, 1959, p. 11.

Chapter 2

1 'Two Realities', *The Collected Poetry of Aldous Huxley*, ed. Donald Watt, London, 1970, p. 20.
2 *The Letters of D. H. Lawrence*, ed. Aldous Huxley, London, 1932, p. xxx.
3 *Letters of Aldous Huxley*, ed. Grover S. Smith, London, 1969, p. 516.
4 C. P. Snow, 'Aldous Huxley – Romantic Pessimist', *New Republic*, 12 January 1959, cxl. p. 19.
5 In Sheldon's view, physique was one of the primary determinants of human behaviour. Briefly, his correlation between types of physique and corresponding varieties of temperament depends on a system of classification in which both physique and temperament are divided into three main categories. In the case of physique these are: *endomorphy*, of which the chief characteristics are a preponderance of fat and a highly developed digestive system; *mesomorphy*, distinguished by a preponderance of muscle and by a high capacity for physical endurance; and *ectomorphy*, where the brain and central nervous system are more highly developed, being accompanied by a thin, delicate, and lightly muscled body. The corresponding categories of temperament are: *viscerotonia*, which manifests itself in sociability, evenness of temper, and a love of comfort, food, and affection; *somatotonia*, characterized by a desire for risk and adventure, and a need for vigorous physical activity; and *cerebrotonia*, where inhibition, self-consciousness, and introversion are the predominant traits. Sheldon's own experiments would seem to indicate the existence of a marked correlation between specific types of physique and corresponding varieties of temperament—but it is only fair to point out that other researchers have expressed grave reservations concerning the extent to which Sheldon's findings have been borne out by subsequent investigations.

For a useful short introduction to Sheldon's theories, see Calvin S. Hall and Gardner Lindzey, *Theories of Personality*, New York, 1970, pp. 338–79.

6 Louis Kronenburger, 'Mr Huxley's New Novel is Savage Satire', *New York Times Book Review*, 14 October 1928, p. 5.

Notes

Chapter 3

1 Gerald Heard, 'The Poignant Prophet', *Kenyon Review*, XXVII, 1965, p. 63.
2 Peter Bowering, *Aldous Huxley: A Study of the Major Novels*, London, 1968, p. 15.
3 *The Works of Thomas Love Peacock*, ed. H. F. B. Brett-Smith and C. E. Jones, London, 1934, Volume III, p. 25.

Chapter 4

1 F. M. Alexander (1869–1955) was an Australian therapist who believed that both physical and mental health were dependant on the maintance of correct posture during the performance of even the most routine physical actions. He developed a technique of 're-educating' his patients by making them unlearn injurious habits of bodily use and learn correct ones instead. Huxley underwent instruction in the Alexander principle during the latter stages of the composition of *Eyeless in Gaza*, and many of the views expressed by Miller in that novel are modelled on those of Alexander.
2 F. R. Leavis, *The Great Tradition*, New Edition, London, 1960, p. 31.

Chapter 5

1 *Boswell's Life of Johnson*, ed. G. B. Hill, Oxford, 1934, Vol. II, p. 319.

Chapter 6

1 For an account of Huxley's involvement with the cinema, see Sybille Bedford, *Aldous Huxley: A Biography*, London, 1974, Vol. II.
2 *The Collected Essays, Journalism, and Letters of George Orwell*, ed. Sonia Orwell and Ian Angus, London, 1968, Vol. IV, p. 479.

Chapter 7

1 R. C. Zaehner, *Mysticism Sacred and Profane*, Oxford, 1957, p. 32.
2 See R. D. Laing, *The Politics of Experience*, London, 1967; also Miriam Siegler, Humphrey Osmond, and Harriet Mann, 'Laing's Models of Madness', *British Journal of Psychiatry*, Vol. 115, II, 1969, pp. 947–58.
3 Laurence Brander, *Aldous Huxley: A Critical Study*, London, 1969.
4 It should be emphasized that it is the furtiveness, not the homosexuality, which is seen as unhealthy. In a letter to Peter Firchow, Christopher Isherwood recalls '... that Huxley gave me a part of *Island* to read in ms and that we discussed it, but since I didn't get to see the whole early draft of the book.... I don't know how much he changed it. All I *do* remember is that I protested to Aldous because he made the heavies (Col. Dipa in his relations with Murugan) homosexual. I pointed out that this was becoming a cliché – homosexual Nazis and other fascists abounded in the literature of the period. Weren't 'good' homosexuals welcome on his island? He saw

the justice of this, of course, and the question is touched on...' Quoted in Firchow, p. 178n.

5 See *Letters*, pp. 734–7 for Huxley's own account of Maria's death.

6 Harold H. Watts, *Aldous Huxley*, New York, 1969, p. 145.

7 Wayne C. Booth, 'Yes, But Are They Really Novels?', *Yale Review*, Vol. LI, 1962, pp. 630–1.

Index

Index

12